ESSAYS IN LONGITUDINAL THINKING

Managing Change with Continuity

About the Editors

Dr. Shailendra Kumar Tamotia, President & CEO of INDAL, an Aditya Birla Group Company, has earlier headed India's largest public sector aluminium company, NALCO, as its CMD. With extensive experience of over 40 years, he has also won a host of prestigious awards including the National Metallurgists Merit Group Award and the Best Industrial Manager's Award.

A leading member of ISTD and presently its National President, Dr. Tamotia is actively involved with several research and management institutes. A Fellow of the All India Management Association, he is also on the Research Councils of the Regional Research Laboratory, Bhubaneswar, National Metallurgical Laboratory, Chairman, CII West Bengal State Council, among others and a Board member of the WEBEL, Kolkata, IPICOL and Central Tool Room and Training Centre, Bhubaneswar.

Vinayshil Gautam is a thinker and a practitioner of the craft of management. Above all he is an institutional builder. As the Founder Director, IIM(K), First Head, Management Department, IIT (Delhi), President, ARTDO International, President, ISTD, Chairman, All India Board Management Education and many other positions he has held, he has always left an indelible impact of his pioneering zeal.

Widely published honoured with awards and travelled. Dr. Gautam has been sought for his management expertise amongst other places in Germany, UAE, Saudi Arabia, Malaysia and some of the best companies in India. He is a member of various Boards in India and Abroad. Currently he is the Dalmia Chair Professor of Management at IIT (Delhi).

ESSAYS IN LONGITUDINAL THINKING

Managing Change with Continuity

Editors
S.K. Tamotia
Vinayshil Gautam

Published for
INDIAN SOCIETY FOR TRAINING AND DEVELOPMENT
by
CONCEPT PUBLISHING COMPANY, NEW DELHI-110059

Cataloging in Publication Data—DK
Courtesy: D.K. Agencies (P) Ltd. <docinfo@dkagencies.com>

Essays in longitudinal thinking : managing change with continuity / editors, S.K. Tamotia, Vinayshil Gautam.
p. cm.
Contributed articles; previously published in the Indian journal of training and development.
Includes bibliographical references.
Includes index.
ISBN 8180691918

1. Management. 2. Personnel management—India. 3. Executives—Training of—India. I. Tamotia, S. K. (Shailendra Kumar) II. Gautam, Vinayshil, 1946-

DDC 658.300 954 21

ISBN: 81-8069-191-8

First Published 2005

Published and Printed by
Ashok Kumar Mittal
Concept Publishing Company
A/15-16, Commercial Block, Mohan Garden
New Delhi-110059 (INDIA)

Phones : 25351460, 25351794
Fax : 091-11-25357103
Email : publishing@conceptpub.com

Preface

Indian Journal of Training and Development (IJTD) began its publication 33 years ago. The uninterrupted publication of our Journal for 33 years is a cause of some satisfaction.

In our 'national hobby' of putting ash on our head we often do not even look at many minor and major achievements of our polity, our society, our institution and even ourselves. We could have obviously done better but what we have done is nothing to be embarrassed about.

Amongst the Societies the place of ISTD is one of legitimate pride. Amongst the Journals in management IJTD is amongst the first rankers. A serious research journal, it has made an impact on the shaping of the management profession and indeed has been shaped by the way management profession has grown in India and abroad.

The Journal has over the years metamorphosed from the earlier focus exclusively on training issues. It recognized that training and development could not be practiced without being related to its context of Human Resource Development in particular and Management in general. Thus it is that it widened and deepened its reach to include contributions from the areas also.

As been noted earlier IJTD is likely a venerable institution. It has had a chain of eminent editors who nursed it with affection and dedication.

It was however left to the managerial insight of Dr. S.K. Tamotia, President, INDAL and also the National President of ISTD to recognize that a cross-section of writing across 33 years would be a veritable treasure house of ideas. Dr. Vinayshil Gautam pitched in to emphasize that the writings and publications which bring out the history of ideas in management in the Indian context were few and far between. The result of this approach you hold in your hand and it is for you to judge.

Nineteen papers were selected over the 33 years period to mark the successive stages of growth of management thought. The names of the authors that came across reads like the most distinguished, the whose-who of the management writing, learning and practice. Nitish R. De (1971); C.K. Prahalad (1971); Barun De (1973); Francis Menezes (1977); Anil K. Khandelwal (1978); S.B.L. Bhardwaj

(1979); Udai Pareek (1981); Dharni P. Sinha (1981); Vinayshil Gautam (1984); Devendra Kumar (1985); Mirza S. Saiyadain (1987); T.V. Rao (1989); B.R. Virmani (1989); M.B. Athreya (1989); R.P. Billimoria (1991); Y.R.K. Reddy (1993); P.N. Singh (1999); M.A. Ogunu (2002) and Padma Iyer (2002). Amongst themselves, writing at different points of time across three decades they represent not only some of the best names in the field but their writings also flag the issues often in a pioneering manner. Several of these papers became trend setters. C.K. Prahalad analyses relationship between "Behavioural Science's Contribution towards Developing Effective Trainers"; Barun De analyses the "Imitation Styles in Indian Management"; S.B.L. Bhardwaj analyses the issues in "Managing Development in the Developing Countries". Vinayshil Gautam's paper on "Select Paradigms of Management in India and the Indian Value System"; and Devendra Kumar's paper on "Transfer of Technology from Lab to Land" are but a few of such texts. This volume is a major contribution in the broad domain of longitudinal thinking in the growth of management literature in India. Reading them in conjunction will show how ideas can feed upon each other and develop as a powerful instrument of leveraging change.

If lateral thinking helps widen the choice of intervention by generating ideas, longitudinal thinking helps ideas to get rooted into practice and embed change in the on going flow of thought and action.

We believe that a volume such as is a major contribution which an institution like ISTD makes to the growth of the profession. That it happens through the instrumentality of IJTD will no doubt bring joy to literally the thousand upon thousands of well wishers of IJTD.

This effort is made in the hope that it will bring joy to all those who seek to understand some lineal aspects of the growth of management literature in India and derive an essence of pride in use of longitudinal thinking to strengthen management action. At the end of the day few tools are more powerful than history of ideas.

To know where we are, we must understand and know where we come from.

This volume is a modest attempt in answering this search from the point of management thought and action in India.

Your reactions on the volume are welcome.

New Delhi
July 3, 2004

Editors

Contents

List of Contributors

Athreya, M.B., Management Advisor, New Delhi.

Bhardwaj, S.B.L., Member, Senior Faculty, Administrative Staff College of India, Hyderabad.

Billimoria, R.P., Chairman, Public Sector Enterprises Selection Board.

De, Barun, Professor, IIMC.

De, Nitish R., Indian Institute of Management, Kolkata.

Gautam, Vinayshil, Centre of Systems and Management Studies, Indian Institute of Technology, Delhi.

Iyer, Padma, Chairperson of Lucknow Chapter of Indian Society for Development and working as Associate Faculty Member, Institute of Entrepreneurship Development, Uttar Pradesh.

Khandelwal, Anil K., Faculty Member, Bank of Baroda.

Kumar, Devendra, Director, Centre for Science for Villages, Wardha.

Menezes, Francis, Board Member of ISABS.

Ogunu, M.A., Senior Lecturer in the Faculty of Education, University of Benin, Benin City, Nigeria.

Pareek, Udai, Indian Institute of Management, Ahmedabad.

Prahalad, C.K., Manager, Management Services Indian Pistons, Chennai.

Rao, T.V., Professor, Indian Institute of Management, Ahmedabad.

Reddy, Y.R.K., ONGC Professor of Strategic Management, Administrative Staff College of India, Hyderabad.

Affiliations of the contributors are as at the time of writing of the paper

Saiyadain, Mirza S., Professor, Indian Institute of Management, Ahmedabad.

Singh, P.N., Chairman, Grid Consultants Pvt. Ltd., Mumbai.

Sinha, Dharni P., Director, Special Studies Division, Administrative Staff College of India, Hyderabad.

Virmani, B.R., Professor of Management and Chairman, Personnel Management and Industrial Relations at the Administrative Staff College of India, Hyderabad.

1

The March of Organisational Development
*An Interim Balance Sheet**

Nitish R. De

Means-Ends Ambience in OD

OD is a comparatively new concept. As such, there is a danger that its newness may lead to an ambiguity in understanding or an overly eager acceptance as a management tool or its rejection on some plea or other. Ideally we would wish to steer clear of all these three possibilities. Beckhard (1969) has provided a terse yet adequate description of OD which with slight alterations reads as follows:

> OD is an effort which is planned
> organisation-wide (autonomous) division-wide
> is managed from the top
> to increase organisational effectiveness and
> health through systematic interventions
> in the organisation's *processes using behavioural sciences knowledge.*

While it is possible to dwell upon each of the emphasized phrases in the description, we shell confine our comments to three points only. *In the first place*, it is necessary to understand that systematic interventions based on behavioural science knowledge preclude the unscientism of using one unique training input only (*e.g.* unstructured group activity). In other words, sensitivity training need not be equated with OD nor need the grid Seminar be coterminous with OD. Special emphasis on chosen inputs that we often come across is usually a

* First published in IJTD in 1971.

reflection of the consultant's own style and experience. *Secondly*, OD is distinguished from Management Development (MD) by at least two major elements. The target of change is not a chosen individual or a few persons as in MD, it is usually inter-dependent work groups. Besides, the objective of the change programme is not, as in MD, the acquisition of some chosen knowledge or skills, but an *expansion* of the individual through the group process resulting in all-round improvement of the object of change. *Thirdly*, in OD, an individual is not looked upon as a means to an end. *Organisational effectiveness and health*, the term used in our description, is much more comprehensive than what an economist looks for in an organisation or what an investor craves for.

Recently in an address P.R. Kamani (1971), Chairman of the group which is in OD field for over three years, expressed his view that the group has to make a conscious movement—from leadership of authority to leadership of shared goals and norms:

- From a state of working under constraint to a state of autonomy and excellence in the temple of work;
- From the primacy of material resources to the primacy of human resources;
- From profit-making to growth-achieving;
- From sensation of pleasure to acquisition of happiness; and
- From self-oriented behaviour to a state of working with and through a functional collectively.

This expression of movement towards a direction is an indicator of what the goals are. There are, no doubt, elements of idealism in the statement but the entire thrust of OD is that such structural and process changes are to be initiated as would assist the human beings associated with an enterprise to realise their potential. In that sense, OD stands for anti-Peter principle: an individual rises to the level of competence and that OD is a means to extend that frontier of competence.

There is thus a re-vamping of traditional organisational goals. The age-old debate between organisational objectives and individual aspirations loses its force when the issue is confronted in the following terms; a synergy of humanness and excellence is possible in an organisation if its activities are organised to provide the requisite opportunity for such an objective (De, 1970 A). If the "why of it" is accepted, OD provides the "how of it".

Application of OD Approach in India

In this section we shall provide a brief resume of the OD work with which the Behavioural Sciences group of the Indian Institute of Management, Calcutta, is associated. While it will be desirable to undertake a description of the OD work so far initiated as well as to offer an evaluation of each project, we shall desist from doing it here. In none of the case, an evaluation is mature, except in the case of the Kamani system, where a tentative appraisal is being carried out (De and Kamani, in preparation). A proper documentation of the OD work though possible will be too voluminous for this medium. However, a brief report is in order.

In early 1968, H.R. Kamani, a member of the family, invited Suresh Srivastava into the organisation. Since then, the major organisation change programme is on. Taking a broad view, the design of the OD approach appears like that shown in the table on the facing page. (Fig. 1.1)

Striking a balance-sheet one will get a picture somewhat akin to Fig. 1.2.

The next major OD programme took roots in the Raw Materials Division of the Tata Iron & Steel Company Limited. While in the Kamani system the initial motivation came from inter-personal problems, in TISCO, concern with organisational issues as reflected in functional conflict brought OD to the ore mines. That was in May 1970 and since then the activities have been extended to the coal mines. Secondly, as contrasted with the Kamani system, the OD programme was launched at two centres of the division and not at the operational Headquarters of the division located at Jamshedpur.

In the span of a year over 200 managerial personnel have taken part in the OD activities at iron ore mines and coal mines. While it is premature to launch into an evaluation of the TISCO programmes, we shall describe in brief some salient features of the total activities.

1. An active and constantly supportive role was played by two of the key persons in the organisation—R.H. Mody, Director in the charge of operations and P.T.K. Panicker, his Chief Personnel aide for the Raw Materials Division. Because of their sustained interest, the activities did not slump into another spate of training programmes. Rather the entire programme became a meaningful activity meant to usher in planned change and development.

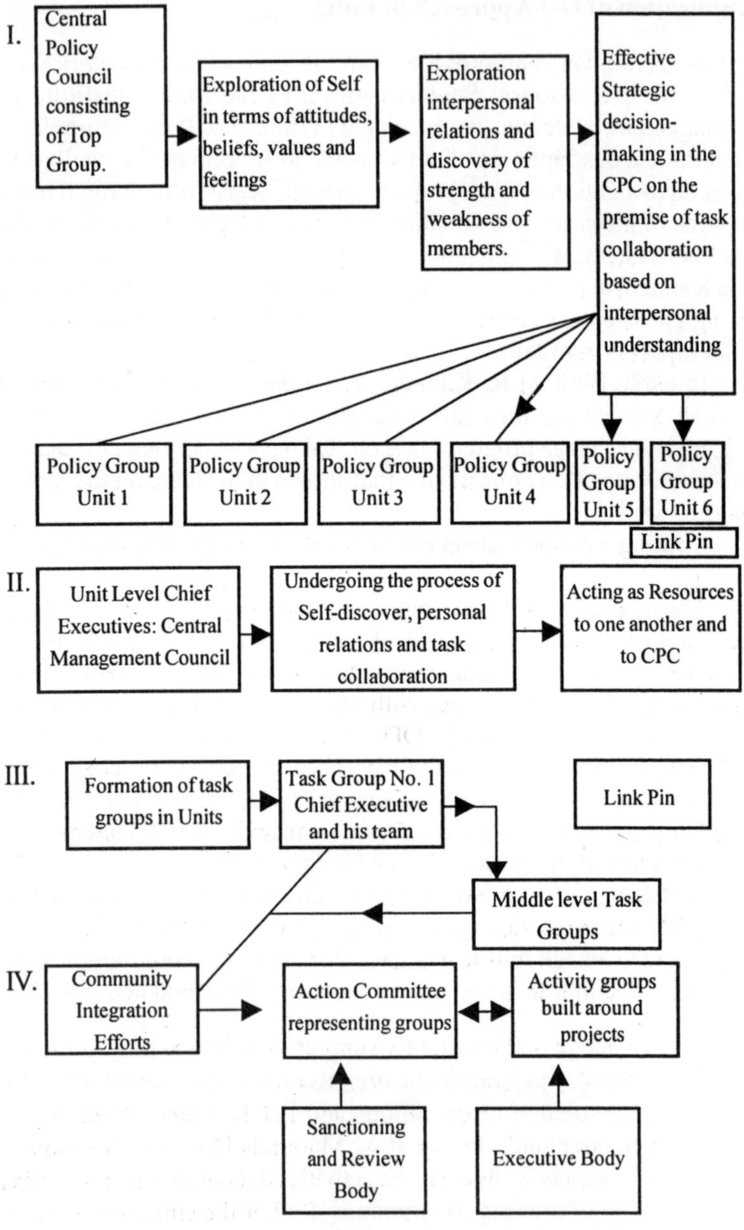

Fig. 1.1: Schematic Model of Kamani Change Programme

Achievement Side: Stabilisation is called for	*Struggle Side: Problems to be overcom*
1. Among colleagues, a culture of authentic communication is established. It is acceptable as a necessary behaviour.	1. Synergy of emotionality an rationality in group working is still a ideal.
2. Between hierarchical levels, openness and trust somewhat established. In some units progress is more than in others.	2. Responsibility and accountability ar still camouflaged by group workin method.
3. Differences—either at the feeling level or at the task level—are explored rather than shoved under the rug.	3. Manipulation at times prevails ov genuine intervention in decisio making.
4. A culture of struggling with the "problem employees" has been fairly firmly established.	4. Forces of dependence and counte dependence still persist at vario levels impeding development norms of inter-dependence.
5. A culture of intrinsic reward is steadily getting accepted.	5. Permissive climate acts as demotivator to some who are strongl extrinsically motivated.
6. More respect for competence is developing.	6. Innovativeness in work activities still lagging while the potenti remains high.
7. In crisis situations, integrative response to leadership has become established.	7. Power struggle and status issue sti bedevil interpersonal relatio blocking optimum task performance
8. Mutuality of interest and emotional acceptance has been established between the Management and the Union Leadership—a key achievement of the OD approach.	8. Gains achieved in interperson understanding get neutralized for lac of system development in good time
9. Decisions concerning human beings are tested against the five principles: (a) Human dignity; (b) No exploitation; (c) Freedom of expression; (d) Management by agreement; and (e) Agreement by persuasion.	9. OD approach at times confused wit "Softy" management and *laissez fair* attitude towards responsibility givin rise to inefficiency and wastefulness
10. Concept of distributive leadership has been gaining acceptance in problem-solving behaviour.	10. The fine balance between tas confrontation and feelin confrontation is still to be establishe
11. Essentials of helping relationship are steadily gaining acceptance at all levels.	11. Too many OD steps introduced at to many places in a short span of tim with limited consulting resourc causing "fade-out" effect and makin re-introduction of measures a mor difficult process
12. A high sense of dedication to the new management philosophy visible in the apex management is constant motivator towards problem-solving behaviour.	

Fig. 1.2: An Interim Balance-Sheet of Kamani OD Project

2. Three top layers of management have been covered by the activities in a planned way. For each group activity, link-pins were provided and almost without fail, the link-pins have been able to generate the initial benign climate that the group needed for productive efforts.
3. The major gains, as reflected in behaviour in work situations are:
   (a) elimination/reduction of inter-personal hostility/apathy;
   (b) greater awareness of the role of and the role pressures on self and the colleagues;
   (c) development of work and behaviour norms in dealing with inter-group issues. The most significant of the achievements was the break-through in resolving a major inter-functional conflict in the iron ore mines;
   (d) significant improvements in three-way communication (vertical down; vertical up; and lateral) among the managerial personnel. Although not totally eliminated, defensive behaviour as reflected in verbal or written communication has abated and correspondingly authentic communication in terms of openness and confrontation has increased;
   (e) an all-round desire to work towards an upward shift of responsibilities on the part of the managerial personnel;
   (f) visible improvements in the empathic role *vis-à-vis* lower level employees. While the legal basis of disciplinary regulations has not changed, in behaviour, some of the key managers have started looking beyond the "legality" issue; and
   (g) functional teamwork, with minimum trappings of formality, has been successfully established.
4. We have found in this case that the variation in the interest, commitment and behaviour in the formal leader of the target system need not necessarily play a significant role in the progress of the change process. In one unit, the top manager who started skeptically became gradually a convert to the OD approach. Technically very sound and administratively decisive and self-assured, this gentleman put his heart and soul, without sacrificing his task orientation, into "helping relationship" with his colleagues. It is our experience that those

among managers who were anxiety-prone, wavering and initially peripheral in their interest in the change programme, slowly and steadily got stimulated through the efforts of this leader.

In another unit, the formal leader was himself wavering and his commitment was visibly limited. In behavioural terms, his habitual behaviour was more in evidence than the new, problem-solving behaviour. He continued to maintain a "kink" in his work-relationship with the colleagues. Despite this distinct ambivalence on the part of the leader, behavioural shift in his subordinates expect in the cases of two, was significant and enduring. As if the "toplessness" of the group had little or no impact on the group, eight months after the OD programme was initiated, collaboration of three members of the top group belonging to operation, engineering and personnel and their subordinates resulted in completion of a project within a record time. The resultant economy was substantial. Yet another instance: before the OD programme, the daily production meeting involving operation, engineering and stores purchase was an exercise in inauthenticity and defensive behaviour. For the past eleven months, these meetings are an informal affair at the pithead and the agreements on the diagnosis of production shortfall, if any, and the action steps to be taken are almost inevitably reached. There are other instances to substantiate the point that despite the different styles of the leaders of the two target systems, the change processes did not turn out to be significantly different.

5. In both the units, the development of a stable collegial leadership has been achieved though partially. But, the dynamics of the evolving process worked out differently in different units. In the first unit, because of the technology involved, the operation wing had established its primacy over the engineering wing. As such, legitimacy of the status of the mining engineers has been behaviourally accepted by the maintenance engineers. On top of that, the leader of the unit, as already mentioned, is a highly competent manager with substantial integrative skills. Thus, it did not become easy to overcome the habit of depending on the high prestige group and take the "back seat" in terms of initiative, drive, risk-taking, in short, innovative behaviour on the part of the

maintenance group. The leader himself gradually realised that he had been to a considerable degree, responsible for fostering a dependent relationship and which, given the state technology, has been functional for the system. But as soon as he realised that the functionality of team-work would depend upon the mutuality of influence process, he took distinctive risks in changing the unilateral influence process through role-modelling, *i.e.*, by effecting change in his own behaviour. It appears that a hierarchically-oriented work group that has its sanction in the characteristics of the technology in use can undergo change should the formal leader take the initial steps in unwinding the process. In this case, the gradual shift has been significantly appropriate as the old technology is going to be superseded by a more mechanised technology as in the second unit.

In the second unit, the formal system was premised on the basis of operation group's legitimacy. But the input of sophisticated augmented operational power to the engineering group. The leader of the target system, whose "loyalty" was more with the operation group, remained vacillating and indecisive, although his "desire" was to see the end of the inter-group conflict. In this case, the initial move came from the formal leaders of the two conflicting groups as soon as they realised that the new technology demanded an "equal status" role for both groups which called for a re-configuration of the systems of group working. The two groups, with the help of process consultants, then worked out the norms of collegial leadership.

6. While it has been our objective in TISCO to help the managerial personnel in organisational diagnosis and action-planning using group-method as a vehicle of change, we have often been struck by (based on one year's observation) stable or quasistable behaviour change at individual level resulting in distinct personal growth type of change. One lady commented to a friend "I don't know what the change programme has done to my husband in his office but I know what it has done to us. Our marriage has been saved." In this particular case, they were alienated from each other and all friendly persuasion in the past ended up in patch-up, no healing. The gentleman, a senior manager, confronted a barrage of work problems with his colleagues during the OD sessions. Conflict often was intense and raw.

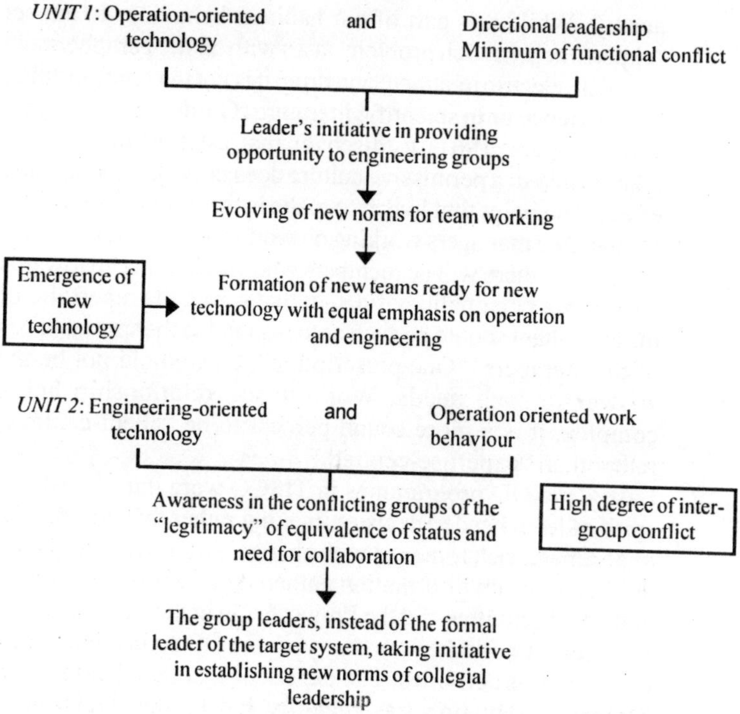

Fig. 1.3: TISCO Model of Changing Norms of Group Working

While working through the issue, led by the Consultant, fellow members entered into an empathic relationship with him. Instead of "prescribing" for him, which is often our habitual behaviour norm, the members gave him "understanding". They struggled to be in his shoes and to a considerable degree succeeded in conveying the message of their struggle. Later on it was found that he took initiative in doing to his wife what his colleagues had done to him earlier. *A rapproachment* became possible and still later on, his work relations with colleagues started improving.

This and similar other instances indicate that the priority problems calls for priority attention. Those who are bedevilled by intra-psychic or inter-personal problems would, in their behaviour, welcome help from colleagues working together in a learning-changing experimentation, which is OD, provided the help is perceived as catering to their "special needs". While it is part of our habitual behaviour to expect "expert" help in such problem cases with all the paraphernalia of couch, electric treatment and drug, it is not uncommon either in experience or in scientific literature (Gordon, 1971; Laing, 1967; Rogers, 1961) to discover that establishing helping relationship in a permissive culture does provide a therapeutic effect. The point that I wish to make is that while for the bulk of changing managers working on work-related behaviour will be in order, there will be members who would proceed towards change *via* personality issues. In that sense, the repertoire of the consultant should be such as to respond to the special needs of the members. "One prescription", OD, would not be the answer to such needs. Work-person relationship being complex, it is a more sound percept to be "client-centred" rather than "expertise-centred."

7. Lastly, the OD programmes in TISCO were introduced in a spirit of level headed decision-making rather than in a huff or as an amateurish romance with change. After over one year's deliberations on information gathered on sensitivity training and allied activities, did the Project begin in the Raw Materials Division. It has taken another year for OD to become a part of the plant's activities. The experience gathered at the Raw Materials Division has recently led to the decision to proliferate OD to the Works. Though time consuming, it seems that for long-range effectiveness, such deliberations are conducive to the system because exploration along with the consultants provides an unique opportunity to build a trust relationship between the client and the consultant, leading to negligible dyo-functional behaviour on either side while the project would be on.

The third major OD project was initiated in the Hindustan Machine Tools Ltd., in June 1970 and since then over 150 senior to middle level managers from all the production units and the Head Offices have been exposed to the change programme. In some locations, as in HMT IV and V, the coverage includes from the top, the Foreman group; in other units it has remained confined to Manager/Deputy Manager level. The plans are that during 1971-72, another 200 managerial personnel would participate in the OD programmes.

As the first major public sector corporation experimenting with OD, the HMT experience may be to particular significance. The first OD project which started with the General Managers and Joint General

Managers, with the active support from the Chairman, paved the way for the crystallisation of the objectives of the OD programmes in HMT. In brief these objectives are:

I. *Collective goals*

(a) Vertical team building;
(b) Horizontal team building;
(c) Staff-line functional integration;
(d) HO-Unit relationship on the basis of openness and mutuality;
(e) Improvement of organisational climate for acceptance of new management techniques, such as value engineering, PERT, performance budgeting, etc., etc.;
(f) Improved inter-personal, intra-group, inter-group and multi-group communication;
(g) Improved mechanisms to manage differences and conflicts.

II. *Individual goals*

(h) Better grasp of one's own responsibility and accountability;
(i) Better utilisation of intrinsic motivational forces;
(j) Competence development;
(k) Better control on one's ownself.

As the goals started evolving during the successive OD thrusts, the strategy adopted by the consultants in matching the goals can be schematically presented here:

Personal style	Working on the road blocks ←	End variables as outlined above: (a) to (k) ←
– Identifying motivational forces – Identifying areas of strength – Identifying areas of inabilities ↓	– Functional – Inter-personal – Inter-group – Multi-units-HO etc.	
Establishing new insights and new behaviours →	Forging new relationships and new norms → Use of GMS, JGMs and Dept. Heads as link pins. →	Developing reoriented action plans and review mechanisms on end variables and use of feedback mechanism.

Fig. 1.4: OD Strategy Adopted in HMT

A Tentative Assessment of HMT Project

In January 1971, after a period of about eight months of the inauguration, the Chairman and his senior colleagues assembled together along with one of the Consultants to review the OD activities. What emerged during the deliberations can be presented in brief:

A. Achievements of the Individual Level

1. *A clear picture of one's own defensive behaviour which is invariably a road-block to work-effectiveness and meaningful relationship.* Gains are indeed differential in that some managers could develop a better insight into their own defensive mechanism than others but overall the depth of awareness became more than what it was before.
2. *Sharper realisation of the areas of competence and inabilities.* Here again, the acknowledgement of the realisation is more open in some cases and more cautious in others.
3. *Awareness of motivation, ideosyncracies, experiences and style of working of others.* This awareness has led to the acceptance of the other persons, although the degree of acceptance is more in some cases than in others.
4. *Breakdown of "stereotypes."* Memory of past history, either in the shape of direct experience or indirect, had in many cases contributed towards the built up of negative images of many managers, causing interferences in interpersonal work-relationship. Coming in closer contact with these persons in an unfreezing climate it became possible to overcome the "stereotype" in some cases, leading to a dramatic improvement in work-relationship.

B. Achievements at the Organisational Level

1. *Given a sense of pride as a member of the HMT organisation and a culture of technical competence, a movement took place from a narrow job predilection towards a broader work concept: expansion of work awareness.*

   The HMT managers, we found, were predominantly task oriented. However, the task orientation had, very often, a narrow focus on the allotted functions or more appropriately upon whatever perception developed about these allotted functions. Thus construed, often responsibility assumed an unitary character leading to conflicts and clashes, in terms of ideas and priorities, with other colleagues. Gradually this unitary concept of work was superseded by a federal concept of work.

2. *There was a movement from dependence/counter-dependence to inter-dependence: Expansion of openness.* As the reality-oriented self-awareness as well as the acceptance of others increased and as a re-orientation towards work took place, caution, diplomacy and competition started getting replaced by concern and care, authenticity and confrontation.
3. *"Pressure" culture gradually yielding to problem-solving culture.* The flux created in the organisation by the economic recession in 1966 and its consequences have established in some of the financially vulnerable units of work culture of high degree of anxiety and "pressure": Management by last minute hurry. Managers placed in key positions having started operating on feedback data on their behaviour have resolutely started moving away from pressure-orientation to problem-solving orientation. Not that the expression of hard feelings was eliminated, but whenever it does occur, exploration becomes possible.
4. *Improvement in inter-personal and inter-group communication.* "Filtering" and distortion have got minimised.
5. *Improved awareness of organisational problems and lessening of scape-goating.* In the past many managers were concerned with "segmented" issues. Now, taking a systemic view of a problem, they could exhibit a more mature understanding of the problem.
6. *Gradual shift from a mechanical concept of the organisation to an organic concept of the organisation.* A more obvious illustration of the shift is the case of a personnel man in a new unit offering to take charge of the stores for a period of six months to relieve the purchase man as his job was critical at that juncture. Under the traditional way of looking of an organisation, this would not be easy even conceivable.
7. *Improved receptivity towards the utilisation of H.O. service/techniques.*

C. Outline for the future

The review meeting also deliberated upon the course of action for the future in the HMT. Some of the agreed upon items are the following:

1. *A master plan for Competence Development.* This will become clear from the following schematic Fig. 1.5:

Task system / Persons	Critical Areas	Less Critical Areas
Competent Managers	Autonomy to be assured and sustained helping feedback necessary.	Plans needed for more effective utilisation of talents.
Less competent Managers	a. Strong supportive action called for. b. At time transfer is indicative. c. Active monitoring mechanism is indicated.	Long/intermediate range planning for the development of the managers.

Fig. 1.5: Strategy for Competence Development

It has been decided that as part of the OD project, a comprehensive inventory of the managerial development needs would be prepared so that appropriate action could be taken on an intermediate range basis.

2. *Need to stabilise the feelings of multiple affiliations and memberships.* While it is widely recognised that supra-attachments have developed among managers beyond the boundaries of self, inter-person, intra-group and inter-group, it is equally necessary to recognise that unless steps are taken to stabilise the spirit of pluralism, habitual behaviour might re-assert itself. This is being achieved in two ways: (a) review sessions of task-related groups of members and (b) continuous interaction of the across-the-function managers constituting a project team and working together on a project evolved by them. Till end December, 1970, there are over fifty project teams working away on short-term concrete projects which are being reviewed by the teams at periodic intervals.
3. *Development of newer varieties of managerial skills.* Three basic areas have been spotted for the time being:

   (a) *Management information system development*: With experience in HMT-V it appears that with a long job cycle time it is necessary for coordinating agencies to develop short-term feedback loop. Such experience-based knowledge will be required to lead to the development of new kinds of information systems.

(b) *Development of new leadership roles*: It is felt that with the evolution of the spirit of team-working a higher level of responsibility is being assumed by the bulk of the managers making it redundant for many senior managers to perform any longer the mediating role among conflicting subordinates. Thus, the new shift towards broader responsibilities in subordinate managers will require a corresponding shift to the old work-role of the integrative managers as well. They will now be called upon to pay increased attention to the management of the interaction between the enterprise and its significant environment and less and less attention to the management of the internal system. Similarly, General Manager of a Unit will be, henceforth, more and more concerned with the management of the interface of the sub-system of which he is the General Manager and its significant environment and less and less with the internal management of the sub-system. A conscious planning of this new role will become an urgent task for the near future.

(c) *Problem of the super-competent managers*: A genuine strength of the HMT system is the high level of task orientation of many managers whose technical skills are commendable. However, since the system is consciously moving towards an open system with emphasis put on the functionally related group working, there is a need for task-oriented managers also to become relationship oriented so that the new forms of management can enlist their support and nurturing.

4. *Development of new motivation for the technology innovators*: It has often been recognised that the growth orientation of the HMT system lies in its ability to move towards products and processes which are more and more knowledge-based. Development of new products and stabilisation of their production technology will thus acquire an essentiality. In the light of this future trend, the personal policies and practices will call for a re-evaluation so that the technology innovators can enjoy a system that will motivate

them towards the challenge rather than inhibit their creative urges. While it is necessary to cater to the extrinsic needs of the innovators just as those of the routine performers, it is quite another matter—calling for skills of sophistication—to develop systems for intrinsic needs to be satisfied.

5. *Creating newer organisational forms in the midst of existing, stable systems*: A new Heavy Press Division has been created within the physical proximity of HMT-V; a new printing press production facility will come into being in the existing premises of HMT-V and a major tractor manufacturing facility will be created at HMT-III. This juxtaposition of existing machine tool manufacturing facilities and the newer, not necessarily related, products often involving newer forms of organisational design, will create the problem inherent in the integration—differentiation processes of complex systems. How much autonomy, for example, will vest in the Managers of the new productive systems so as to enable them to deviate from the systems and norms that are already in existence and are found to be functional for the existing product lines? This and related issues will require to be confronted in near future.
6. *Provision of living links in communication*: Apart from the traumatic experiences of the labour-management de-relations dramatised in the series of incidents that took place in HMT-I and HMT-II in the latter part of 1970, it became quite evident of the sensitized change-prone managers that the communication gaps that existed between different layers of the employees was the widest between the lower echelons of the management and the workers. The analysis also revealed that while the communication between the executive system (that wing of the management that deals with the industrial relation problems) and the representative system (the trade union leadership) was being maintained, although at times in a tenuous form, there existed little or none within the executive system in so far as the base of the communication pyramid was concerned, namely, the workers. Willy nilly, it was believed that the representative system assumed upon itself the role of the communicator with the workers which was substantially correct in theory and practice. But there are many unique properties of internal communication within an executive system (comprising of a manager and his entire

subordinate command) which could neither be relegated to the representative system nor could it be effectively performed by any one other than those who occupy executive roles in the enterprise system. It was felt that this neglected side of the organic system could no longer be allowed to persist and that serious collective effort would require to be devoted in the management of the effective communication system.

7. *The need for proliferating the OD approach to Union-Management relations*: Along with the deliberations on the communication gap, it came to be realised that in the long run the OD thrust could not be legitimized unless its spirit could be enshrined in the union-management relations as well.

   While no concrete proposals could be mooted at this phase, it was felt that the Consultant's assistance would become imperative to convert a distributive bargaining orientation into an integrative orientation without in anyway jeopardizing the identity of the Union or the legitimacy of its representative role. It was felt that the Kamani Engineering experiment (De and Kamani, in preparation) could indeed provide the embryo of an idea that needed to be incubated.

8. *Need to foster development of behavioural norms that could overcome the forces of "cluster" leadership*: It is, we believe, a tribute to the open system approach that has steadily gained acceptance in the HMT system that some of the Managers could bring out into the open the problems associated with clustered leadership within a sub-system. These could be the forces of casteism or of regionlism, or of other subtle variations that are in currency in India today. While there is an intellectual recognition that such forces might stand in the way of the synergy of organisational and individual effectiveness, in behavioural terms, in many an organized situation, its existence is not seriously challenged.

   In the HMT, at least in one unit, the managers could recognise the debilitating effect of such pressures and welcomed the prospect of working through the problem. There is, thus, an awareness of the need that as the work-related issues would be gradually confronted and resolved, tradition-based attitudinal and behavioural stereotypes would demand priority attention.

9. *Fostering a neo-culture in the system whereby the Head Office service functionaries could become the "helpers" and the unit functionaries could assume the role of control.*

While it was realised that such issues as the development of an integrative industrial relations system of the establishment of behavioural norms that would destroy the "corrupt" aspects of clusterism are indeed long-term projects, these are, none-the-less equally significant in terms of priority allocation, precisely because, longer cycle time problems, if delayed, would on the one hand prolong the cycle time and on the other would further complicate the already complex issue. In the same context it was felt that new orientation was called for in the Head-quarters-Field relationship, contrary to what is firmly established in most modern corporations. In tune with the concept of specialised services that the Chairman had already established in the Headquarters, it was felt that the "service" concept of the Headquarters role should be developed along with the "self-control" role of the Units with a high degree of commitment on both sides. What is being conceived of can be presented in the from of a diagram:

SERVICE

TRUST (left) / MISTRUST (right)

I. *HQ-Field Relationship* Provision of ideas by the HQ and rendering of help by HQ on the basis of mutuality and reciprocity.	III. *HQ-Field Relationship* Help rendered by HQ on a formalistic basis of requisition and not mutuality. Service-mistrust dynamics calls for "correct" behaviour rather than functional (i.e. innovative) behaviour.
II. *Field-HQ Relationship* Field resorts to monitoring activities as an aid to effectiveness and the open system that exists provides systematic data to HQ to seek help.	IV. *Field-HQ Relationship* Field resorts to defensive control mechanism with priority on guarded reporting system for HQ control purposes. Help sought would depend upon whether "authority" would be impaired.

CONTROL

Fig. 1.6: Complementarilty in HQ Services—Field Relationship Dynamics

It is not difficult to perceive that Boxes I and II are complementary just as are the boxes III and IV. The goal, as visualised in the HMT system, is to establish norms leading to Boxes I and II. It may, however, be pointed out that we are not specifically referring to the line organisation that runs through the HQ-Field continuum: We are concerned more with the autonomous staff organisations located in the HQ *vis-à-vis* the line set-up that commands the field.

10. *Lastly, there is a need to stabilise the changes ushered in and then further the frontier of change through the creation of a cadre of change agents*: Management of a major system-change demands, in addition to other facilities, a cadre of gate-keepers, not only to informally audit the results of change, but also to generate energies as a "human dynamo" to fight against the relapse to habitual behaviour and to become a sensitive "human radar" to record latent and/or inarticulate issues which, but for timely intervention, could dampen the rate of progress of change. An awareness is developing in the HMT system that while the organisational development unit will continue to spear-head the programme of change, active agents of change will need to be located in each unit so that their role will need to be legitimized in the spirit of helping relationship.

A fourth corporation where, encouraged by the preliminary reports obtained from the HMT system, OD intervention was inducted is the Hindustan Aeronautics Ltd., at its Hyderabad Division. Here the first phase was initiated in December, 1970, primarily on account of the permissive climate gradually built up in the system under the leadership of P.C. Lal, who until recently was the Chairman of the Complex and the direct interest evinced by the General Manager of the Unit, R.M. Nayar. It is indeed too early to even undertake a rudimentary assessment of the effects and we shall not go into any such venture. However, encouraged by the initial responses received, the HAL System is planning to actively try out the OD in other sub-systems of the HAL Complex in May, 1971.

Project that have been cleared for implementation: Encouraged by the results of some of the on-going OD activities, the following enterprises have decided to experiment with the OD approach in near future:

Name	*Location*	*Tentative Initial Steps Planned for*
1. Orient Paper Mills	Brajrajnagar	April, 1971
2. Bokaro Steel	Bokaro	April, 1971
3. Tata Engineering & Locomotive	Jamshedpur	May, 1971
4. State Bank of India	Central Staff Training College, Hyderabad	May, 1971
5. Indian Aluminium	Belur	May, 1971
6. Hindustan Steel	Bhilai	June, 1971
7. Indian Detonators	Hyderabad and Rourkela	August, 1971

Before we move to the next section, we may provide here a highly impressionistic current status of the OD achievements in the three organisations where they are in existence for a period of ten months to thirty-six months. The data for such an assessment have come from a number of sources: (a) author's own observation of behaviour; (b) experiences shared with him on first on second-hand basis; (c) observations made by persons belonging to the organisations but who did not take part in the experiments and; (d) observations of my colleagues who have participated in these projects. Let me add that it

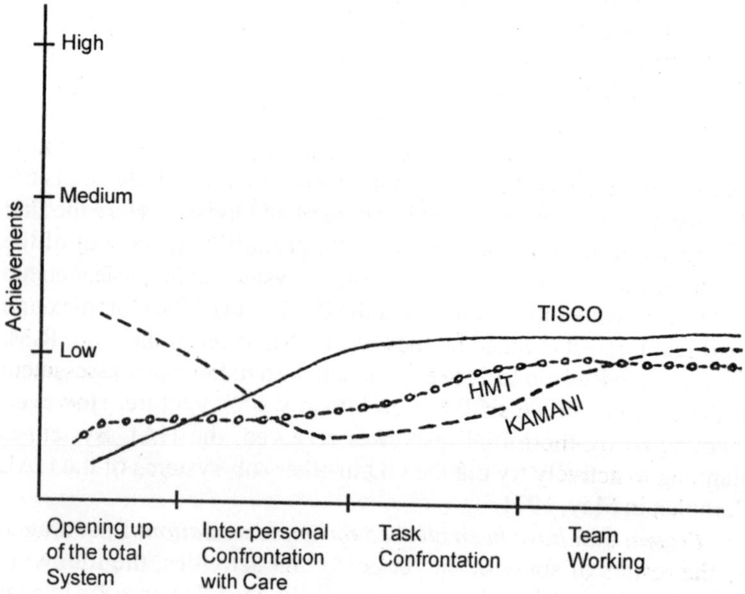

Fig. 1.7: The State of Development of the Three OD Projects

is not our objective to enter into an invidious comparison of the three organisations. We do look upon the tentative evaluation as a process event, as it stands now. In the diagram given below, we have taken only four variables on the horizontal axis in order to present a non-complicated picture. We do not claim that these four are the most significant among the relevant variables:

The differential process events as they appear can at best be looked upon as a compound of (a) of characteristics of the managers manning the system, (b) the characteristics of the technology and the organisational culture, (c) the characteristics of the Counsultants who have worked with the systems as well and (d) the strategies of intervention adopted by them.

Typical Organisational Problems which are Responding to the OD Approach

In this section, we shall, on the basis of our organisational diagnostic studies in India, present some the recurrent problems that stand in the way of organisational excellence. Bulk of the propositions have been culled from another source (De, 1971). It is our experience, though limited by the element of time, that these process events are steadily and encouragingly responding to the OD intervention initiated so far.

1. Attitudes and values of the top leadership of organized activities have a significant flavour of habitual behaviour. Present glories and past successes shelter them against sensitivity and reception of feedback. To a certain degree their responses to a new event or a situation indicates a reactive, as opposed to, a proactive behaviour.
2. The existence of cluster or divisive leadership at the operational level often leads to a stronger sentient group (homogeneous emotional bond) as opposed to a functional task group.
3. Task inter-dependence and inter-penetration remain often unreflected in behaviour. There is often the phenomena of buck-passing and scape-goating. Poor team work is often visible in production meetings and progress review meetings.
4. Individual responsibility and initiative are often hamstrung by impersonal cheeks and balances.
5. Upward communication is often a reflection of the perception of the superior's priorities in likes and dislikes, except when it originates with the representative system.

6. There is a strong tendency to reduce communication in writing with a low priority for face-to-face communication. It is reflective of the degree of existence of interpersonal distrust.
7. Very often there exists a chasm within the executive system communication primarily on account of low commitment to the practice of new skills. Transference of past experiences has a high uncritical acceptance at the executive level.
8. Very often, the existence of communication between the executive system and the representative system becomes an excuse for poor inter-hierarchy communication within the executive system.
9. Usually there exists some form of directive-type conflict resolution mechanism almost with the total exclusion of systems of resolving interpersonal conflict at the affective level.
10. Rather than developing a planned system for the generation and utilisation of knowledge, it is often left to haphazard developments thus leading to disillusionment and apathy at junior level which is often confused with the problem of generation gap.
11. Productivity towards solution-mindedness added to the need for anxiety-reduction often leads to the development of mechanical forms of organisational structures and processes making it expensive in human and other invisible cost to become adaptive to environmental pressures.
12. Existence of a high degree of polarisation in commitment. There are a few over committed members in the system, as if, to compensate for a large cadre of the under-committed. The "get ahead" group very often clings to the *status quo* as it usually works in its favour whereas the "get along" group very often initiates or supports an *anti status quo* movement. Such a conflict often gets reflected in a power struggle over the control of extrinsic rewards.
13. There is often a short time-perspective for the managerial priorities which result in a "double-fault" problem-solving orientation:

    (a) the routine gets precedence over the non-routine; and
    (b) fire-fighting activities get precedence over the fire preventing activities.

14. Existence of low reality orientation in executive behaviour. Self-oriented behaviour usually dominates over the self-aware

behaviour, with the result that realistic self-assessment and owning up of one's own strength as well as inabilities do not get reflected in behaviour.

15. In the matter of comforting with an actively changing environment, with the routine-oriented, security-conscious and anonymity-seeking, propensity show up rather stubbornly in a desire to adapt passively to the environment. At the extremities are the minority who either respond to the challenges of the environment with the instinct of a controlling parent ego-state or with that of a destructive child ego-state. The active adult as a problem-solver does not usually show up as the executive agent.
16. There exists, almost invariably, a consistent human conflict between one's own public self and the concealed self on the one hand and the public self and the blind self on the other with the consequence that the intrapsychic conflict overshadows work-rationality and emotionality often contaminating both.
17. Inculcation of a narrow concept of product sovereignty to the utter neglect of the process development often adds to an optimistic illusion of what the ends are or should be.

These propositions are by no means an exhaustive catalogue nor do they claim to any degree of finality in organisational diagnosis. However, their recurrence in many a financially sound organisation with a consistent record of achievement come to us as a matter of some concern. There is a lurking fear that such a concept of results, however sophistically conceived, will delay the dawn of the consciousness that a viable organisation, given the current state of knowledge in human sciences, is entirely consistent with the concept of a whole man.

While we cannot claim that the OD intervention has brought about such an achievement, yet we indeed are gratified by the yet-to-be complete development process of a number of internal change agents working in their own organisations. Building on their myriad strengths and skills, which were in existence prior to their commitment to OD, they have been able to, in a short period, sharpen their own life goal in a meaningful way. Also they are in a happy position to enter into helping relationship with many others and all those activities are becoming possible not on the basis of given authority or allotted status but on the premise of empathy and personal growth. I shall mention just a few names, not because they are the only ones, but because I have personal knowledge of their developmental history:

1. V.S. Baliga	...	Chief Engineer, Tata Iron Ore Mines, Noamundi
2. Col. S.P. Bhattacharya	...	EME Base Workshop, Agra
3. Y.V. Chavan	...	President, Kamani Employees' Union, Bombay
4. H.R. Kamani	...	Deputy Managing Director, Kamani Group of Organisations, Bombay
5. Navnit Kamani	...	Finance Director, Kamani Group of Organisations, Bombay
6. T.V. Manuskhani	...	General Manager, HMT-IV, Kalamassery
7. S.N. Pandey	...	Chief Personnel & Welfare Officer, Tata Iron Ore Mines, Noamundi
8. Maj. Gen. R.N. Sen	...	Deputy Master General of Ordanances, Army HQ, New Delhi
9. R.N. Sharma	...	Chief Mining Engineer, Tata Collieries, Jamadoba
10. D. Thankappan	...	General Secretary, Kamani Employees Union, Bombay
11. M.S.S. Varadan	...	Chief, OD Unit, HMT HQ, Bangalore

Factors that Inhibit Effective OD Intervention

The foregoing description and analyses may create the impression that the OD interventions have had a smooth, success story in India, wherever applied. It is only fair to mention that there is no basis for such an assessment. Over the past three years our record of failure is no less impressive! Ruminating over these failure cases we may now be able to codify some of the forces that inhibit the progress of OD (De, 1970B).

1. In the first place, an authority-figure of the target system must provide an active support to the change programme. His lack of interest or sluggish support or his inability to comprehend, at least to some measure, what the OD intervention is all about, may indeed become a stumbling block to the experiment.

   The active role, including the struggle he put up with to win over the resistance and allay the anxiety of many a colleague, that H.R. Kamani played over a period of three years, the proactive involvement that R.N. Sharma manifested in his behaviour in TISCO collieries, the overseeing support the sympathy that R.H. Mody and P.T.K. Panicker provided for the Raw Materials Division change programme and the scientific inquisitiveness and active interest in the process change that S.M. Patil showed in the HMT projects are the key to the stabilisation of the OD programmes.

- By the same token, some of our failure experiences show that the initial gains in a productive system in Calcutta region evoking interest and enthusiasm of the participants were lost because the target system centrally controlled by the Headquarters could not secure the support of the Divisional Manager. Two months' efforts were lost.
- In the case of another Calcutta-based international organisation the authority-figure indicated a vague support to the incipient change programme and he himself remained too distant all the while, thereby contributing to the sagging of interest of those inside the organisation who took the initiative.

  It will be seen that we have experienced two categories of support: (a) authority-figures in an active participation as did Hasmukh Kamani, Navnit Kamani, T.V. Mansukhani and R.N. Sharma; and (b) authority-figures in a supportive role as did S.M. Patil, R.H. Mody and R.M. Nayar.

2. Unless the authority-figure has a professional interest in the Consultant and his activities and the relationship assume the nature of a trusting relationship, the change programme would languish.
   - In the case of an international agency the change programme "flopped" primarily because the head of the origanisation had no professional interest in the Consultant although a warm personal relationship existed.
   - In another organisation, attempts at inducting the change programme with the support of a Consultant, received a lukewarm reception because of, among other reasons, the lack of any trusting relationship between the principal client and the Consultant. The Consultant then went into a state of hibernation in so far as this project was concerned. And instead he concerned himself with some other projects with encouraging results which came to the notice of the client. At this stage, that is a period of one year after the abortive first try, the client approached the Consultant for a series of seminars on aspects of organisational diagnosis. These series of interactions slowly and steadily built up a bond of confidence between the two that has recently consummated into an OD project.

3. Should the authority-figure be extrinsically motivated to needle with a change programme and the intrinsic motivation remains low, the change programme is likely to fail.
   - In a public sector corporation the chief of a target system enlisted the task team. While the OD project was launched it became evident that the chief was primarily motivated by a desire to "overcome" the opposition to his authority for the fulfilment of which objective he did not receive enough "support" from the Consultants. This was the "Waterloo" of the OD venture.
   - In an international organisation the situational contingencies favoured an OD thrust. The second and the third level of hierarchy, after the initial fear of the unknown was overcome provided enthusiastic support to the OD efforts. There was distinct evidence of a "thaw" in the relations between the fighting executives of an important operating department. The "acting" Chief Executive duly "noted" the progress and even reported it to the Consultant with the feeling of appreciation.

     However, after a period of six months the Chief Executive became "cool" to the project. On enquiry he frankly confided that the "patron" in the parent company had decided to defter a decision on his "acting" status. So, the OD must wait!
4. Should the "contact person" (*i.e.* one who brings in the Consultant) be one who does not enjoy enough prestige in the system nor does he enjoy the confidence of the authority-figure, the OD efforts are not likely to succeed in the enterprise.
   - In a public sector plant the OD efforts did not take roots primarily because the contact persons was not effective with the top brass. So the "guineapings" were the "small shots" whose frustration was deep after each shot of OD intervention. The project was dead-locked. At this juncture a high status executive came in contact with the Consultant. Now onwards, the Consultant was found professionally competent and attitude-wise "committed" and the OD efforts henceforth, started receiving "priority".
5. The OD type change programme, if confused with the usual training activities, will lose its effectiveness. The distinction

between the two should be conceptually clear from the very start.

- In a public sector service organisation the Training Manager organized a series of sensitivity training programmes while the inarticulate premise in his mind was that he had embarked upon an organisational change programme. His consternation was great when he had discovered that his brand of OD was what the state of sensitivity training was in early 1950s.
- In recent months, because of certain publicity that some of the OD projects had received, a steady flow of request poured in asking for a series of "OD lectures" in these enterprises for the benefit of the "young executives". It requires a super-diplomatic effort to convey the message that the "OD pill", in terms of efficacy, does not behave exactly in the same manner as the "birth control pill".

6. OD efforts are most likely to "fail" should the interventions be aimed at the lower echelon of the management while the inter-dependent and inter-acting higher echelon is plagued by forces of mistrust, competition and authoritarianism.
   - In a medium sized enterprise the Chairman and his three functional colleagues have been merely maintaining a semblance of unity while their assistants were brought together by the "lion-hearted" Training Manager to an exposure to OD. With their respective loyalties remaining intact, these assistants only succeeded in the articulation of the conflict which existed at the top, of which they were only too conscious. The bosses could not be confronted with the issue because they were indeed busy with work!
   - In another organisation, the top management having found a "loyal" Purchase Manager to look after certain important aspects of financial management in disregard of the sentiments and views of the legitimate functionary, it became extremely difficult to establish a task group out of these managers because a culture of mistrust, personal loyalty and secrecy had been in existence for a long while which was beyond the capability of this group to deal with.

7. Whatever be the immediate motivation for invitation to an OD intervention, unless the top management is mentally prepared to risk, at some point, a confrontation with its own operant values so as to cause a redistribution of power of the decision-making processes keeping in tune with the dictates of the changing circumstances, the OD thrust will sooner or later be blunted.
   - In the Kamani system the willingness and the ability of the top management to constantly examine the need for a shift in the power base can be pin-pointed as a major factor for the OD to become a living phenomenon in the system.
   - In an industrial organisation the initial thrust of the OD intervention having had some measure of success (improvement of inter-group working, authentic communication and resolution of some long-standing interpersonal conflit), attempts were made to extend the frontier of the project, by organizing a field-Headquarter confrontation on the control dimension of the management. The Chief Executive, initially keen on improving the work relations between the units, became most reluctant to agree on the second phase of the project. He pleaded business commitments and a delay of the project. Nothing has since been heard on the proposed second phase.
8. Lastly, unrealistic expectations on the part of the largest system, in terms of spectacular gains within a short space of time, are likely to cause impatience with the OD progress and then a gradual slackening off of enthusiasm.

   Major system-change programme which encompasses a re-evaluation of attitudes and values as reflected in behaviour and the recasting of work-systems and process is indeed a long-term project, apart from the basic premise that planned change is a continuing process. Whether it is Glacier Metal or Horwood Manufacturing, or Alcan, or TRW System, the real pay-off lies in long-term effects of the change efforts. While it is desirable that a continuous monitoring of effects—even short-term—should be undertaken as an integral of the OD project, a "trader approach" to the OD intervention is not the most functional.

Current Strategy for the OD Movement

Having acquired some experience, we are now seeking to develop a module for the OD dispersion in organized activities. Thies is not to suggest that a universal capsule is under preparation. We want to retain a good measure of flexibility and yet some degree of uniformity of approach is conceivable given the state of our experience. Some elements of our approach can be spelled out here:

1. Development of an OD model for learning for some of the key executive development programmes organized by the IIMC. The Behavioural Sciences Group offer a few key programes, on a repeat basis, for a variety of organisations: Some of these programmes are (a) the Managerial Leadership and Conflict Resolution, (b) Organisational Design, (c) New Perspectives in Industrial Relations and (d) Leadership Development for Trade Union Activists.

   A major input in these programmes is the element of experiential learning from behavioural manifestations both for the faculty and the participants as a collective entity. The idea is that we should not only "preach" the message but should devise the programme in such a way that the "message" acquires "meaning" through the process of model and authentic behaviour. These programmes almost invariably evoke a genuine interest in some of the participants who wish to pursue.
2. The next stage is that whenever an interest is shown and initiative is taken by a prospective client, we do plan a one-day or even a half-a-day seminar for the top leaders of the target system, presenting concepts and cases, in order to clarify the ideas about OD. Here also we seek to retain the flavour of OD in a "here and now" learning focus by blending process-product orientation in such a manner that the intellectual curiousity is met but the "threat" of an unfreezing process is minimised.

   One element of this seminar is to lead the participants to an open-system diagnosis of the organisational problems, as distinct from the issues, with process help available from the Consultants so that there is a "mini-experience" of OD in addition to cognitive exposure.
3. Should the response to the exploratory seminar be encouraging, we plan for a series of dialogues between the client and the

Consultant so that the dangers and pitfalls are openly explored and understood. Both parties avail of these opportunities to reach out for mutual understanding in terms of attitudes, values and priorities. Efforts are made to reach a psychological contract during this phase. The doubts of the skeptics will have to be confronted during this phase.

Priorities in our Approach to OD Thrust

The decade of the seventies have shifted our emphasis on the priorities for the OD work. While it is undeniable that all sectors of the organized activities in India deserve to be planned for the synergy effect of efficiency and humanness, because of the limitation of resources and capabilities, we are in the midst of a reappraisal of our OD strategy. To the extent that our ideas have crystallized, they may be shared here:

1. A need to shift our emphasis on the "key impact groups" for the national development.
   (a) A most crucial sector seems to be the top civil servants in the States and the Centre who are concerned with the policy level decisions and higher-level integrative role. This cadre includes the bureaucrats as well as the technocrats. Recently, Indira Gandhi exhorted the Central Government Secretaries to work on the plans and programmes of development as a collective entity rather than as a horde of functionaries, each with his own perceptions and priorities. This is no mere homily, should we consider the reality that in 1970-71 there was a short fall of Rs. 160 crores in development expenditure due to the differences among ministries (Nayar, 1971). We believe that the recognition of the problem and its public expression at a high national forum is the fist problem-solving movement towards resolution. However, for the pronouncement to be operative, certain action-steps are indicated which the OD intervention can fulfil.
   (b) Simultaneously, it will be a necessary concomitant to expose the younger set of civil servants to the "experience" of problem-solving orientation as distinct from the shackle of the habitual behaviour. This group, though bound by the limits set by the higher echelon, continues to enjoy a measure of autonomy in the use of

the executive power. Already a collaborative effort is afoot between us and the Indian Institute of Public Administration to launch such a programme of OD.

(c) It is necessary, we believe, to concentrate our energies on such vital industrial sectors as steel, heavy engineering, machine tools, heavy chemicals, etc. Here too, we would prefer to converge upon a few enterprises before we move on to others. The Kamani experience shows that hurry does not pay and that the stabilisation-efforts are move critical than the initiation-efforts.

(d) Using our already popular mechanism of the programme for the Trade Union Activists, we would prefer to carry the OD intervention to the virgin field of trade union effectiveness.

(e) We would like to help the small scale industry sector, particularly where concentration of such efforts is available, like an industrial estate.

(f) We would also progressively move on to the field of education, particularly the secondary education. Already an OD project on in a higher secondary school in Bombay. Should we find the results encouraging we would like to increase our effort in this areas of national development.

2. Another major priority venture would be to devote attention to the creation of a cadre of internal change agents throughout the vital sectors of the organized activities. We have listed out about a dozen names earlier and a potential dozen is at hand. But for the gigantic efforts that are needed, this number is most inadequate.

   We have, keeping the future demand in view, devised a three-phase programme spread over a period of one year for the development of internal OD specialists. We visualise that during the 1970s India would require at least 150 such specialists and this is an effort that demands inter-institutional collaboration.

This is indeed an ambitious project but the encouragement for such a project has come from our limited experimentation within the Behavioural Sciences Group. This group in the IIMC is highly autonomous within the Institute system and there is an equal amount of freedom for the faculty members within the group. The group operates on the basis of collectively evolved and shared norms with no sanctioning authority behind them other than the moral-normative orientation that Etzioni speaks about (Etzioni, 1964). Faculty members are free to develop their own interests and specialisations but because of the permissive climate that operates with almost a total absence of organisational hierarchy, all members of the group except for one have got themselves immersed in OD work. The development of such a preference is, by itself, an OD project.

To provide an illustration: Dharni P. Sinha a dedicated student of Anthropology with wide field experiences in India, the U.S.A. and New Guinea, joined the group in 1968. So did Reginald C. Mascarenhas whose background is Political Science and the interests are in the area of autonomy and control as political processes. Both of them have moved into the field of OD, initially as learner in a climate of colleagueship. In a period of two years, through a process of rigorous learning experience with colleagues support, both of them have moved into leadership role on OD initiative, one in TISCO project and the other in HMT project.

We believe that the air of freedom along with the experience of a group culture of openness in giving and receiving feedback, confrontation on emotional and task plane and making the practice of "helping relationship" (Rogers, 1961) a living reality have all converged to make the group an OD team which is constantly seeking to learn and grow.

In addition to mutual help and support in individual efforts of research and consultancy, a major aid to our OD effort is the collective "clinicing" culture that the has been established in the group.

Project	*Co-ordinating Consultant(s)*		*Clinicing Council*
Kamanis	Suresh Srivastva	Nitish R. De.	Functions:
TISCO	Dharni P. Sinha	Dilip Q. Lahiri	1. Development of OD strategy
HMT	Reggie C. Mascarenhas	Nitish R. De.	2. Sharing of Data
TELCO	Mrityunjay B. Athreya	Nitish R. De	3. Review of Consultants' role
Bokaro Steel	Mritunjay B. Athreya	Kamini Adhikari	4. Review of Progress/Failure
HAL	Nitish R. De	Krishna Swaminathan	5. Programmes of Development for Faculty
INDAL	Nitish R. De	Bhupendra K. Shrivastava	6. Allocation/Reallocation of Human Resources.
HSL Bhilai	Nitish R. De	Mrityunjay B. Athreya	

In sum, we believe that the OD strategy portends well for the future of human systems. The results, though encouraging, are still confined to a few cases of industrial organisations. Its scope seems to be far and wide. This also appears to be the challenge for the coming decades.

It is our experience that the excitement of participation in the amoving drama of change and renewal, as OD is, is itself a tonic for our self-renewal and self-actualisation. We believe that such an action programme is one sure way to negate the effects of anomie in the world of academia.

REFERENCES

1. De. Nitis R. (1970A): "Person to Reperson Non-person," Magazine Section, *The Sunday Statesman*, May 24, Clacutta.
2. De. Nitish R. (1970B): "The Impact of Behavioural Sciences on. Administraion: From the Conception of Charge to the Reality of Changing," (mimeo), *Asian Institute of Educational Planning and Administration*, New Delhi.
3. De. Nitish R. (1971): "The Rle of Process Consulation in Change Programmes," (mimeo), *Indian Institute of Management*, Calcutta.
4. De. Nitish R. and Kamani, H.R.; "*Conflict and Confrontation: An Approach Towards Synergistic Organisation*," in preparation.
5. Etzioni, A. (1964): "*Modern Organisations*, New Jersey, Prentice Hall.
6. Gordon, James S. (1971): "R.D. Laing: In Search of a New Psychiatry," *The Atlantic*, January.
7. Kamani, P.R. (1971): "*The Birth of a New Management Philosophy*," Indian Institute of Management, Calcutta.
8. Laing, R.D. (1967): "The Politics of Experience," New York, Ballantine Books.
9. Nayar, Kuldip (1971): "Collective Responsibilities of Secretaries," *The Statesman*, March 24, Calcutta.
10. Rogers, Carl R. (1961): "*On Becoming a Person*," Boston, Houghton-Miffin.

2

Behavioural Science's Contribution Towards Developing Effective Trainers*

C.K. Prahalad

In the last two decades, developments in the areas of quantitative methods and behavioural sciences have revolutionized management research, education and to an extent, practice. While the quantitative disciplines provided tools for gaining an in depth understanding of the complex business systems and a certain facility to manipulate them at a conceptual level, the behavioural sciences have greatly increased our understanding of man, his role in the business system and his contribution to its effectiveness. The former has increased the "rationality content" of decisions and the later managements' ability to implement them. Both these disciplines are contributing to several spheres of action and problems in management. Behavioural science, for example has been active in the area of education and training as instruments for improving management practice.

This chapter is intended to present briefly the contribution of behavioural sciences to the training function and more specifically to the development of effective trainers.

Scope of Training

When we talk about training, we seem to intuitively restrict the scope of the activity to management training. In the last few years, with the increasing emphasis on human relations training, the scope is further restricted to behaviourally oriented programmes. At times, one talks

* First published in IJTD in 1971.

of apprentice training or front thing apart. This is an artificial limitation of the scope of training. Fig. 2.1 represents the scope of training in an organisation in the form of a grid.

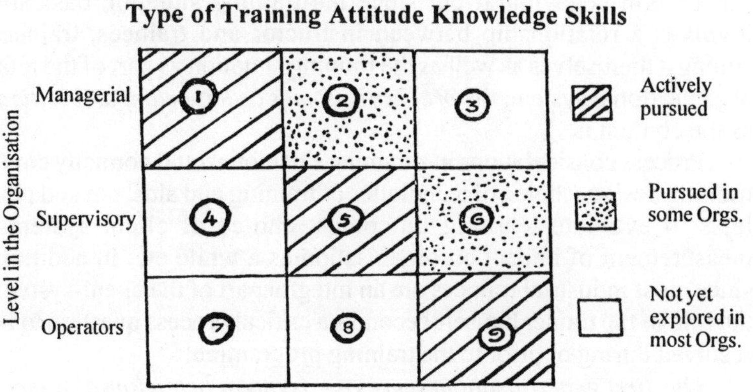

Fig. 2.1: The Training Grid

The concentration of most training effort has been confined to behaviourally oriented, small group training for managerial staff (box 1), techniques or tools oriented programmes for supervisory personnel (box 5) and skill training for operators and other shop personnel. In many organisations, training at the workmen level is considered distinct from the other two levels. For our purpose, we shall consider the scope of training to include the entire grid.

Content/Process Dilemma

The contribution of behavioural sciences in managerial training (Box 1) is apparent for two reasons. Firstly, the training content itself is behaviourally oriented-leadership styles, conflict management, interpersonal effectiveness and so on. Secondly, most of the trainers for these programmes either drawn from outside the organisation or from within, are behavioural Scientists or those familiar with it. The same situation would exist if we considered boxes (4) and (7).

But when we consider training in statistical quality control: Operations research, Fortran programming, skills at setting a machine or in using inspection, equipment, the content is not behaviourally oriented.

The content is distinctly different from what it is attitude training. But all training involves two aspects (a) the content, what is taught and (b) the process—how it is taught. The learning outcome desired can be non-behavioural but since the training situation basically involves a relationship between instructor and trainees, trainees amongst themselves as well as the training situation as part of the total organisational system, the *process becomes as important and critical* as the content is.

Process considerations in a training situation would normally cover training design, choice of techniques of training and aids, pre and post tests to evaluate learning outcomes, choice of client systems, measurement of impact on organisation as a while etc. In addition, since most industrial trainees are an integral part of the client-system, the role of the trainer himself becomes a critical process question to be resolved during or prior to the training programme.

Our first generalisation, therefore, is that a behavioural science understanding is necessary and critical irrespective of the level or type of training attempted.

Purpose of Training

Training in an organisation can be undertaken with three basic objectives—*viz.*

(a) "Routine" training like induction, company and product information training etc. The objective here is one of transfer of information.

(b) "Problem solving" training which is based on problems that the organisation faces—Problem areas like poor quality, high inventories, bad deliveries etc. might be solved by systematic training of staff at different levels in the organisation in SQC, inventory control concepts and computrised production planning respectively. This involves active identification of problem areas, developing an integrated course of action for its resolution, training being a part. For example, the quality control problem might require machine replacement; use of SQC charts and sampling plans, revision of specifications, change of tool profiles etc. Training in SQC principles becomes just one of the series of actions necessary.

(c) Training for "Organisational Effectiveness" involves a complete integration of training with other activities of the organisation and a deliberate use of training and its related functions to seek out organisational problems, develop organisational solutions and use training as an instrument to implement them. While problem solving approach treats problems on an *adhoc* basis, the organisational effectiveness approach is based on clearly defined organisational objectives, actual performance, short falls and is a more inclusive concept and a long-term activity.

Training is moving away from the "routine training approach" to problem solving approach. This implies that in addition to a process understanding of training, an understanding of the process of problem solving and its integration with other activities is necessary. The actual potential of training can be realised only if a problem solving if not an organisational effectiveness approach is taken.

Behavioural scientists have made available a vast amount of empirical data and conceptual understanding of the process of planned and deliberate innovation and problem solving and methods of managing and improving organisational systems.

Our second generalisation therefore is that for training function to be effective, a behavioural science understanding of planned and deliberate innovation for problem solving and increasing effectiveness of organisations is essential.

Role of the Trainer

If our concept of training is one that looks at training as an aid to increasing organisational effectiveness, inevitably, the primary function of training becomes one of the introducing change in the organisation and that of the trainer, a change agent.

Trainer as a change agent has to resolve for himself several issues. Some of these pressing problems are:

(*i*) *Perception of Roles in the Organisation*

Change agents play a variety of roles—researchers, consultants, teachers, line managers and counsellors. They have to play all these roles selectively and shift from one to another. This calls for a certain degree of clarity of roles; an ability to shift roles, an understanding of its implications to themselves as well as their client systems. This becomes all the more necessary if the change agent is part of the client system as all industrial trainers are. It is also critical that the client system which is the organisation perceives his role just as clearly. There is a great need for role definition for himself as well as an understanding of it by the client system.

(*ii*) *Goals in a Changing System*

The change agent, who is part of a changing dynamic system must at once be a part of change as well as influence and direct it towards organisational goals. This calls for an ability to differentiate personal goals from organisational goals; an ability to define it and shift emphasis as one goes along.

(*iii*) *Models for Change*

The trainer needs to conceptualise the process of change for the client system and selectively use interventions based on the model. This involves integrating several instruments of change—Procedural, cultural, and organisational. He has to also outline for himself and the organisation the method for implementing these.

(*iv*) *Credibility and Legitimacy*

The trainer can give credibility for his role with respect to the client system as well as legitimacy in the organisation only if he is able to demonstrate his own ability for renewal and change. Influence as a change agent, in its absence is minimal if not dysfunctional. Schematically, his problem can be illustrated as in Fig. 2.2.

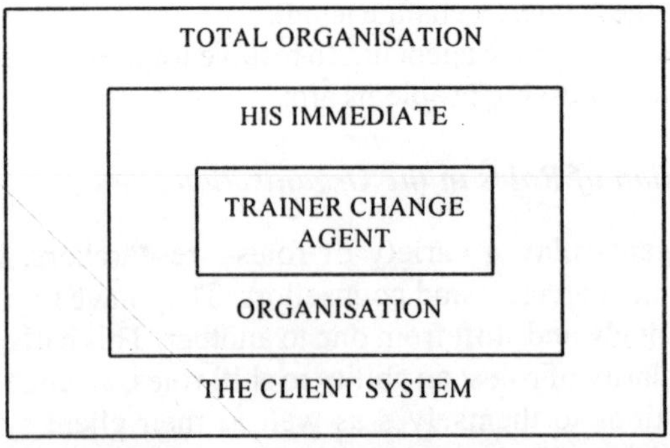

Fig. 2.2: Schematic of Trainers Role in the Organisation

A Trainer should be able to demonstrate his own ability to change as well as that of his immediate organisation, say the training department before he influence the client system. This calls for a high level of understanding of Self, ones motivations, and authentic relationships with others.

These call for a very high degree of self-awareness, acquisition of skills of change agent. *Our third generation therefore is that behavioural science background self-awareness and skills in develop adequate self-awareness and skills in introducing change in organisations.*

Implicit in our discussion so far is the underlying theme that as training includes all levels and types and since it is one of the key instruments in increasing organisational effectiveness, the effectiveness of a trainer is to be measured not on a programme but on the basis of long term changes in organisation effectiveness, level of team work and oneness of purpose. Evaluation in these terms, implies extensive use of behavioural Sciences.

Our fourth generalisation therefore is that behavioural science background is necessary for evaluation of trainer effectiveness.

Now to some experiences with trainers in India.

II

These observations are based primarily on my exposure as faculty member to approximately 50 trainers in Mitra (Management Institute for Training and Research in Asia) workshops for trainers conducted over the last 3 years and my contracts with fellow trainers over time.

Behavioural Science for Trainers

Trainers, as we all know, are a very heterogenous lot and as a rule since the training function is new, most of the trainers have had no formal background in behavioural sciences. The need for a sound behavioural science undertaking for becoming effective as a trainer has been emphasized earlier. As such the critical need today is to develop a "Behavioural Sciences for Trainers" package covering the essential aspect of the advances in the area. This, I see as the need of the hour. In fact MITRA is working on a programme which will provide trainers who have had no formal behavioural Science training an adequate insight and orientation.

Perception of Role

Most trainers perceived their role in a way that restricts the scope of their work. Often, the role is defined in terms of conducting or arranging for a series of programmes. This includes a larger concept of training as a problem solving or an organisational development activity. In other words, there seems to be an inclination to shy away from the main stream of organisational activity and isolate oneself. As a consequence, the organisation also looks at training as a function with a limited scope. In fact this is vicious circle. In the last ISTD-MITRA programme for trainers conducted in Silversands, Mahabalipuram, the trainers were given a MITRA exercise called "Exercise Future."

These attempts to evaluate changes likely to occur, as perceived by the trainees, in seven areas: (i) educational needs, (ii) reward structure, (iii) interpersonal ability, (iv) computer effects, (v) environment (vi) organisational structure and (vii) organisational objectives and their perceived control over them. These areas can be grouped as "Individual's Concerns" (i), (ii) and (iii) and the rest "Organisational Concerns." We found that the trainees perceived substantial changes in all the seven areas but felt that they could control to an extent the changes that concern them as individuals but have no control at all on changes in the organisation. This is so contrary to our concept of a trainer and his role as a change agent in the organisation.

Approach to training

Yet another major problem area seems to be the conflict in roles experienced by a trainer in a training programme. In short, we have found that the trainer finds, it difficult to play the role of a trainee in a learning situation, say in a trainer workshop. In fact a major problem in such situations is to effectively deal with perceived status incogruence by this trainees. There is tendency for developing emotional barriers to learning. This leads to a curious situation where trainers are not wholly committed to training themselves.

Concern with Techniques

Several trainers seem to be preoccupied with developing an ability with the mechanics of new training techniques and not concerned with its implications or in acquiring an adequate background, to use it—

behavioural and other. Most trainees programmes also emphasise only the mechanics of training techniques rather than provide insights.

Reluctance to "Use Oneself"

Most trainers do not devote attention to the fact that they are by themselves a resource in a training situation and as such must learn how to "use themselves". They perceive themselves not as an integral part of the learning experience but as a "detached outsider" watching the participants acquire the attitudes or skills. This is both an unrealistic and dysfunctional approach. Most trainees learn by observing the trainer and he normally "role-models" for the trainee. If the trainees perceive his detachment as non-involvement or disinterestedness, the consequences could be damaging.

Summing up as trainers we have to be concerned with three aspects to become effective *viz.*

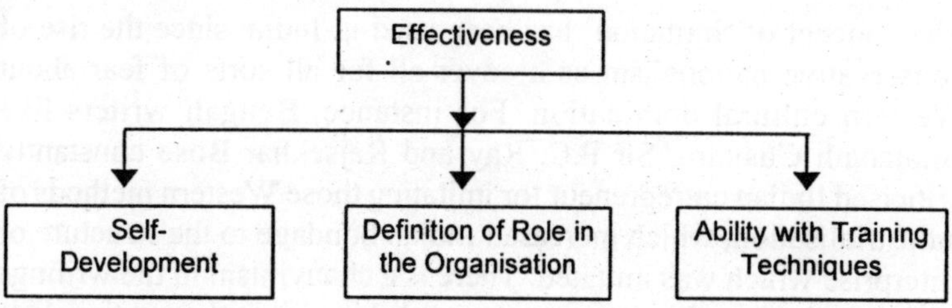

One would not be far off the mark if he said that our preoccupation so far has been with training techniques *per se* and not the other two. Behavioural Sciences once again can help us develop self-insight as well as define our role in the organisation resulting in better use of training techniques.

Our fifth generalisation, is therefore that behavioural science education and development of skills in this area is a prerequisite for trainer effectiveness as defined above.

3

Imitation Styles in Indian Management*

Barun De

The Critique of Imitation: A Counter Dependent Reaction to Colonial Dependence

The concept of 'imitation' has been used in India, since the rise of conservative nationalism as a cover-all for all sorts of fear about Western cultural domination. For instance, Bengali writers like Bholanath Chandra, Sir P.C. Ray and Rajsekhar Bose constantly criticised Indian entrepreneur for imitating those Western methods of industrialisation, which increased Indian bondage to the structure of enterprise which was imitated. There is a chauvinism in the writings of these people—despite their outstanding merit and as nationalists and anti-imperialists—which relates to their essentially narrow view of the markets in which they expected Bengali enterprise to operate. Bholanath Chandra, was a 19th century journalist, who wanted Indians to prosper, and one day become independent and dominate in the economic scene. Acharya Prafulla Chandra Ray was a teacher of Chemistry and entrepreneur who wanted his students to get jobs in which they could apply their knowledge. He diagnosed this joblessness as being due to the constricting effect of not only British imperial economic structure, (implicit in the peculiar form of cartalisation known as the managing agency system), but also due to the economic enterprise of non-Bengali merchants, who by their competitive merits were able to dominate the Bengali economic scene. Rajsekhar Bose, another chemist, and far more humorous follower in Ray's footsteps was more 'modernised' in so far that he focused on the endogenous faults of the

* First published in IJTD in 1973.

Bengalis and their reasons for non-competitiveness with other Indians. But the sum total of the charges, for instance that these three people, who spanned one and a half century between the birth of Bholanath and death of Rajsekhar—which is the one and a half centuries, during which attempts were made for industrialisation of India under the aegis of British rules—their message; be yourselves—do not ape the conquerors—strike out your own paths. This is the content of much of the present charges that the controllers of enterprise in India today are imitators. The charge is that these controllers instead of being themselves ape foreign methods, technology and cultural style in business.

Before we take up the more fundamental question whether they do ape, or whether they creatively adapt, let us look at the historical content of the charge. It represents the non-rational part of a national response to colonial exploitation.

What was happening in the one and the half centuries was that Britain was interested in the development of India only to the extent that the latter could produce a raw material base for "the workshop of the world". Any develoment of finished products, which did not compete with the metropolitan industrial sector in Britain was considered healthy, since it increased colonial complementarities for the world market of the British Empire. But in development of finished products, or even some processed raw materials, which did compete with production in the white colonies of the Empire, or Britain itself, was considered to be unhealthy, since it struck at the basic reason for British colonialism, *i.e.* the diffusion of prosperity among the middle classes and working classes of British, whom we may term the "palace guard" and "the palace slaves" of the imperial court. Metropolitan colonialism's policy premise had a dialectical consequence: it created among its colonial beneficiaries the urge for emulation and competition. India merchants who had started out as "compradors", *i.e.* dependent on the metropolitan producer, soon felt that they could multiply their profits, by entering into competitive production themselves. When they showed signs of success, such as Dwarkanath Tagore in his Assam steamship, or Raniganj coal ventures in the 1830s or 1840s, or J.N. Tata in his cotton-carrying steamship enterprise in the 1890s or in his attempt to build up an iron and steel industry at Bhilai, or people such as Jytorindranath Tagore or V. Chidambaram Pillai, whose memories was recently referred to by Mrs. Gandhi at a memorial meeting in Tuticorin, then British cartelised interests moved in to scotch their comparative advantages. This they did by radical and temporary lowering of costs or by pooling of resources to limit capital supply to the Indian competitors. In this situation the British colonial government extended its support to the mercantile interests of its own race, instead of being impartial (as the State was expected to be in a period when *laissez faire* dominated Indian national economic ideology).

It was in the context of this economic process that Indian writers carried on a two-pronged demand Swadeshi. The first prong of this ideology was economic: develop indigenous industrialisation and deny yourselves the benefits of foreign production, even if it is more sophisticated. The second prong was social: in pursuance of this denial, do not emulate the objects of your boycott—try to be yourselves. The second prong led directly to the call to eschew aping. The Swadeshi ideologist did not only talk of the second prong. This programme was more total in its social and economic dimensions. When today the charge is made that the controllers of the Indian enterprise ape the West, then it is often made without reference to the first prong to which I have referred, and when this is done the charge, lacking totality, also lacks content. While the Bengali managerial ideology has implicitly tended to follow the premises of P.C. Ray and Rajsekhar Bose, the managerial ideology of western and southern India has developed on different lines.

There, first the Parsees, then the Jains of Gujarat, latterly the Chettiars in Tamiland, and Maratha families, such as the Kirloskars have tended to act more on the first than the second prong. In their industrial, though still comprador heyday in the mid-19th century, the Parsees were clearly the imitators of British enterprise: in a period of entrepreneurial consolidation during the 20th century, the Gujarati magnate of Ahmedabad or Baroda or Bulsar has clearly drawn on a cultural style and managerial ideas, derived from MIT, Harvard, the Wharton School in Pennsylvania and the Tavistock Institute in London; and of late the leading Chettiar families have tended to get their younger generation educated in U.S. entrepreneurial methods for their improvement. Whether these methods have led to the improvement of Indian industry in general, or only to their own personal wealth is a question that I do not propose to take up just now. But, the apparent fact is that their cultural styles appear to be more successful than those of the more petty-bourgeois chauvinism of Bengalis—measured, at least in terms of productivity, annual rate of increase of profits, and entrepreneurial stability. This may be one reason why the charge of aping is heard more in Calcutta than in Ahmedabad, where the imitation of Western ideas has become merged and internalised with the Gujarati entrepreneurial style.

I wish to put before you two questions. Is cultural imitation necessarily wrong, if it leads to success and efficiency; is the charge that it is wrong really not a function of resentment against those who seem to be successful because they imitate? Tentatively, for the purposes of discussion at least I would like to take the position, that the entire criticism of aping is based on the psychological feeling of deprivation from the cake of economic profits.

The Purpose and Content of Creative Imitation

Actually, I have raised a red herring in order to show what some people may interpret our general question to mean and why I think they are wrong. All aping is imitation, but all imitation is not aping. Social and economic history is replete with examples of creative imitation. The Anglo-Saxon subjects of Norman Conquest creatively imitated French values: English culture in the 15th and 16th centuries benefited from contact with the Indian renaissance, not only culturally but also economically in terms of accounting practices, and the very chauvinist saying, which was common in early 20th century Bengal that

> "an Englishman Italianate is a devil incarnate a Bengali Anglicised is a devil maximised"

is not historically correct even though Anglicised Bengali gentlemen may perceptually appear to be like devils maximised, when they speak with clipped accents (sporting ties and side whiskers) to their petty-bourgeois clerical staff!

Nearer our times, the examples of the U.S.A. and Japan creatively imitating Britain and Germany in the 19th century, are too well known for elaboration. The economic historian Alexandar Gerschenkron has placed this problem in the much broader framework of latecomers trying to catch up and outpace their earlier rivals in economic development. Creative imitation is one of the cultural phenomena through which all late comers have to go, when they race to make up for last time. If we can identify such a period now in our country's movement for capital accumulation, then I think managers need not be too worried about creative imitation.

However the question now arises what part of imitation is creative? How can we identify creative element in imitation? If imitation satisfies two criteria, then perhaps we may call it creative: (a) if it is internalised within the imitating cultural style, in such a way that the end-product appears to possess certain strong values, which are not necessarily dependent on the cultural or economic system of the culture which is being imitated; and (b) if that end-product is capable of sustaining a rate of prosperity and growth, which leads to success; then the end-product may be called a creative imitation.

Let us view two Indian groups mentioned above in the light of these criteria. The Parsee merchants of the mid-19th century (great though their wealth may have been, compared to that of their contemporary *banias*) were not able to produce a culture, which by and large was a part of the India of their time. The Jeejeebhoys, the Petits and the Wadias developed a style of life, which, though it contributed much, philanthrophically to the bourgeois civil life of Bombay, did not fit in at all (in its initial Anglicisation, and later Frenchification) with the life of the Gujarati and Marathi mercantile groups or industrial working class. Their achievements are monuments of the imposition of Victorianism in Bombay, *i.e.* the beautification of the bourgeois Fort area, and the growth of the slumminess of Central Bombay. This was an entrepreneurial style which resulted in their success, but not in the general improvement of prosperity or the lower middle classes and the industrial workers of Bombay. On the other hand the Gujarati industrial entrepreneurs, according to all the stories that we hear—I have not been to Ahmedabad myself—were able to contribute more to the general uplift of conditions in Gujarat. This does not mean that there is no marked dualism between Old Ahmedabad and Shahibaug standards of living or that the magnates do not exploit the work force. That is a condition of capitalism. However the Gujarati entrepreneurial style has led to the diffusion of their knowhow to classes, which were previously only on the fringes of prosperity, such as the cattle cultivators of Kaira, or the agriculture marketers in many other districts, and to the development of many small-scale industries along the railway lines radiating from Ahmedabad. Creativity lies in diffusing the benefits of prosperity to a wider arena than those in which it originates. Whether that creativity is imitative or not, is hardly to the point. Viewed in these terms, a corollary would of course be that, creativity is a more important goal than either imitation of ideas, styles and techniques taken from the outside world, or than emphasis on one's own innate values.

Inevitability of Information Sharing and One Criterion for Media-Selection

One final point, before other themes are discussed by participants. Is it really possible to be creative without referring to the fruits of knowledge in the rest of the world, isolating oneself to one's own local or national traditions? All things being equal, this seems impossible: modern civilisation, *i.e.* industrial cultures which was based either on the economic profits of capitalism, or on the essentially political premise of Communism, are essentially interdependent. No technologically progress is possible without either acquisition of general knowledge from the rest of the world, or even in the last resort, dissemination of this knowledge—at a price—by the originators. Viewed even in limited terms, this is the meaning of the Patent Laws, or the inevitable growth of multi-national business corporations, or of bilateral trade treaties between nations. In Communist countries this essential tendency for the centralisation of human efforts was accepted as a premise by Karl Marx, given institutional form in the International Associations of the Working Class of the world, and is still built into, for instance, the structure of COMECON, or of the present tendency for Friendship Treaties between Communist and non-Communist nations. Information sharing is a fact of economic life.

Similarly, in social matters. For the present argument it is not even necessary for me to take the position that the mode of production determine social structure since after all, social structure is also an element in the mode of production. However, it is clear that both in matters of economic organisation as well as of cultural style, a certain degree of emulation, and where innate talents are not immediately available, then imitation is necessary.

When it comes to the case of an underdeveloped country, underdeveloped precisely because of the development of a country which once dominated it, then the inevitability of imitation becomes all the more clear. There is an information gap in such countries, largely because the opportunities of development, which would have created the demand for more information, had been historically restricted. Hence not only information but also modes of behaviour and technology have to be quickly assembled. Independence makes it necessary for the newly developing nation to draw experience of other countries, and if necessary to imitate. This is true also of underdeveloped countries, which never come under foreign political domination, such as Japan, or the core of China.

In this inevitable process of imitation the language of the country at the time of Independence, or of revivalisation, is an important medium. Information or acceptance of new modes of behavioural or technology are mediated through the language of the State. When India became independent, the common language of the educated elite was English; much of the cultural style was a result of this. This English language opened the minds of the educated elite to the Western world, principally the English speaking world. One criterion for the effectiveness of the language medium for such invitation, is the economic and social power of different countries in that language speaking group. In the context of world events in the twenty years after the end of the Second World War, it is understandable that the U.S.A. should have dominated the horizons of the Indian imitators more than Great Britain, which in that period in the last resort became an appendage of the U.S. world economic system. Our assumption in this argument is that the imitations was carried out by capitalists whose motivation was not to bring about a radical revolution in Indian life, but to build up a "stable" economic system on the basis of what is known as "mixed economy".

Conclusions

These are only some general theoretical points through which we may approach the problem of imitation styles in Indian management. Like most theories it has not been made applicable to actual realities of managerial behaviour in different parts of India. In this sense it is what is called a "simple model" *i.e.* an abstract construct for simplification of the problem, so that bit-by-bit more realities can be fed into the model; in the process, the model may be "successively approximated" to realities which it sets out to explain. If, in this process, the model alter appear irrelevant, so much all the better; it will have served its purpose; at least its possibility as an explanation of the problem it approaches will have been eliminated. But if the reality, which I expect the managers present today to state (perhaps as a result of provocation offered by my model) tends to agree with the model, then we will be one step closer to understanding the problem.

That step will be the realisation that the objectives of training managers is not to impose on them a set pattern of values, derived from either outside, or inside, the country. The first necessity in training is to decide which values can be taken as given, in a democratic society, and then to bring the trainees up fair and square with the particular problems of their own organisation and of their profession, so as to make them realise how these values should be utilised for the better management and profit within national objectives of that organisation or profession. Whether a person is an imitator or not, his first necessity is to improve the functioning of the specific system of work within which he earns his living. The skills of management as distinct from proprietary entrepreneurship can best be deployed in performing that limited purpose, rather than in mistakenly going for the Utopian ideal of an initially total change in values.

Discussion

Roy: Can creativity be imitated? I have my own doubts. To be creative, one explores: trying to solve a particular problem in a particular environment, in a particular way. This process, like learning, is largely a personal one. Our "self" needs to be pitted against our own environment. The danger of imitation is that it short-circuits the grind, the personal-experience phenomenon. Without this one does not learn. In the imitative process we are "borrowing" from past situations and or other peoples' success. This being so, imitation cannot be creative especially because the environment is different.

Dr. De: It is true that we learn through our own experiences: "self". This is at all times doing something. In the process of doing one is continually learning from experience but this experience is often outside one's self. Here, one learns from outside. Learning also means adapting actions to the behaviour of other people. Sometimes there is not enough to think and plan time and one is forced to make a split-second decision, and then the tendency to imitate comes in. We sometimes follow the lead set by other people and sometimes adapt. The experiences which we adapt which are outside us are not part of our culture. Nevertheless such imitation becomes creative. You can say that this kind of imitation is the self's learning process.

Khandke: We have agreed that creativity is necessary: the argument is whether we should be "creatively" creative or, "imitatively" creative. Applying the process of survival, you have the option to pursue what you are doing either on own or by adaptation. You could be sometimes natural and sometimes initiative.

Dr. De: Yes, choose when to imitate and when to adapt from lessons of the past or from others.

Roy: Though one learns from the past, from one's own and other people's experiences, to be creative one has to look into the future. About this neither we nor the others have the experience. If India is to progress past experiences are of limited value only, although no doubt we should "study" the examples of other countries, without imitating.

Khandke: We must measure past actions in relation to what to do in the future.

Roy: Only point is that unsuccessful people remain prisoners of the past. Japan became successful when it became unique, when she chose a line of thought which no one had chosen before. A conscious choice was made to do something differently—there was no imitation.

Saraogi: Every business situation calls for creativity. In a business environment one is continually imitating and adapting, and in turn being creative. This is how we survive. Creativeness comes when you have broken the "routine" barrier.

Khandke: Achievement being the goal, imitation is intrinsic in achieving certain objectives. Whether such imitation is being creative or not will be judged by the result: is one surviving or not surviving?

Rangnekar: Creative process begins like this: First, we have a problem, then we try and find a solution sometimes even by thinking of something not directly related to the problem itself. For example, before printing press was invented, the inventor had seen grapes being crushed in a press. From there he got the idea of a Printing Press. The same solution did not occur to thousands of others who had been seeing grapes being crushed. You have to see the problem and idea together.

Consider the concept of the Commissar and the Yogi. In the past every Manager was expected to be a good Commissar, not a Yogi. Imitation and creativity are both necessary but we seem to have imitated the styles of the others, notably the U.S.A. In our country the Commissar, *i.e.* administrator has become more important than the Yogi, *i.e.* the creator. In all aspects of life we find this problem, the Yogi has taken a backseat. When our Managers see a problem, their immediate impulse is to imitate to find out how others coped with a similar problem. Everybody wants to follow the course that others followed.

Khandke: Industry has produced a generation of Commissars, which was useful for administration but not for innovation. Yogis are necessary for innovations and creativity.

Saraogi: It is not creativity alone why some succeed and others do not. What we need is a different style of management which is clear about its objectives.

De: If we try to examine whether there is any imitation in adaptation, it would be worthwhile finding out the rules behind creativity. Take the case of those Indian Industrialists who broke into new lines. The influence on them was mainly British (since theirs was the dominant culture on India), but there were those who tried to learn to necessarily from the British but generally from 'outside'. What they were learning was culturally a different product. They then started learning from Japan—and those who learnt from Japan learnt about cheap products. Then Indians started going, not to England or Japan, but to U.S.A. for education. They learnt about market diversification from the U.S.A. which was a new concept for us but not in the States. Going into the roots of creativity, we find it in the people who break away from the traditional forms, employ skill and capacity for perseverance to become creative.

Nalkur: People imitate sub-consciously, *e.g.* even in clothes. Whether imitation is creative or adaptive depends on whether the imitation will be successful or not and on the individual himself, *i.e.* whether he blindly imitates.

Imitation is human, but it should be conscious and not blind. It is correct so long as it meets the objectives and solves the problem concerned. Unconscious or blind imitation is wrong and should be avoided.

Lal: If a developing country imitates a good example and develops rapidly and productively there is nothing wrong with it if it leads to prosperity and success.

De: One must however make a difference between imitation and aping. We all agree with that to ape is wrong. It leads nowhere.

Creativity is important, although, unfortunately we have not in our discussion gone deeper into the question; "What is the creator of creativity?" Creativity is a necessity, not only for development, but also for survival since non-creativity leads to decadence and failure. What are our necessities in this respect in the context of a national perspective? An entrepreneur may have a different perspective here to the manager but there will have to be a point where the two must meet in a national perspective. The problem of how to arrive at this national perspective will however remain.

4

Experiences and Experiments

*ISABS and TA**

Francis Menezes

The Indian Society for Applied Behavioural Science (ISABS) was formed on December 5, 1971, at the Tata Management Training Centre, Poona by a group of concerned applied behavioural scientists. Twenty of them were present at this meeting. The objectives of the Society are:

Objectives

1. To provide opportunities for fulfilling the affiliative needs of those who share common interests in experience-based learning.
2. To share and develop professional skills.
3. To advance conceptual and cognitive knowledge in the field, and to further opportunity for conceptual enrichment and updating.
4. To develop professional services to as yet unserved areas of public interest.
5. To organize training programmes for professional development of new entrants.
6. To develop and set professional norms for its members.

* First published in IJTD in 1977.

Membership

The ISABS has two categories of membership, *viz.*, professional members and associates.

The professional membership is open to persons who are active in laboratory education, sensitivity training, and related methods of experience-based learning as well as broader applications of behavioural science.

The Society also has associate members consisting of persons who are interested in the advancement of laboratory training, sensitivity training, and related methods of experience-based learning as well as broader applications of behavioural science.

The present board of the ISABS consists of:

1. Pulin K. Garg, Executive Director
2. Somnath Chattopadhyay, Dean of Interns
3. Mrs. Indira J. Parikh, Treasurer
4. Mrs. Purnima Sinha, Editor (ex officio), ISABS Journal
5. Dharni P. Sinha
6. Sujit Bhattacharjee
7. Gouranga Chattopadhyay
8. Francis A. Menezes
9. Dennyson Pereira
10. Parayag Mehta

In its five years of existence, the Society has grown exceedingly fast and is recognized as the spokesman for applied behavioural science, both in India and abroad. In fact, some international organisations such as the IAASS have suggested a possibility of a relationship between the international organisation and ISABS.

Every year ISABS holds an internship programme to train potential trainers. This is its core programme and is meant for would-be professional members. The internship covers three years. In Phase I the intern begins looking at himself and his role as a trainer, and his relationship with others in a group. By the time he reaches Phase II, he is ready to work as co-trainer in unstructured training laboratories.

Interns learn to discuss group processes, to create learning situations, to understand the dynamics and relationships of feelings, thoughts and values in a group, and to understand himself, his strengths and weaknesses, and his effectiveness as a trainer and as a person.

Each phase covers a fortnight broken by two days when an annual conference is held. At the last conference in Bangalore, the subject was "T-Groups and Indian Culture". Papers are read by professional members from all over India and reactions are sought from colleagues attending the conference.

Concurrent with the Internship programme, one-week laboratories are conducted on themes such as managerial effectiveness, organisation development, personal growth and community development.

The personal growth programme is obviously focused on the individual's growth and is not necessarily related to organisations, while the other programmes concentrate on making participants more effective as managers or as in the case of OD to understand change and growth, in organisations. Some OD programmes emphasize change agent skills.

ISABS publishes a journal every quarter, when reports of new experiments and experiences appear. There are also a few reports on research conducted by members besides some stories of success in organisation development efforts.

There is no doubt that ISABS is a growing and dynamic organisation. Certainly every young person who would like to work in the field of applied behavioural science sees the professional membership of ISABS as a goal worth seeking; sometimes, unfortunately I might add, even as an end in itself.

TA in India

What is Transactional Analysis?

TA is a theory and practice of human experience and communication invented by Eric Berne in the mid-fifties and perfected by him and others since then. In his book *Transactional Analysis in Psychotherapy,* Berne writes that TA is "a systematic consistent theory of personality and social dynamics derived from clinical experience, and an actionistic, rational, form of therapy which is suitable for, easily understood by, and naturally adapted to the great majority of psychiatric patients".

Why the Word "Transaction"?

A transaction is some kind of a business deal in which one person gives something to another and in exchange gets something back. Berne saw that in transactions people not only exchanged material goods but also a lot of other elements such as recognition of one another. Berne described these elements as "strokes", using the analogy of the physical stroking which given to children when they are young and which if withheld will cause the death of the child. Thus, a transaction is an exchange of strokes which takes place when two people communicate with each other in one message and response between them.

What is TA All About?

In TA, we analyse the transactions of people. The full analysis covers structural analysis, transactional analysis proper, game analysis, and script analysis.

The book which brought TA into limelight is Eric Berne's *Games People Play*; this has been translated into many languages. Tom Harris' book *I'm OK, You're OK* is another popular introduction to TA.

For a clear, well-presented, methodical study of TA *Born to Win* and it's accompanying workbook *Winning with People* by Muriel James and Dorothy Jongeward are recommended. Also, for use in teaching situations and for serious use in the home the same authors' book *The People Book is good.*

The most scientific and technical introduction to TA is given in *Transactional Analysis in Psychotherapy* by Eric Berne. On TA as a form of group therapy, see Berne's *The Principles of Group Treatment* and the *Structure and Dynamics of Organisations and Groups*. Also recommended for scientific study is the Monograph Series of the Midwest Institute for Human Understanding (4004 Huffman Rd, Medina, Oh. 44256) by Bill and Marty Holloway.

Life-scripts are covered extensively in Eric Berne's *What Do You Say After You Say Hello*?, and in Claude Steiner's *Scripts People Love*. Steiner used the script matrix in working with addicts and he reported on this in *Games Alcoholics Play*.

TA in business environments is dealt with in Dorothy Jongeward's *Everybody Wins* and, a business man's introduction to TA is in Jut Meininger's *Success Through Transactional Analysis*. Another suggestion is Muriel James' *OK Boss*.

Unlike unstructured groups, transactional analysis is a conceptual approach to learning about oneself and other people and is not threatening to the learner. TA is being used widely in the United

States business organisations and other institutions with a fair amount of success. The movement is new to India and there are hardly 4 or 5 people who have accredition from the International Transactional Analysis Association (ITAA). More and more trainers abroad in the field of organisation behaviour are using transactional analysis as a key instrument in their training. Some professional members of ISABS are also familiar with TA and use it in their group work. TA is specially effective in programmes on effective communication and counselling, but one may also predict that it will have an important and legitimate place in most training involving the management of human resourcers.

5

Challenges of Training in Banks*

Anil K. Khandelwal

Introduction

Banking Industry in India is engaged in a unique experiment inasmuch as it has taken up the non-traditional task of developing such key sectors of the economy as agriculture, exports, transport, and small-scale industries. Further, banks are not only trying to minimise economic disparities but also engaged in rehabilitating the poor and exploited classes by providing them financial and technical assistance. In fact the public policy has shifted the focus of banking from a supportive role in development to a catalytic agent of change; from class banking to mass banking. Thus both the philosophy and function of banking have assumed new dimensions in the past few years. The urgency for revamping the scope and improving the quality of training of banking personnel can hardly be over-emphasized in such a situation.

According to an estimate by the NIBM, the total number of training personnel is likely to rise from 230,000 in 1970 to 497,000 in 1980 and to 730,000 by 1985. Thus the management of banks are faced with the acute problem of getting suitable personnel for meeting the growing demands of mass banking and attuning them to the proletarian needs and attitudes of new types of customers.

The greatest challenge facing Indian banking is the area of "Integrated Rural Development" through larger attention to backward areas, greater help to neglected sectors, and rectification of regional imbalances. A properly motivated and suitably trained personnel alone can face this challenge of change.

---

* First published in IJTD in 1978.

It is true that training is no panacea for all organisational ills. Objectively conceived and sincerely imparted training can certainly equip an individual to prove worthy of the expectations. Training should neither be a casual phenomenon nor holidaying for a selected few or even all. In turn, it has to be process of human development for the fulfilment of defined objectives.

In fact training should be considered as a rare opportunity (especially when the resources for training are so meagre in relation to the needs) and hence it is imperative that training needs are properly assessed and critical areas affecting either customer service or business of the bank/profit are properly identified.

An effort, therefore, is made in this paper to:

1. Suggest how to identify training needs in a bank;
2. Point out deficiencies in the existing process of training;
3. Identify critical areas/levels in hierarchy which need priority in imparting training;
4. Suggest ways and means to make the training function dynamic in a bank.

Identification of Training Needs

Banks are facing a great challenge in the areas of identification of training needs at organisational level, occupational level, and individual level because of the growing number of branches and increase in the number of employees in recent years on account of implementation of massive expansion plans. Due to manifold activities undertaken by banks and increase in the area of operations, the need for training at each level, right from top to bottom point of hierarchy, is all the more crucial. The task is so great that priorities have to be established in order that crucial levels in the hierarchy which can make or mar the operational efficiency receive training first.

There could be different methods of determining training needs of personnel at different levels. Also, the training needs of same categories of staff could be different. For example, training needs of the clerical staff at branches and head offices are as follows:

(a) At Branches

(i) Customer Service
(ii) Job knowledge including the various rules and regulations governing day to day banking.

(b) At Head Office

(i) Noting and drafting.
(ii) Job knowledge on practical banking.
(iii) Processing proposals and implementation of various policies of the bank.

Similarly, training needs of various kinds of branch managers are different.

The training needs of banking personnel have to be related to the thrusts and emphasis proposed in business plan such as agricultural financing with special reference to World Bank projects, Rural Employment Scheme, stepping up the credit/deposit ratio in rural areas, increasing coverage under DRI advance scheme, active assistance of bank in the government's poverty eradication programme.

For identifying training needs, the following activities and information would be most useful:

1. Business plan and policy guidelines.
2. Potential available as a result of environmental data.
3. Cluster of accounts such as craftsman, sheep breeds etc. indicating specialized activities.
4. Deficiencies observed in control statements, proposals.
5. Complaints from staff and clients.
6. Inspection and Audit reports.
7. Diagnosis as a result of human observation.
8. Self-appraisal.

Deficiencies in the Existing Training System

1. Training should be a continuous activity but in the context of limited capacity of few training centres, there has been a great need to utilize the training capacity in full. However,

paradoxically utilisation in most of the banks is found to be much lower. Hence those engaged in training activities should try to solve this paradox.

2. Job rotation is not regular and periodical in most of the bank branches with the result that planning for training of employees is not done well in advance. The branch manager takes the training function casually due to various reasons, *viz.*, lack of adequate staff in the branches, lack of his own training and non-visibility of circumstances. The selection of training for a particular programme is not always rational. Thus training is sometimes used as a reward for those who show interest and willingness in work. This leaves the slow-pacers in the background and they continue as slow-pacers and later on become problem employees.
3. Another notable problem is that the present system of training does not lay emphasis on "attitudinal training". It is mainly job orientated. Due to lack of training in attitudes, the customer service poses a major problem. Attitudinal training will be very useful from the customer service angle if bankmen take interest in the problems of customers, give them advice on banking matters, give personalized service and, in general, develop cordial relations with them.
4. The training centres are usually ill-equipped in terms of latest literature on banking. Important periodicals (like *Reserve Bank of India Bulletin*) and papers are usually conspicuous by their absence. Hence the environment in the training centre seldom gives the trainees a feel of academic atmosphere. Thus they are not adequately motivated to learn.
5. At present, things are not very satisfactory in regard to faculty in training centres of banks. No training programme can be better than the trainer himself and unless the trainer is properly selected the whole activity will prove a flop, right from the beginning.

Suitable organisational policy should be developed to plan a career for training of banking personnel so that the best persons are attracted to the training profession. It is not uncommon to find placement of such officers in training centres who are rejected from operations or whose integrity itself is doubtful.

The banks will have to change their entire approach to training and will have to ensure that persons with necessary experience, knowledge and enthusiasm are asked to shoulder the responsibility of training. Placement in training centres should be considered as a reward rather punishment. This alone would give a respectable status to the training function.

Critical Areas of Training

The critical areas which need priority attention of bank management are identified as under:

1. *Training of Subordinate Staff*

The subordinate staff in banks constitutes on an average 25 per cent of the total staff strength. The smooth work flow as well as efficient customer service largely depends on this cadre. It is very important and relevant, therefore, that efforts are made to make this cadre duty conscious in regard to imparting better and effective customer service. There is a lot of criticism about delay in various transactions in banks. At times, this is attributed to delays in the flow of various books/vouchers to respective departments. Various important papers and filed are frequently not available. To overcome all these day-to-day operational problems and to ensure speedy and effective customer service, it is necessary that a formal training programme is arranged for this cadre with a view to inculcating in them a concern for efficient customer service and an awakening to this fact that their apathy can cause dislocation in work and consequent frustration in customers.

The experiment of imparting training to the subordinate staff was tried by one of the associates of State Bank. The objective of the course was to familiarize the subordinate staff with the work flow, their role in organisation, and customer service. As a part of the programme an inter-face was also held with the identified customers who had lodged complaints regarding poor customer service. The participants thus had first hand feedback from the constituents. The participants were addressed by members of top management as well as their own union leaders on the role of the subordinate staff in providing effective customer service. The participants felt highly motivated and interviews with their respective branch managers revealed that after training there was a feeling of concern in them for the customer. More banks should try this experiment with proper organisational support and with a view to involving the lowest in the hierarchy in ensuring effective customer service.

2. *Training of Newly Recruited Clerks*

Persons with brilliant academic background join banking service these days. This consequently throws a great challenge for bank management to train them properly so that they are suitably inducted in the organisation. Most of the banks are now exposing the newly recruited clerks to induction programmes during which the participants are acquainted with the bank organisation, their career, and various functions of a bank. The experience and interviews with the newly recruited clerks reveals, however, that the present content of the induction programme with its emphasis on routine is procedure-oriented and does not provide the beginner an opportunity to understand his role in totality. The time of induction could be best utilized in exposing the newly recruited clerks to come into contact with customers. The newly recruited clerks could even be taken to loan camps where they could assess the credit needs of the borrower. The experiment of a bank in asking the trainees to conduct to door-to-door survey of customers' preference, customer satisfaction level, and the expectations of the customers from the bank has been found very successful. This inculcates in them customer consciousness which is likely to have an everlasting impact on their mind about the importance of customer service.

3. *Training of Supervisory Staff*

With the massive expansion plans undertaken as also to fulfil their socio-economic obligations, the banks are now providing very good opportunities to its staff for promotion. Thus within four to five years of service in clerical cadre one gets a fair chance of promotion to the officers cadre. But this promotion is abrupt ... abrupt in the sense that during the short span of clerical period a person gets no opportunity of doing supervisory work. The induction programmes for newly promoted officers also do not lay much emphasis on developing supervisory skills or bringing about change in attitudes. Thus the banks are left to be managed by poorly equipped supervisory staff which frequently results in a poor customer service and indiscipline. It is, therefore, suggested that the course content at this point of training should be such as to inculcate the needed supervisory skills in the employees. The course content could be basic management principles, public relations techniques, human relations, group dynamics, etc.

4. *Training of Managers*

Another critical area of training is the training of managers of bigger branches of banks. The problems of a bigger branch are more of administration of tasks, employees as well as skills in public relations. The big branch managers should be exposed to long duration courses in personnel management, industrial relations, and public relations. Most of the banks complain lack of trained and all-round managers to man big urban and metropolitan centres. The branches at these centres do not come up to the desired expectations due to lack of managerial skills in the branch managers. It is, therefore, necessary that due attention should be paid for all-round development of these managers by exposing them to suitable internal/external courses. The methodology for training in such courses should be proper blending of theory with practice with a little more emphasis towards practical day-to-day problems. There should be more and more input of behavioural sciences in the training programmes. The teaching techniques for such courses should include role play, case studies, etc., rather than routine lectures. Managers with proven record of successful handling of administrative problems should frequently be invited to training colleges to share their experience and expertise with the trainees.

5. *Training of Senior Management Personnel*

Most of the senior management personnel such as Regional Managers, Assistant General Managers, Incharge of the Regions/Zones are those who have put in 20-25 years of service in a bank and are product of traditional and exploitative culture. Some of these executives continue to manage affairs in a way which is not only highly traditional and orthodox in the present environment but at times creates lots of inconsistency, subjectivity, and irrationality in the decision-making process. Training of these executives is very vital and crucial because the development of Region/Zone depends upon their skill and expertise.

They should be imparted training in management and exposed frequently to various modern methods of management.

6. *Training of Trainers*

The success of a training programme largely depends upon the trainer. Therefore, the problem of training of "trainers" assumes added significance in the modern business setting. Since most of the training needs of bank employees at various levels are related to "attitudinal" problems it is very necessary that the trainer should possess up-to-date theoretical and conceptual knowledge of economic development in general and banking in particular. The trainer should in particular be conversant with the latest techniques of teaching for better training effectiveness. The following steps may be taken to achieve the aforesaid goals:

- (i) The trainer should be afforded facilities to visit training centres of other banks and to study the techniques of training adopted by them.
- (ii) He should be asked to visit problem branches of the banks to have a first-hand knowledge of the issues which hamper the progress of a branch. This will help in preparing case studies for use in training.
- (iii) He should be deputed to courses on "group psychology learning" and teaching processes and behaviour patterns.
- (iv) Trainers should also be associated with the process of identification of training needs of the employees.

7. *Training of Directly Recruited Officers*

Commercial banks started direct recruitment of officers on a large scale after nationalisation in 1969. This was with a view of facing new challenges and meeting new demands arising out of the new policy of the government. In a study conducted by the author[1], it was revealed that these directly recruited officers who have a good family background and brilliant academic career soon get frustrated on the jobs because—

- (i) they feel that they are not properly inducted and are given hum-drum jobs which require little application of their intelligence and experience;

(ii) they feel that there is no recognition of their abilities and that placement on the job is not consistent with their interest, aptitude, and background.

The foregoing analysis is indicative of the fact that if these directly recruited officers are given properly structured training, suiting their ability, they would feel more homely on their jobs. In most of the banks, the directly recruited officers are sent to the branches under the care of those who have little concern about the potentiality and aptitude of these persons. Thus, instead of rendering systematic training they use them as regular officers. It is very essential that directly recruited officers are given to follow a fixed schedule of training which should be class-matched and followed up with proper postings and job assignments. This area of training is really very crucial and banks are advised to take suitable steps to ensure that directly recruited officers are trained to assume responsibilities without loss of time. That would avoid frustration on the one hand and raise productivity of banking operations on the other.

8. *Training of Rural Branch Managers*

Rural banking has thrown the greatest challenge to commercial banks in terms of service. To achieve this gigantic task, what we need today is a new breed of rural branch managers who combine youthful enthusiasm, dedication, and multi-disciplined competence. This poses a great problem of training of personnel posted in rural areas. The rural bank officials will have to shed their urban complex and mould themselves in such a way that they are not considered as alien. They will have to develop a high level of task orientation and immense capacities to sacrifice luxuries of life and adopt to stresses and strains caused by cross-currents of opinions in the peculiar social environment.

Once the problem of basic attitudes is clear, it is possible to plan the training inputs which should constitute inculcation of the knowledge and skill to survey the village farms, households, correlate relevant data, process the data to assess the potential and constraints, formulate bankable schemes, appraise loan proposals, arrange supplies and services, etc. The training, in fact, should seek to build up the requisite inter-personal competence, communication skill, and the ability to work in a team.

The training of rural branch officials can be effective only when they are exposed to the rural environment. This can be done by field training on specific assignments or imparting training in a rural setting itself so that trainees can have a first-hand experience of village life.

Making Training Functions Dynamic in Banks

The task of training in banks is very tremendous and calls for committed efforts at all levels rather than more lip service by opening Training Centres. It is quite fashionable now to have a training centre and have a ritual of sending people for training just because some sort of training activity is to be kept going. Training in such an environment often becomes a routine and fails to satisfy the genuine development needs of the enterprise. It does not produce the required changes in the behaviour of trainees. Someone has rightly pointed out that training in some organisations is treated merely as a "Call Girl" to be ushered in when needed than a "House Wife". To make training really effective and worthy of the money spent on it, the role of top management becomes very crucial. They have to treat training as a truly professional endeavour and have faithful commitment towards the results which can be achieved and which may bring about a change in organisational and individual behaviour. They should accept that training is a responsibility which cuts across all functional and organisational lines. The responsibility for training is in fact with all the layers of management and it is not merely the responsibility of Training and Personnel Managers.

Another factor which can go a long way in bringing results out of training is to assign the task of training to a really capable and outstanding faculty. One very disturbing feature which at times is observed in banks is deputation of operationally rejected officers to Training Centres. It is questionable whether such persons can be of any real use in Centres meant to provide a worthwhile training. The training function is not to be considered an activity of the sparable by sparable and for sparables. The banks will have to professionalize training. As such they must select the best professionally qualified personnel with aptitude for training to manage Training Centres. They can also locate experienced and successful branch officials and place them for training jobs. To make a career worthwhile in this area banks will have to take necessary steps for making placement in Training Centres/Training Departments as rewarding. They will have to involve training personnel right from recruitment decisions to placement decisions. Without such an integrated approach, training will never achieve its real purpose and it will remain a mere waste of time and money.

Another important factor which can contribute to training effectiveness in Indian banks is to decentralize training and development function. For this purpose, it will be necessary to place professionally qualified persons with adequate experience in banking operations to look after such a cell. The creation of such a cell at regional level is essential with an effective mechanism to assess training needs of employees at various levels in the region and identify training gaps so that they can suitably plan and design courses to match the requirements of the bank's development plans as also to link the training needs with career path planning of individuals. They can also maintain effective liaison with the branch managers and guide them in training and development activities, *viz.*, job rotation, identification of training needs, etc. The functions of such a cell could be as under:

1. To provide expertise to line management to ensure that employees are recruited from sources most likely to produce the number, quality, and experience required for efficiency.
2. To ensure that training is so imparted that each individual can acquire the knowledge, skills, an attitude required to do his/her job effectively.
3. To see that individuals are so trained that they are prepared for future roles (as far as these can be foreseen).
4. To build up a system of placement through which training and experience is utilized to the best advantage of the organisation and the banking community. The trained personnel should be asked to carry out duties which are clearly defined and seeking to achieve objectives which have been discussed and agreed between them and their branch for department and which contribute towards the coordinated objectives of the bank as a whole.
5. To have adequate arrangements for communication, upward and downward, including open channels for the expression of individual views.

Each of these aims will be best achieved if line managers have the skill to handle them within the general guidelines laid down by the top management. Hence the role of such a cell will be most crucial in energizing the individuals to do their best for the organization and motivate them to convert their latent potentials to the skill which will prove useful to achieve organizational objectives.

Conclusions

As indicated earlier, training is no panacea for all the organisational ills. It is merely one segment of the total management development activities of a bank. Top management personnel at times show skepticism about the utility of training. The rationale of spending huge organisational resources in terms of men and money is questioned, forgetting that training cannot become a substitute for managerial ineffectiveness. Poor measure of performance, poor supervision and unsuitable organisational structures are mistaken for training needs. However the result of training can be spectacular when corresponding changes in organisational pattern and administration accompany training efforts. Training is merely a tool and has to be used as such. One should expect neither more nor less from it, but use it to the maximum. The problem of integrating training with the banking business has to identified, understood, and tackled. Lastly, to make training really effective a suitable status will have to be given to this function. The training department in banks should be placed under very senior and really competent officers to bestow it with the degree of credibility and respectability it really deserves. No short-cuts or casualness can click.

NOTE

1. Directly recruited officers in Banks—Square pegs in round holes" by Anil K. Khandelwal, Prajman, *NIBM Journal*, January-March, 1976 issue.

6

Managing Development in the Developing Countries*

S.B.L. Bhardwaj

Planned Development: Scope and Infirmities

Development of the less developed countries (LDCs) has emerged as a critical concern during the second half of the present century. Several interacting factors have contributed to this emergence some of which may be identified as follows:

1. The quest for dignity and national well-being by countries that have become independent in the wake of Second World War.
2. Global upsurge of a humanistic ethos; a realisation of interdependence of nations and peoples; and a perception of poverty, hunger, ignorance, and disease as challenges to human dignity and threats to international peace and stability: a realisation that these problems of deprivation and misery call for concerted effort by all nations—rich and poor.
3. Emergence of international and regional agencies for providing developmental aid and technical assistance, under the auspices of the U.N., or other bodies.
4. Enlightened self-interest of the richer nations that have come to realize that their own economic growth and affluent lifestyle depends on the economic development and political stability

* First published in IJTD in 1979.

of poorer nations: this has led to bilateral or multilateral developmental assistance.

5. Gradual evolution of insights into the goals, processes, and alternative strategies of planned national development, based on the experience of agencies and countries involved in development efforts.

The Goals of Development: Changing Definitions

Although some broad understanding of the general goals of country development has always existed, there is no agreed international definition of what is Development? The meaning and thrust of development seems to have changed from time to time, among the aid-giving nations and international agencies. Thus, in the 1950s, development was equated with *economic growth*: an increase in the output of goods and services. In the 1960s, the main thrust was on sustaining the momentum of economic growth through some changes in technical and institutional arrangements to ensure an increase in *productivity capacity*. The focus in the 1970s has been on increase in *welfare*, especially with respect to segments of population living below the poverty line, thus implying major transformations. In the social and economic structures of the developing countries.[1]

The Report by the UN Committee on Development Planning, at the start of the Second Development Decade says: "It cannot be over-emphasized that what development implies for developing countries is not simply an increase in productive capacity but major transformations in their social and economic structures...The ultimate purpose of development is *to provide opportunities for a better life to all sections of the population*." Some parameters of "better life" mentioned in this Report are: elimination of inequalities in the distribution of wealth and income; doing away with mass poverty and social injustice; creating new employment opportunities; providing more food, and better education and health facilities, etc.

Thus, the emphasis in development, at least in the eyes of most donor countries and development agencies, has shifted from economic growth to "Quality of Life", in the 1970s. The overt or implied inclusion of "human rights" status of a developing country as a factor in deciding upon the nature and quantum of developmental aid and assistance by the donor western democracies has created serious complications in the development effort of many recipient LDCs. As an illustration, the

Carter Administration is linking up US contributions to the World Bank and Inter-American Development Bank, and bilateral aid to Third World countries, with considerations of Human Rights. This has had repercussions on the developmental aid policies of other rich nations of the West.

The concept of Human Rights emerged in the seventeenth century, and has been refined and re-defined since then. Ian Brownlis has presented an anthology of statements on Human Rights in his publication entitled *Basic Documents on Human Rights* (Clarendon Press, 1971). The ILO has brought out two significant documents linking up "basic needs" with "human rights".[2] But, perhaps the best definition of Human Rights is contained in the two U.N. Covenants: The Economic, Social and Cultural Rights Covenant; and The Civic and Political Rights Covenant.

Some of the significant Economic, Social, and Cultural Rights embedded in the U.N. Covenant are:

- Gaining one's living by work, freely chosen or accepted.
- Enjoying just and favourable conditions of work; fair wages.
- Rights to form Trade Unions.
- Social Security.
- Adequate standard of living for self and family, which includes: adequate food, clothing, housing etc.; continuous improvement of living conditions.
- Freedom from hunger, for which the ratifying states undertake to improve methods of food production and distribution through agrarian reforms enabling most efficient development and utilisation of natural resources.
- Enjoyment of highest attainable standard of physical and mental health, with special reference to child care.
- Right to education.
- Cultural rights; the rights of faith and worship.

Included among the Civic Rights in the UN Covenant are the following:

- Protection of life and liberty.
- Protection from torture or degrading punishment.
- Protection of privacy.
- Protection from retrospective punishment.

- Freedom of opinion.
- Equality under law.

Some of the Political Rights covered under the Covenant are as follows:

- Right to peaceful assembly.
- Right to form trade unions.
- Freedom of self-expression.
- Right to take part in the conduct of public affairs.
- Protection of the rights of ethnic, religious, linguistic minorities.
- Liberty of movement.

There is evidence of some disillusionment about the achievements of the LDCs in terms of national development *vis-à-vis* human rights.[3] Some developmental gains in terms of economic growth become meaningless in the face of contravention or denial of some of the economic and social rights. Similarly, denial of some basic political rights seems to adversely affect the development process by an absence of mass participation.

The Amnesty International examining a limited aspect (political prisoners) of the Human Rights record of many developing countries of Asia, Africa, and Latin America finds it to be none too bright—in the case of 37 out of 58 developing countries receiving World Bank assistance, and 27 out of 36 countries getting IDA credits. The Human Rights defaulters, among the developing countries, range all the way from per capita GNP of $ 5,000 per annum to $ 100 per annum.

It is generally known that decades of developmental effort in the LDCs has failed to alleviate the poverty, hunger, and misery of sizeable sections of the population of these countries. Most of the fruits of development seem to have been appropriated by the elites. It is often said, with considerable truth, that the rich have become richer, and the poor have been reduced to greater poverty.

In summary, the following basic propositions pertaining to development may be stated:

1. Within the framework of basic human rights, each developing country should evolve its own model of development, consistent with its socio-cultural, political, and natural

resource realities, and based on the principles of equity, "distributional justice", and human dignity.
2. National development is a total and integrated process, in which economic, technological, socio-cultural, ecological, and political aspects have to be woven together into an organic whole.
3. Mass participation in the development process is a pre-requisite for effective national development.
4. The successful management of development calls for appropriate structural arrangements, inputs, managerial skills, action strategies and mature political leadership and institutions.
5. The choice of (and creation of) appropriate technology is critical to the process of economic development.
6. The ultimate test of the success of development effort lies in the overall improvement of the quality of life of all segments of the population, particularly those living around and below the poverty line.

Some General Factors in Ineffective Development

In numerous national, regional, and international conferences and symposia, questions have been raised about the causes of failures and shortcomings of the developmental effort in the LDCs. Some of these factors resulting in miscarriage or under-achievement of development are briefly indicated below:

1. Over-ambitious developmental goals, beyond the resources and/or existing technological and managerial skills available within the country.
2. Excessive dependence on foreign aid; disadvantageous contracts with multinationals and other foreign collaborators with regard to transfer of technology, and profit transfer; errors in choice of technology.
3. Urban and elitist bias in development strategies; an inappropriate mix between industrial development and agricultural development; neglect of the small-scale, medium-scale, and agro-industries.
4. Either neglect of the "welfare" and "human rights" aspect of development, or disproportionately high resource allocation to welfare programmes/projects.

5. Iniquities in distribution of the gains of development by favouring politically advantageous segments of population, and neglecting the minorities and the poorest.
6. Failure to create a compatible infrastructure (transportation, roads, communication, energy, etc.) in keeping with the plans for economic development.
7. Failure to develop human resources matching the developmental plans and needs of the country: inadequacies of the indigenous educational systems.
8. Inadequate involvement/participation of the masses in the development process, at both the planning and implementation stages, creating attitudes of excessive "dependence" among the people, thus failing to foster local initiative and self-help.
9. Political instability, uncertainties, discontinuities; inefficient management of international relations.
10. Failure to develop indigenous sophistication in development concepts and skills; uncritical borrowing of alien development models with little efforts at adaptation and innovation; inability to learn from own successes and failures in development, and from the experience of other developing countries; cultural incompatibility of borrowed models, institutions, and strategies.
11. Errors in the pace of change, and the timing of change.

Managerial Failures of Development Administration

It is now recognized that the major set-back in achieving development goals in a developing country arises from *Implementation Failure.* Various causes of such failure are now understood reasonably well, and some of them have been indicated in this section.

The public service administrators, in most developing countries, seem to display the following symptoms, responsible for their relative ineffectiveness:

1. Pervasive inertia, with occasional brief spurts of all-planned activity.
2. A pre-occupation with status, career interests, and excessive concern with trivial organisational issues.
3. Rigid patterns of behaviour in relation to organisational hierarchy, demarcation of authority, channels of communication, rules and procedures.

4. Willingness to disregard or circumvent inconvenient formalities, when vested interests are involved.
5. Alternating between wasteful spending, and penny-wise parsimony.
6. Abdicating independent thinking and critical appraisal, once public decisions (howsoever wrong) are made or announced.
7. Lack of sophisticated management skills necessary for planning and implementation of development activities; ineffective and unimaginative control systems, and poor critiquing skills, poor project management know-how, etc.
8. Empire-building; wasteful competitiveness where collaboration is demanded by the situation.

Certain attitudes of "public sector managers" (which term includes: public service administrators, members of statutory boards and corporations, and Executives of state-owned enterprises), which contribute to their ineffectiveness as managers of development, arise from the cultural ethos of the transitional society to which they belong. Some of the these culturally-embedded behaviours have been examined in several studies, such as those by Heeger, Andreski and Field,[4] and are briefly indicated below:

1. Thanks to attitudes to tolerance in the society at large, public sector managers are characterized by corruption, nepotism, and selfish opportunism, leading to the managers having a vested interest in sustaining inertia and inefficiency in their own organisation, often manifesting itself in the form of deliberately induced delays in decision-making.
2. Managers in the public sector are influential figures in the society, and have extra-organisational loyalties to the section of the society to which they belong (ethnic group, religious group, linguistic group, etc.). They are prone to dispensing favours to their own communities in return for support in any bid for greater power and authority, or protection in the face of any threat to their position. In the context of general feelings of insecurity, these managers tend to build networks of mutual support.

Whereas it is true that managerial behaviour reflects the realities of a national climate of sectionalism, patronage, and political conflict, this fact by itself constitutes only a partial, inadequate, and exaggerated explanation of managerial inadequacies.

Yet another factor, contributing to ineffectiveness of development managers emanates from the incompatibility between the indigenous socio-cultural norms and the cultural characteristics of institutional forms borrowed from alien societies. The cultural contradictions are particularly marked in government departments of developing countries modelled on western bureaucratic systems, which are based on: a clearly structured hierarchy of authority; a division of responsibility based upon clearly defined tasks and roles; a set of regulations applied uniformly to all; the principle of impersonality of each office. Very often these bureaucratic norms, transplanted from the West, go against the very ethos of a developing society. Public sector managers are thus enmeshed in a cultural dilemma, and choose soft options likely to alleviate their feelings of insecurity: they lead a schizophrenic existence. Development managers seem to live in a twilight zone where they are judged on the one hand by their ability to uphold the principles of organisational discipline and rationality, and on the other by their ability to respond to day-to-day personal and political pressures which require them to ignore or circumvent organisational norms and regulations.

Structural Weakness in Development Administration

Most governments of developing countries are aware of the fact that a potent source of "implementation failure" of national development plans lies in the structural weakness of the public administration apparatus. The characteristic response of these governments to this problem have taken the form of "administrative reforms". In many developing countries, permanent departments or statutory bodies have been set up to overcome this problem. From time to time special commissions have been created to report on structural weaknesses and suggest remedial reorganisation.[5]

Among the numerous structural weaknesses identified by various administrative reforms bodies, the following deserve special attention:

1. *Authoritarian and centralized style of decision-making*

Decisions are monopolized by heads of ministries and departments, with little or no consultation, decentralisation or delegation. This leads to serious delays in decisions, and unawareness of the consequences of decision. Executives and functionaries, lower down the hierarchy, develop attitudes of abject dependence, and avoid taking initiative or *bona fide* risks. The top man plays the role of the prescribing father, and development of subordinates is often based on notions of paternalism and benevolence. Yesmanship and blind conformity dominate the system.

2. *Parochial departmentalism and territorial rivalries*

Organisational loyalties are to particular departments, ministries, or corporations, which lead to unhealthy rivalries and competition for power, resources, and visibility. New responsibilities are avoided unless they are perceived as offering opportunities for enhancing departmental resources. Shared responsibility with other departments or agencies is seen as a potential threat to departmental autonomy. The result of this "departmentalism" is: delay, duplication, and buck-passing, and lack of coordination at local and regional levels. A large number of case studies from various developing nations illustrate how narrow ministerial/departmental loyalties hurt the cause of effective area development.

3. *Rigid adherence to close regulations and procedures*

Such inflexible and unimaginative procedural rituals inhibit the prospect of accommodating new problems and opportunities within existing organisational forms. The development process calls for innovation and speedy reaction to unforeseen situations: this is thwarted by public system, "red tapism", and labyrinthine procedures.

4. *Low sensitivity to client reactions*

The public administration system in most developing countries is characteristically impervious to the aspirations, needs, and feelings of the client system they are expected to serve. This aloofness and insensitivity is partly due to elitist attitudes modelled on colonial rulers of the past, with little or no identification with the poor and the deprived, and implicit intolerance of communal, ethnic, or linguistic "out groups". Other factors contributing to this unresponsiveness are: poor interagency coordination, high rivalry among departments/agencies, centralized control, and rigid procedures.

Political Weaknesses Affecting Development Administration

Apart from ineffective behavioural modes of development managers, and structural weaknesses of public systems, another significant source of development failure, or under-achievement, is the political environment in which these managers are obliged to operate.

The political climate of many developing countries of Asia, Africa, and Latin America is characterized by: political uncertainty; intra-military conflict; cabinet purges; immature or vacillating political leadership; inner conflict and competition among ministers; inflexible demand for political loyalty; and a political tendency to make scapegoats of public system managers in the event of any failures or political scandals.[6]

The public system managers often receive scant respect and capricious treatment from their political masters. Their managerial energies are often wasted on irrelevant activities. They have to spend disproportionate time in dancing attendance on the political gods. There is frequent political interference, asking them to carry out the politically motivated wishes of their superiors, even to the extent of short-circuiting or circumventing established organisational procedures or regulations. Their feelings of insecurity are further aggravated by constant organisational changes and experimentation.

Under the circumstances described above, it is nearly impossible for a development manager to discharge his primary responsibilities in an effective and conscientious manner. He soon realizes that, for sheer self-preservation, he must calculate the political implications and risks involved in his managerial decisions. This results in a cautious approach to problem-evasions rather than an aggressive and entrepreneurial approach to problem-solving.

Summary

In this section, we have examined the changing goals of national development in the LDCs: from economic growth to improved "quality of life" for the masses living in poverty, ignorance, and neglect. Some basic propositions for effective developmental strategies have been outlined and errors commonly committed by developing countries enumerated. Apart from these strategic shortcomings, a few chronic causes of "implementation failure" have also been reviewed. These include: inappropriate values, attitudes, and behaviours of public service administrators; incompatibility between the norms of borrowed western bureaucratic systems and the indigenous ethos of the developing nations; some structural weaknesses of the public administration apparatus in these countries; and political aberrations and interference which adversely affect the public service administrators.

But the process of planned national development cannot be rendered more effective merely by a correction of the errors and deficiencies noted above. What needed is a massive and continuous educational effort to support the development process. Such an effort must involve all segments of the population, all agencies directly or indirectly involved in the development exercise.

Education for Development

Towards Dignity and Participation

Planned national development is too serious a business to be left entirely to the political decision-makers and public service administrators. Unless the common citizen, in the urban as well in the rural areas, has a broad understanding of the goals of development, identifies himself with these goals and aspirations; cooperates in the implementation of development plans and projects; receives continuous and objective information about the achievements and shortfalls of developmental efforts; visible perceives the gains of development within his own hamlet, village, or town; and takes initiative in bettering his own lot and improving his style of living unless all this happens, developmental efforts could not to be said to have succeeded. This highlights the need for continuous "Development Education", which is not to be confused with cheap political propaganda.

Development of the individual, national socio-economic development, institutional building and organisation development: all these are organic and interdependent elements of any worthwhile plans of national development: it would be futile to debate which aspect of development leads to which, although the primacy of economic development (with distributional justice) has often been emphasized. Whichever be the development model chosen by a country, whatever the priorities and strategies for implementation of the chosen model—the common citizen has a right to know the alternative approaches to development, and the criteria for choice among these alternative. He must be given a clear understanding of what is expected of him in terms of his personal contribution to the national development efforts.

Development must not be perceived by the political masters of a developing nation as an act of public benevolence or charity, or paternalistic munificence. "Development with dignity" is a basic human right of all citizens of a country. This proposition, however, leads to a basic dilemma of development *vis-à-vis* the vulnerable, underprivileged, poor and backward sections of the population in a developing country. Undoubtedly some "negative discrimination" and protection would be essential in the early stages of development of the ignorant, the neglected, and the discriminated against. But such protection should not degenerate into a disabling pampering, attitudes of over-dependence, or loss of dignity and self-generated efforts at betterment. For these underprivileged sectors of society, we would need: "education for dignity and self-reliance", rather than parennial protectionism. Nothing degrades like sloth-generating charity and unearned doles.

All people must fully participate in national development: the elites, as well as the rural poor, without any discrimination based on class, caste, community, race, religion, language, or region. But participation implies a feeling of belongingness and appropriate participatory skills. It would be the responsibility of a country's educational system, and its media of mass communication to impart and reinforce these participative values, attitudes, and skills. National development must constitute a basic orientation of the curriculum at the primary, secondary, and higher levels of education. Agencies involved in adult education programmes, literacy programmes, social and family welfare programmes, must weave their activities round the theme of national development with emphasis on self-betterment, participation, collaboration, improvisation.

Education and Training of Change Agents

Apart from general educational programmes in development, whether formal or informal, aimed at the children, youth, and adult segments of population, we need specialized programmes, on a continuous basis, for training the change agents. To develop a nation implies making changes in its economic activity, social, and cultural institutions, public administration, and the lives of individuals. Hence a massive educational programme needs to be formulated and implemented, geared to "Management Development" at macro and micro levels.

Some of the target groups, for which training programmes in management of development may have to be designed, are suggested below:

1. Political leaders and legislators.
2. Public system administrators (Federal and State) including officers in: administrative services, irrigation and water management; agriculture and horticulture; development planners at State and federal levels; urban development and habitat planning; fisheries; animal husbandry, poultry farming, and diary development; health and hospital management: family planning; social welfare; tribal development; education; police and civil defence; forestry; flood control and water management; transport (airlines, railways shipping, and road transport); engineering services (public works departments); cooperatives; environmental control; power, etc.
3. Officers of financial Institutions and banks.
4. Professional working in mass media of communication (radio, TV, the press).
5. Local administration officers; officials of public utilities systems.
6. Managers of public and private sector enterprises.
7. Voluntary welfare agencies.
8. Young entrepreneurs; small-scale industry managers.
9. University and college teachers and students.
10. Trade union leaders.

The content of these educational and training programmes will depend upon the specific roles (present and potential) of the particular target group in respect of national development. Some programme contents are indicated below:

1. *Programme for Political Leaders and Legislators*

The content of educational programmes for this group may include: meaning and scope of planned national development; models of development; planning process; policy formulation; investment decision; resource generation and taxation; choice of technology;

resource management; monitoring and control of development projects; economic development and social change; developmental legislation; communication for development; mass involvement and participation; development of backward areas; eradication of poverty and employment generation; development strategies of other developing countries; indicators of socio-economic development; foreign aid agencies and procedures; negotiation strategies; etc.

2. *Programme for Public System Administrators*

The training programmes for this diverse group (in the form of basic courses in public administration and periodic refresher courses) may cover the following topics: the national development plans; the planning process; policy formulation, development legislation; the economic environment; the socio-political environment; choice of technology; management processes; human resource management; public relations and participation; local self-government; rural sociology and the psychology of poverty, project formulation, implementation, and monitoring; data collection and processing; managerial economics and resource management; management of conflict; etc.

3. *Programmes for Managers of Financial Institutions and Banks*

National development financing; term-lending; working capital management; developing entrepreneurs; rural banking; financial needs of the cooperative sector; risk-taking; etc.

4. *Programme in Communication for Development*

Communication as an instrument of continuous education; the process of attitude change; role of mass media in socio-economic change; effective strategies and media for rural communication; evaluation of impact of developmental communication on urban and rural target populations; communication and "quality of life"; communication for national integration; lifestyles of other developing countries; communication for agricultural development; fostering participation and self help, etc.

5. *Programmes for Local Administration and Public Utilities*

The management process; delegation, accountability, and control goals and strategies of national development; role of urban and rural civic bodies in national development; manpower planning and personnel management financial planning and management; office management; efficiency concepts and systems; client relations and public relations; urban and rural housing and habitat; management of delivery systems; slum improvement and eradication; etc.

6. *Programmes for Mangers of Public and Private Sector Enterprises*

The social responsibility of business; business ethics; ecological responsibility, pollution control, and conservation of resources, choice of technology and employment generation; facilitating healthy and mature trade unions; organisational growth and effectiveness; integrated rural development; rural marketing and distribution; developing agro-based industries; developing new entrepreneurs and ancillaries; development of backward areas; helping the handicapped; transfer of managerial skills to farmers; research and development for appropriate rural technology; alternative sources of energy; etc.

7. *Programmes for Voluntary Agencies*

The nature and scope of welfare target populations for welfare; recruitment and development of welfare workers; welfare programmes and national development; welfare and self-help; skills and values of helping relationship; counselling skills; strategies or welfare; sustaining the gains of welfare; evaluation of welfare programmes; raising resources for welfare programmes; liaison with governmental and voluntary agencies; the psychology of the welfare recipient; organizing for welfare; financial management and controls; etc.

8. *Programmes in Entrepreneurship*

Entrepreneurship and development; environment opportunities for entrepreneurial ventures; resource generation; planning, organizing, directing, controlling, and staffing; styles of supervision and leadership; financial management; materials and operations management; quality control; packaging; marketing management; management of personnel; investment decisions; choice of technology; industrial legislation; processes and procedures for setting up a new enterprise; expansion and diversification; corporate taxation; safety and welfare; etc.

9. *Programmes for Teachers and Students*

National development plans; national service schemes, their natural and scope; quality of life; the economics, sociology, and psychology of poverty; management of change; integrated rural development; agricultural activities; ecological and social habitat; social work; adult literacy programmes and skills; savings and investment caring for the sick and the aged; planned parenthood population control; women welfare; brining science and technology to rural citizens; slum improvement and eradication; preservation of wild life; liaising with official and voluntary agencies engaged in development projects; demographic data collection; etc.

10. *Programmes for Trade Union Leaders*

National and International history of trade unionism; changing roles of trade unions and national integration; trade unions and national development; worker education; national wage policy; social responsibility of business; trade unions and the customer; industrial policy and legislation; welfare and safety; financial management corporate financial statements; productivity bargaining; negotiation strategies; leadership roles and styles; trade union movement in other developing and developed countries; the ILO, its roles, achievements, and shortcomings; etc.

The nature and content of the various educational programmes, indicated above, are suggestive rather than exhaustive. These can be further refined in terms of learning goals, strategies, design and methodology. The central thesis of the above discussion is that national development is a serious and complex business, and calls for multiple strategies, sustained enthusiasm and a sense of mission, harnessing of all possible resources, and a deep commitment and participation by all segments of population. National development is not a private and mystical sport of the political leaders and public system administrators. It is everybody's concern.

Summary and Conclusions

This paper has briefly reviewed the scope and strategies of planned national development in the developing countries. The final goal of development is the improvement of quality of life and realisation of basic economic, social, cultural, civic, and political rights of the citizens. Development is thus a total, integrated, and continuous process. This process, by its very nature, is never complete: there would always be new hills to climb and new horizons to scan.

If one looks at the vicissitudes of the developmental efforts of the developing countries of Asia, Africa, and Latin America over the past two or three decades, one realizes that there are many models of development, differing priorities, and varied strategies. There cannot be a single universal model applicable to all developing countries. Each country has to choose its own developmental style and modalities, suited to its socio-cultural realities, its political ideologies and institutions, its endowment of natural resources, the genius and skills of its people, and its vision of a good life and a viable future.

Whatever be the developmental choices and approaches of a developing country, the ultimate test of the success of its efforts towards planned national development would be in terms of: eradication of poverty and ignorance; adequate and nutritious food; adequate housing for all segments of the population; effective health services, control over disease, and improved life expectancy; population control; environmental control and preservation of ecological balances; provision of adequate productive and gainful work to all citizens in the working age groups; economic growth through improved production of goods and services, and sustained productivity; constant improvement in the standard of living of all segments of population; sustained protection of the fundamental human rights of all citizens, irrespective of colour, class, caste, creed, race, region, language, or sex; and continuous human resource development.

There have been many failures in the actual achievement of developmental efforts of the developing countries. One of the major shortcomings has been that the gains of development have been usurped by the elites and the favoured sections of the population, and the common citizen (particularly in rural areas) is none the better for these ambitious plans and projects, and continues to grovel in poverty, hunger, disease, and ignorance. Another major failure has been the creation of attitudes of total dependence and subservience in the masses. Very often, the goals of development have been unrealistic, over-ambitious, and flashy. Sustained mass participation has rarely been generated.

The "implementation failures" of planned development have been variously ascribed to: political instability, caprice, and nagging interference; structural weaknesses of the development machinery;

behavioural failures and skill deficiencies of public service administrators and public enterprise executives; deeply ingrained cultural values and norms of the society which are antithetical to a development ethos; etc.

This paper has suggested that, apart from making necessary corrections in the behaviours of the political decision-makers and developmental administrators, successful national development can only be attained through a pervasive and sustained mass participation. This calls for a massive "Education for Development". Some target populations for this educational effort have been identified, and tentative suggestions have been offered regarding the content of specialized educational and training programmes for these groups.

NOTES

1. See, "Human Rights, Economic Development, and Aid to the Third World: an Analysis and Proposal for Action", Douglas Williams, *O.D.I. Review*, No. 1, 1978.
2. *Employment, Growth & Basic Needs*, By the Director of ILO, 1976; and *Meeting Basic Needs—Strategies for Eradicating Mass Poverty and Unemployment—Conclusions of World Employment Conference*, I.L.O., 1976.
3. See, *Economic Growth & Social Equity in Developing Countries*, Irma Adelman & Cynthia Taft Morris, Standford University Press, 1973.
4. The Politics of Underdevelopment, Gerld A. Heeger, London, Macmillan, 1947; *The African Predicament*, Stanislav Andreski, London; and *Search for Security*, Margaret Field, London, Feber & Faber, 1960.
5. *Recommendations and Conclusions of Administrative Reforms Commissions—A Compendium*; New Delhi, Manager of Publications, 1970; *Korea's Administrative Reforms Commission*, C. Kie-ok, Madison, Wisconsin, University of Wiscosin, 1978; and *Inter-regional Seminar on Major Administrative Reforms in Developing Countries* (25 October-2 November, 1971), New York, United Nations, 1973.
6. See, "What's Wrong with Managers," John Howell, *O.D.I. Review*, 1978, No. 1.

7

Training of OD Facilitators*

Udai Pareek

The success of organisation development depends on the effective use of and coordination between external consultants and internal change agentry function. Both the external consultants and the internal change agents are facilitators in the process of organisation development. We shall call them OD facilitators, because their function is to facilitate the process of OD. Both the external and the internal facilitators have specific functions to perform, a few of them being common, and some others being different, which supplement each other. Before commenting on the kind of training needed to develop effective OD facilitators let us look at their functions and critical attributes they should possess.

External Facilitator

One or a team of consultants come from outside. One of the conditions of OD is that applied behavioural science experts are employed for OD work. This is not only useful, but also is necessary. The consultant's role is that of an expert who has a process specialized and who also has experience in several fields in which the organisation wants to bring about change. There are some advantages in having outside consultants for some time. The internal persons, even though they may have the necessary expertise, are likely to be inhibited and have their own perception of the problem. Also, they may be restrained by the internal dynamics. This may make the internal people less effective.

* First published in IJTD in 1981.

Therefore, even the organisations with a very high quality of expertise in a particular field invite outside consultants for some time. The following functions are performed by the consultant(s).

(*i*) *Implanting Function*

The External Facilitator (EF) is not to supplant the internal expertise available but supplements and implants such expertise. It is necessary that the EF carries along with him the various people at different stages of the process of organisation change. Then, the consultant is able to make change a part of the organisation.

(*ii*) *Transcending Function*

One great advantage of the EF is that he is not bound by the constraints of the organisations. He takes an overall view. He transcends both the ecology of the organisation, *i.e.*, the various units and departments to be able to take an overall view of the organisation, as well as transcends the time and people into the future of the organisation. This transcending function makes the role of the EF more creative. He thinks about the total organisation not only as it is now but as it is likely to be in the future. This helps give a wider perspective to organisational understanding.

(*iii*) *Alternative Generating Function*

The EF is not as much for working out a specific solution as for helping the organisation develop the capability of evolving solutions. The EF does this by generating several alternatives out of which the organisation can choose one or two. The more the consultant generates and helps generate several alternatives, the more creative and useful his role is, and the more the organisation develops the ability to design interventions and ways of solving problems.

(*iv*) *Process of Facilitating Function*

The EF is primarily a process facilitator. He has to be perceptive of the reality in the organisation. There is nothing like an ideal or the best solution. Even if one solution may be technically the best one, the EF may see the repercussions of the solution, and may like to make the necessary modifications to suit the situation. The EF also helps in developing various roles as the change programme proceeds and change is being implemented. The process facilitating role helps the EF move towards self-liquidation. He helps the relevant people in the organisation take over the role as the programme is being implemented.

(v) *Shock-absorbing Function*

During the planning of change and making necessary recommendations many unpleasant feedback may be required to be given to the organisation. It is difficult for internal people to do so. They cannot take the risk necessary to make some things explicit. The EF can take such a risk. He can afford to absorb the shock created by the change and can help the system confront the reality and discuss certain processes which may be quite unpleasant but without which it may not be possible to move towards the solution.

(vi) *Resource-sharing Function*

The EF brings with his background the latest knowledge and a wide variety of experience, which he uses in making organisational change effective. He collects such resources and shares them with the internal people so that the knowledge can be utilized for making the change effective.

(vii) *Resource-building Function*

The EF helps in generating resources within the organisation by building the necessary expertise as he works with the organisation. This does not mean that he makes people dependent on him. By sharing his knowledge and experience and by continuously discussing with the concerned people he helps in building internal resources.

(viii) *Self-liquidating Function*

By building internal expertise and resources he is working towards withdrawal from the organisation and liquidating his role and indispensability. In many cases, the EFs enjoy the influencing function so much that they may continue to play this role in the organisation. This is bad both for the organisation and the consultants. The EF deliberately refrains from using undue influence on internal executive decisions. And as the work of the organisational change is over he takes definite and deliberate steps to withdraw and wean the organisation from depending on him. The self-liquidating role is very difficult. Once an EF is successful and effective, he may have the temptation to continue to influence the organisational decisions. If the EF is not perceptive enough that in his eagerness to be helpful he is making the organisation dependent on him, and he enjoys this dependency, the results may be bad for the organisation as well as for the consultants.

Internal Facilitator

For any OD effort, it is necessary that an internal facilitator is either available or is developed in a process of OD. The OD effort will not be successful and effective unless internal expertise in facilitating change is properly developed in the organisation. The internal facilitator (IF) supplants several functions of EF and at the same time performs some functions which only an EF can do. The following functions are, as far as internal facilitators are concerned.

(i) Specialist Function

An IF is seen as an internal expert to whom many problems can be referred. He provides the necessary professional expertise to deal with process problems. In due course of time, he acquires a special status in the organisation, and deals with highly complex problems requiring specialist attention. For most other problems, he develops necessary expertise amongst other people to take care of these.

(ii) Intervention Designing Function

IF has to design interventions to deal with various problems and issues in the organisation. He should not be satisfied with what he has learnt during his training but should himself design new interventions and try them out for solving problems. Some of these interventions may be structured in the form of exercises, games, etc. and some of them may be unstructured.

(iii) Diagnostic and Feedback Function

One function expected of IF in all organisations is to undertake on-going activities to serve organisational health and other dimensions and to provide continuous feedback to the organisation for possible action. This would involve designing instruments, or selecting them from available ones, using instruments for collecting data, analysing and interpreting data, and providing feedback various levels in the appropriate form in which it can be understood and used.

(iv) Action-research Function

Whenever a specific problem is posed by one sub-system in an organisation, the IF may sit with the concerned people and devise ways to dealing with the problem. This is action research. Action research involves the use of scientific methods of diagnosing a problem and working out alternative solutions, in collaboration with the practitioners who are facing and experiencing the problem. Action research starts with the identification of problem, and ends with evaluation of the action plan, and replanning in the light of such evaluation.

(v) Inviting-Function

IF faces unusual problems and comes across situations he might not have encountered in the past. This requires a function of continuously inviting diagnostic methods, interventions and other aspects in order to deal with problems.

(vi) Catalyst Function

An OD facilitator, whether an external or an internal, primarily plays a catalytic role. He is a means of energising others for action. He helps people get involved and work on the problem themselves. This function is both a critical and a difficult one.

Critical Attributes of OD Facilitators

In the light of the brief mention of some of the functions of the OD facilitators it may be obvious that they would need a variety of attributes. We suggest the following attributes to the OD facilitators:

(*i*) *Empathy*

The OD facilitator needs to have great empathy for other people so that he may be able to understand and appreciate different points of view, and empathize the difficulties of other people.

(*ii*) *Ambiguity Management*

An OD facilitator works in situations which are not properly defined and which, over time, present some new dimensions. These create ambiguities. The OD facilitator has to deal with such ambiguities.

(*iii*) *Value in Change*

One critical attribute of facilitator is his values of changing. One who values *status quo* cannot become a good OD facilitator. The OD facilitator looks for improvement all the time, and values change for improving the various dimensions of organisational life.

(*iv*) *Process Skills*

An OD facilitator primarily is a process worker. He works on different process of organisations. He has to know how conflicts arise, how collaboration takes place, how people get motivated, etc. etc.

(*v*) *Action-represent Competence*

An OD facilitator needs both competence of research to solve the problems, as well as the skill of involving people concerned in the solution of the problems. He should know how to prepare various instruments for collecting data, how to interpret data, and how to value action taken for solving problems.

The Foci of Training of OD Facilitators

In order to develop the critical attributes in OD facilitators systematic training programmes need to be organised. We suggest the following aspects for designing the programmes for the training of OD facilitators.

(i) Personal Growth

An OD facilitator has to first deal with himself and work through his young process of approach and avoidance behaviour, the defences he uses, his competitive and collaborative tendencies, and his general style of working with people. An OD facilitator needs to grow himself and continuously as he continues to work in this role.

(ii) Organisation Theory and Dynamics

Since OD facilitators work in the organisational context, their understanding of the relevant organisation theory and the dynamics of working of organisations is necessary.

(iii) Process Work

Since an OD facilitator uses applied behavioural science methodologies, his training in process competency is very important. His skills in dealing with small group processes and organisational processes are critical. For example, he should be able to deal with processes of conflict and competition in smaller groups and generate the process of collaboration. Such process competence will be continuously needed.

(iv) Intervention Designing

The OD facilitator should be trained in designing and developing various kinds of interventions, including structured exercises, simulation games, exercises to involve groups in the problems they are facing, etc. He should also be trained in designing unstructured interventions to deal with people, both of smaller groups and organisations. While he may have a special inclination and preference for some interventions, he should have enough knowledge and experience of several interventions, so that he may have a wider choice.

(v) *Action-Research Competence*

The OD facilitator should have training both in research competence, (diagnosing a problem, collecting data, analysing data and interpreting them, developing instrument for data collection, techniques of data analysis, interpretation of data, clinical methods of collecting unobtrusive measures, etc.) and ways of involving people in such research process. This is action research. He has to learn both the technology of research as well as the values of participatory problem.

Several ways can be used in providing training to OD facilitators. One model is followed by Indian Society for Applied Behavioural Science in offering a phased training programme in the form of internship. This programme requires the participants to undergo intensive training for two weeks for 3 summers, and working on specific aspects for 2 years in between the summer programmes. An organisation can design a training programme if it has sufficient number of OD facilitators. The programme may consist of the basic lab for OD facilitators for about 10 days followed by specific well-directed activities, and intensive models of training spread over a 2-year period. There may be 5 to 6 such modules each of about one week duration interspersed with readings and action plans. Or, several institutions can be combined to develop an OD programme for their internal facilitators. Whatever the arrangements are, it is necessary to ensure that the five dimensions mentioned above are properly designed in the training programmes.

8

Emerging Perspectives in Organisational Development

*Indian Experience**

Dharni P. Sinha

The first OD experiment in India dates back to 1968-69 with the Kamani Group of companies (December 1971). The Tata Iron and Steel Company (Sinha, 1973) and the Hindustan Machine Tools (Varadan, 1974). In a paper entitled 'The March of Organisation Development: An Interim Balance-Sheet', Nitish De reviewed the status of OD experience in India in 1971. In Kamanis, he noted that OD had led the central policy council to explore the inter-personal relations and discover strengths and weaknesses of members which, in turn, helped the company make effective strategic decisions. Also it was seen that OD had contributed to the development of collegiate culture, between and across levels in the organisation. It was further pointed out that synergy in group work was still an ideal manipulation; forces of dependence and counter-dependence, permissiveness, power struggle, and an overall culture of "softoe" management were the burning issues confronting the organisation. In TISCO, Organisation Development involved group methods and team-building as a major intervention, in the raw materials division. Its thrust was to build commitments and a balance between engineering-oriented technology and operation-oriented work behaviour. This eventually led to restructuring of the top management team in the mines division of the company (Sinha 1973). The burning issue, however, was to consolidate

* First published in IJTD in 1981.

the gains of process change and bridge perceptual gap between Chief Executive at headquarters and the top team in the field. In HMT, the first public sector corporation to experiment with OD, the initial strategy was vertical and horizontal team-building, staff-line functional integration, improvement of organisational climate, and development of mechanisms to manage differences and conflicts. Besides the above three major OD interventions in the country, several other organisations which initiated OD efforts by 1971, included Orient Paper Mills, Bokaro Steel, Indian Aluminium, Hindustan Steel and State Bank of India.

The interim balance-sheets of organisation development in these organisations reflected primarily change in their organisation processes. The interventions were aimed at improving the organisation climate, personnel effectiveness of magnets, teamwork, inter-departmental problems and improvement in the human systems of the organisations. The following chart summarises the state of development of these three OD projects in 1971.

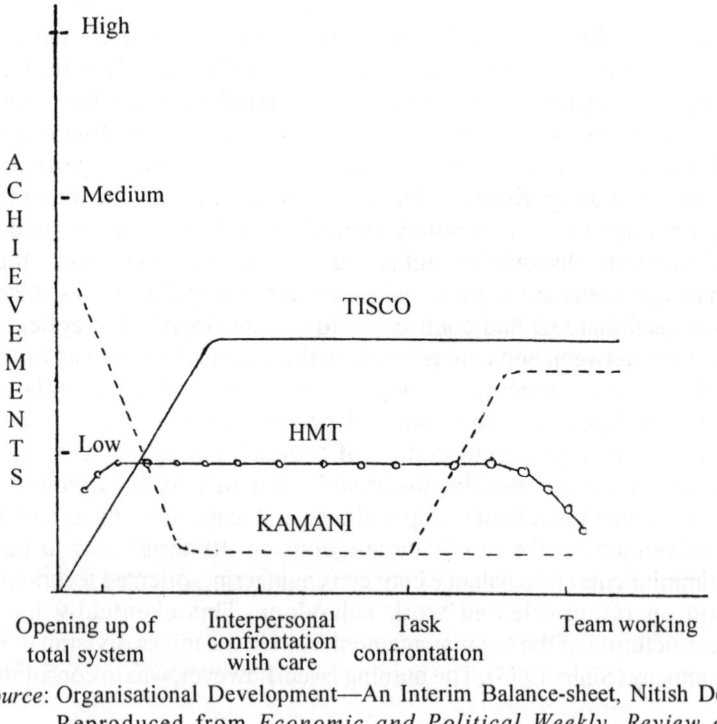

Source: Organisational Development—An Interim Balance-sheet, Nitish De, Reproduced from *Economic and Political Weekly, Review of Management*, 6 (22), May 29, 1971.

It is obvious that while OD interventions seemed to have moved smoothly in TISCO and HMT (perhaps required new interventions), in the Kamanis it had a fluctuating fortune. The achievement, in either case, however, was only between low and medium. To summarise, the organisation development experiments in India, during 1968-71, reflected the following major orientations:

1. Effort to improve human systems in the organisation focusing on personal development of managers, team-building of managerial task groups and inter-departmental problem-solving,
2. Involvement of the top management, sometimes direct, sometimes indirect,
3. Using process interventions and group as a vehicle for change, and
4. Attempt to link process change with structure, task and performance improvement.

It may also be mentioned that the early interventions in OD used T-group as a major technology for organisational change. This was true in Kamani, TISCO, as well as in HMT wherever needed, the technology was supplemented by structured simulation and task forces for problem-solving.

The early experience of OD experiments in India may be traced to two major sources. One, the laboratory training movement and the other, the survey research and feedback methodology. It reflected the impact of Ralf Lynton of the SIET Institute and Warren Dennie of the Indian Institute of Management, Calcutta, who spent a good deal of time establishing behavioural science profession in India. Douglas McGregor also contributed to it with a brief spell of work with Indian Professionals and industries in 1966. An early exposure to National Training Laboratories of Indian Behaviour Scientists determined to a large extent the orientation of early OD interventions in India.

The years between 1972 and 1975 saw several innovations in OD experiments in India. Some of them which stand out were:

(i) An emphasis on organisation diagnosis as a prerequisite to OD intervention,
(ii) An effort to build bridges between organisation process and organisation structure interventions, and

(iii) Continuation of organisation-based behavioural science training for personal growth, team-building and organisation change.

During this period, this author was involved in initiating major OD interventions in Indian Explosives Ltd. and Bharat Caking Coal Ltd. and in both the cases a good deal of time was spent on understanding the organisation, diagnosing their needs and providing systematic feedback to the key groups in the organisations for setting up change goals and intervention priorities. However, the technology of organisation diagnosis was basically an observation of, and interview with, a cross-section of population representing various sub-systems, levels, and functions in the organisation. The following four diagnostic questions were formulated for such interviews:

(i) What are you proud of in your organisations?
(ii) What are you concerned about in this organisation and what are you worried about?
(iii) What makes you work in this organisation and what keeps you going?
(iv) If you were the Chief Executive and had all the powers to effect change, what would you change?

Based on the interview data, a brief diagnostic report was prepared, describing organisation in terms of its strengths, weaknesses, motivation and morale, strains and stresses, and desired directions of change. This diagnostic report was used a vehicle for further dialogue and discussion with the client system. The discussion and critique determined the organisational priorities for effecting organisational change, and generated commitment to change plans.

In the case of the Indian Explosives the organisation diagnosis became a major OD intervention. It contributed to organisation-wide awareness of organisational problems and priorities; motivated forces for and against change; and helped identify the priority areas for OD intervention. The first intervention was to improve the organisational processes, using T-group for unfreezing, team-building and inter-departmental problem-solving. In Bharat Coking Coal Ltd., the diagnosis showed that the organisational priority was to develop an effective organisational priority was to develop an effective organisation structure and clarify the roles before the working on the organisation process and people. In retrospect, the decision to use organisation restructuring as a primary intervention for organisation development in BCCL worked very effectively. It provided a solid base for changing the organisational behaviour.

In a similar experiment with the State Bank of India, major interventions identified by the top management was organisation redesign. However, the bank experienced problems in implementing the new structure which did not seen acceptable to its managers. Therefore, a strategy was undertaken which, in a way, strengthened the structural interventions made earlier in the bank.

Some of the OD experiments initiated before 1971 took different turns during this period. Kamani experienced increasing internal stress and strain; HMT extended the process intervention to task-oriented, union-management interface workshop, work redesign, value engineering and organisational planning interventions. In TISCO, after process intervention which led to reorganisation of the top management team, the internal mechanism for OD monitoring was initiated by the head of personnel that led to a continued effort within the company. However, where training as a major strategy of organisation development was used, for example, in TELCO, Bokaro Steel, HAD and INDAL, it enabled the management development but OD innovations during this period were undertaken with temporary organisations, such as conference task groups, (Pareek, 1979) and project group in public corporations (De, 1975). Besides industrial organisations, OD was initiated in education system (Sinha, 1979) as well as in hospital system (Muss, 1973).

In the third and current phase—during the last five years (1976-80); OD experiments in India have covered a wider ground, diversified strategies, and multiple technologies for planned system-wide change. OD has now focused not only on changing organisation by improving its processes and structure, but on development of systems, goals and objectives, as well as effective interface with its environment. The new experiments with organisations, such as ITC Ltd., IDL Chemicals, Vazir Sultan Tobacco Co., Bharat Heavy Electricals Ltd., Larsen and Toubro Ltd. and a variety of banks and public systems have given a totally new thrust to organisation development. These reflect the learning from the failures and successes of the past as well as recent innovations in technology of organisation development.

Organisation Diagnosis: The Key Word in OD

The technology of organisation diagnosis today draws upon not only observations and interviews but also sophisticated instruments, such as questionnaire survey, brainstorming, structured SWOT analysis, analysis of present structure and past records and performance, survey of the client-system and environment, and interface of technical systems with human systems. In ITC, for example, the diagnosis was done by massive organisation survey through structured questionnaire which reached almost every manager and key employees. The analysis of the questionnaire data was supported by interviews with key managers. A brief report of twelve pages, summarised the diagnosis and provided feedback emerging out of the survey to the corporate board of the company. In IDL Chemicals, the diagnosis was conducted with the help of a detailed study of organisation performance data, an extensive survey of organisation, climate, a questionnaire-based managerial profiling, an in-depth interview with the key managers, ending with a structured presentation of organisation diagnosis in a two-day workshop for the top management. The output of the workshop was to identify priority action areas.

The key word in organisation development today is organisation diagnosis, which in itself is an intervention, integrating the organisational data and individual perceptions and generating involvement which enable effective implementation of change programme. Organisation diagnosis does not only generate valid information which is necessary, but its interpretation, reinterpretation and acceptance by the organisation leaders entrust them with the responsibility of managing OD interventions. Organisation diagnosis has to be widely shared; if not, OD effort would remain confined to coping with resistance to change.

There are various ways of presenting the diagnosis. The most obvious one is highlighting the strengths, weakness, opportunities and threats, called SWOT analysis, in the organisation. The second is to analyse the data in terms of leadership, organisation structure, organisation culture, technology and environment. A third approach is by drawing performance profiles of the organisation in terms of hard core data, as well as in terms of perceptions of the people, showing bumps, depressions, growth, and decline, followed by open discussion with the top management group to understand what these mean for the organisation. Still another way to project diagnosis is to make a very simple analysis of the organisation process and organisation purpose, task and performance. As shown in the model below, the organisation process may be adequate or inadequate, the organisation purpose may be clear or unclear.

Organization Process

	Adequate	*Inadequate*
Clear	Healthy Organisation	Uncommitted/Vulnerable Organisation
Unclear	Wasteful Organisation	Declining Organisation

Organisation Diagnosis Model

Looking at the model, one has to identify the box where the organisation stands today and discuss the factors responsible for the same.

Yet another way of presenting organisation diagnosis is to use the systems framework of Rencsis Likert (System 1—Autocratic, System 2—Benevolent Authoritative, System 3—Consultative, and System 4—Participative) and thus identify the organisation in terms of its present system of management and the ideal system, as perceived by the managers. There are 43 variables to measure the management system (Likert, 1967). Basically, the organisation diagnosis is an exercise in survey feedback. The feedback, however, has to result in setting up of the organisational change goals and deciding on the priority areas of action and OD interventions.

Begin Where the Client is

Of late, I have learnt not to go for organisation diagnosis unless the client-system, at least the top management, is aware of its objective. Neither an intelligent diagnosis nor a sound plan for OD intervention can be successful unless output variable and organisational objectives are clearly articulated and accepted by the top management.

Sometimes an organisation leader seeks OD intervention without really being very clear about its output, what does he want it for? And, if you ask the client why does he need OD? What are his output goals, he may sometimes respond: "You are the export, you tell us what the objectives should be; you have worked with many organisations, and you tell us what we should be doing?" When the client throws the ball in the consultant's court, it becomes difficult to really tackle it. If you make an attempt to give the objectives, based on your past experience, you may get into the trap of doing what the client should do. If you let it evolve in an unstructured way, the process becomes time-consuming and wasteful. What is, therefore, required is to enable the top management to reflect, examine, question the present goals that they have in mind and through participative process, facilitate the setting up of output objectives for the OD intervention in the organisation. As an OD consultant, my ground rule is "begin where the client is and not where you are". The client may be in genuine need to learn from you your experience in other organisation; or may be wanting to seek your help in setting objectives. If you respond without enabling the client to think through, you may create a situation where you will have to carry the burden of failure or success of organisation development in his company. To avoid this, it may be pragmatic to meet the client-needs midway, and that is what I generally do.

Once the output objectives are set, the diagnostic data are collected, descriptive profile is prepared, presented, discussed, modified, and agreed to with the client-system, a broad organisation diagnosis emerges. To my mind, diagnosis is an art of recognising the presence of specified problems beneath recurrence of manifested systems collected in the survey; it involves interpretation, inference that a consultant and client jointly arrive at through analysis, critiquing, and finally, by a fine sense of intuition. It is hard to explain as to what is intuition. It is something that flashes across one's mind, when one looks at organisation data in a gestalt perspective. I also believe that intuition comes from experience of working with large number of systems, as well as from the consulting skills, particularly of raising the right kind of questions. To give an illustration, let me recount one personal experience.

Several years ago, a large public sector corporation (which will be anonymous) was constantly facing intra-union rivalries, and approached me for organisational sensing. Sensing is technically a quick diagnosis which can later be tested by intensive survey. While analysis the interview data. I came across clusters of managers having different view-points and perceptions about the organisation. In a structured meeting, I placed the data in a diagrammatic form, and asked the question if the profile made any sense. After some initial hesitancy, one manager raised a point ... "there is no need of taking their (one cluster) viewpoint into account, those are the MD's view". I quickly asked: "Are your views in consonance with those of the Technical Director (which was obviously another centre of power)?" There was embarrassment. Then, I raised another question: "Do these two clusters have anything to do with the two groups of unions in the company?" This brought a long silence. And, what followed was a real critique of the managerial groupings and their reflection on the employees' unions. This was an intuitive statement.

There is yet another lesson from some of my failure experiences in OD. The organisation diagnosis has to be accepted by the chief executive, the top management team, as well as the key managers of the company, and this has to be done by structured exploration with the critical client groups. Most large corporations have a system of presentation, critiquing of organisational plans and performance and I find it useful to use that forum for presenting the diagnostic profile and collecting their views, agreements, disagreements and questions, which generate their involvement and commitment to the change goals. These presentations invariably conclude with a question: "With this organisation profile, what should the client-system do differently to achieve the output objectives, the change goals?" Sometimes, in the diagnosis itself, one may collect ideas about what the client system should do to achieve the change goals. Sometimes, it can be generated through discussions. Sometimes the consultant, based on diagnostic data presents a profile of organisational intervention and a list of possible interventions which could be used to achieve the specified objectives. This presentation includes the objectives of intervention as also it its focus; in other words, the organisational level where the intervention should take place. The objective of the intervention could be to sharpen the organisational system, to improve organisational processes. The level at which the intervention can take place could be individual or individuals; groups, teams and departments; intergroup and organisation; and organisation-environment interface. The OD intervention model that emerges from this conceptual consideration is presented in Table 8.1.

Table 8.1: OD Intervention Model

	Individual(s)	*Group (s)*	*Intergroups and Organisation*	*Organisation environment*
Process	Counselling: Individual feedback; Interpersonal Competence; Management Profiling Personal Growth Labs.	Team-Building; Data feedback; Process Consultation; T-group.	Sensing Meeting; Intergroup image Building; Survey feedback; Organisation Diagnosis; Third party peace making.	Survey feedback; interface meeting; Open system planning.
Structure	Role analysis; Job-Redesign; Job-profile.	Role negotiation; Work redesign.	Organisation Redesign – Basic and Shape – Technology	Organisation Redesign-Strategy and environment.
System	Personnel system; Performance appraisal; Career planning.	Work planning, Socio-Technical System.	System Development across management functions.	Feedback system from stock holder; client-customers/community, government.
Objectives and goal	Job objectives, goal setting and review.	Team objectives; goal setting and review.	Organisation Objectives, long range planning. Performance review, Survey Research.	Strategic planning.

Having agreed on the diagnosis, the top management is provided with the above model of OD interventions. In a Seminar, the details of each intervention and its implications are explained; and then it is left to the client-system to decide the choice of primary, secondary and ultimate interventions.

The choice of OD interventions is basically determined by the inter-play of two factors: (i) the objective of change, and (ii) the focus or level of change. The priorities of change also determine the series order and flow of interventions which may be required for total system-wide change. There has to be agreement on the time commitment as well. OD is a long-range strategy of change and it has to have a span of three to five years. It is, therefore, very much necessary that one should be clear about the dimension of time involved in reaching the change goals. Once agreed, an OD intervention plan would emerge which has to be monitored on and corrections made as interventions progress. It is also helpful to place the overall change plans on a PERT, with critical paths, right in the beginning, so that the client-system has a total perspective of OD.

OD: Essentially a Management Intervention

As seen earlier, the objective setting, organisation diagnosis and commitment to change goals constitute the first and the most critical phase of organisational development efforts today. This in itself, is an OD intervention; it creates an awareness of where the organisation is and where the organisation ought to be going. This also sharpens the change goals; and enables the client-system to make a decision to go or not to go in for long-range strategy for OD. During the last five years, this has been critical OD in IIC, IDL Chemicals, VST and other Corporations. I have followed the above process, almost religiously, wherever called upon to initiate OD. In an already established OD organisation, for example, in HMT, there have been several reviews the resetting of change goals. Today, OD at a unit of HMT carried out survey research on organisational problems which provide effective inputs to the top management for reviewing organisational objectives and change goals (Rao, 1980).

Having agreed to an OD plan, the next critical step in organisation development is to ensure its implementation. It is of utmost importance that intervention plans are carried out as scheduled and committed to by the top management of the company. While initiating OD interventions, one must ensure that the internal resources as well as external resources are available to the company. Internal resources consist of the time, the manpower, the finance, the resource-persons, the chief executive, the top team, and the internal change-agent (if necessary); the external resources would include consultant or consulting team, change technology, etc. If any change has to be made in the OD plans, it should have a mutual agreement between the client and the consultant. However, the active role in the implementation process must rest with the chief executive and the top management team of the company. Otherwise, the organisation will perceive this not as a management intervention but as a consultant's intervention or research/training activity. This has been effectively adhered to in several recent OD projects in India. However, it is also equally true that in several organisations, OD interventions have stopped short of going beyond the management development training.

Need for Regular Monitoring/Review

To ensure success of OD interventions, it is necessary that there is an on-going monitoring and review of plans and outputs. OD is a long-range strategy, only if they see some steady progress and small returns towards the change objectives. A regular review of progress towards outputs variables *vis-à-vis* organisational process, that is, in the behaviour and performance of people, as well as in development of systems, structure and goals would strengthen the OD process. Review should include progress of OD intervention plan as well. In the beginning, this monitoring must be done every six months. After two years, it may be phased out as an annual review. Most organisation leaders are not only concerned about what they have achieved but also how they have achieved and what kinds of interventions have facilitated the organisation. I believe that these intervention reports should be prepared quarterly so that the chief executive and the top management team are kept abreast of what is happening in the organisation.

During the past thirteen years, OD has moved from the phase of technology (*i.e.*, T-group) based invention to system-based intervention. OD has also matured in terms of diagnostic tools, and acquired a wide range of technologies to deal with organisational needs and priorities. OD continues to be a behavioural science-based strategy, of system-wide planned change. However where behavioural science knowledge is unable to meet organisational needs, OD consultants have learnt to seek the help of other specialists. OD is not the panacea for all organisational ills but it certainly enables for an organisation to remain on the road to progress.

REFERENCES

De, Nitish (1971), The March of Organisation Development: An Interim Balance Sheet, *Economic and Political Weekly,* 6, 22.

Huss, Caroll (1973), *Participative Management in Hospital System,* New Delhi, Voluntary Health Association of India.

Pareek, Udai (1979), Some Ethno-auto Biographical: Notes of Consulting, *In Consultants and Consulting Styles (Ed.,)* Dharni Sinha, pp. 129-47.

9

Select Paradigms of Management in India and the Indian Value System*

Vinayshil Gautam

The management function focusing on optimisation of all resources be they human, financial or material, has no option but to look at the cultural reality to understand more clearly the parameters of its operation, constraints in its way and the facilitators which it may convert to productive use it is, therefore, natural that a closer look be taken at the instrinsic Indian value system by those who have to operate with reference to the India national frame.

Writings on Indian identity are several and varied Megasthenes, Huen Tsang, Al Beruni, Ibn Batuta and multiple others attempted to identify the common denominator of the "Indian" and understand his shared values and traits. Nevertheless, attempts to reduce the element of randomness of the Indian experience to managerial frames of comprehension in the field of culture have eluded many. It is not unoften that the superficial has been mistaken of the substantive and the incidental for the fundamental. The problem typically has been of perceptions in the value frame of the interpreters rather than the interpreters carrying out their activity in the value frame of the people they are trying to understand. Illustratively the Orientalist Movement of the late eighteenth and early nineteenth century was not so much a discovery of the Indian mind *per se* as registering yet again by the western mind of the Indian realities. Similarly, several anthropological explorations of the Indianness carried out by people who were seeking to discover the Indian rather than to understand it have been caught up

---

* First published in IJTD in 1984.

in the clap trap of emphasising the caste, the village community, the rituals or whatever. Whereas these explorations may be interesting and valid to an alien mind exploring Indian ethos, its relevance as such for the Indian situation itself remains to be established and operationalised.

Sudhir Kakkar (*Indian Childhood*, Oxford University Press, 1979, Delhi). Raymond L. Owens and Ashish Nandy (*The New Vaisyas*, Allied Publishing Pvt. Ltd., 1977, Delhi), Vinayshil Gautam (*Enterprise and Society*, Concept Publishing Co., 1979, Delhi), doctoral thesis of Indira J. Parikh on "Emergence of Work Identity in Indian Organisation," works done by Prakash Tandon, Ishwar Dayal, Pradip Khandwalla, Shankar Sen Gupta, L.P. Vidyarthi, Eric Erikson and others did make seminal contributions to identify Indian value system relevant to management function. The fact however remains that even if put together all these studies, outstanding as they are, would not still be in a position yet to throw up a unified connected and integrated picture of the Indian mind. Accordingly many more studies would have to be carried out before that stage is reached. Till then a recognition of the larger effort being undertaken by people from diverse disciplinary background of Anthropology, History, Psychology, Economic and such other relevant pursuits which may contribute in this direction have to be accorded.

One is conscious of the tentative nature of some of the conclusions being put forward in the pages which follow but if there is a place for impressionistic statement of a practitioner and field worker in the line, one seeks to put forward no greater claims than that.

In the course of one of his Sri Ram Lectures presented at the Punjab Agriculture University, Prakash Tandon had set these explorations in perspective by pointing out that any generalisation in this direction would be a hazardous exercise because of the extreme diversity of patterns of industrial development in various parts of the country and difficulties of definition regarding what constitutes a managerial job. Perhaps a part answer, he thought, could be attempted by seeking to set the historical scene against which Indian executive operates. He pointed out that the young Indian executive had come directly from the tradition of the covenanted managers of the East India Company Civil Services, so called, because the men used to sign a convenant before taking up employment in India. A product of somewhat mixed parentage, the modern management trainee, he thought might appear to be somewhat out of place in a traditional society and some may even appear as non-Indian. But perhaps, the manager could also be called a new India: more mobile than his parents and less markedly regional in type than they were. Mobility usually began with their fathers who were the first or the second generation of professional men of India. He was educated often away from his home, safe at his school and university in any other part of India and perhaps he had been abroad. He thus represented the first of a type that was a synthesis of the cultures of different regions of India. In many ways he could be said to represent what Loyyd and Sussane Rudolph have talked of as the modernity of tradition in their celebrated book (*Modernity of Tradition*) on the Indian developmental process. The positive element of Indian tradition and its creative potential, is unfortunately, not often enough emphasized in the India context. A concern for the Indian value system and the Indian mind may appear in the managerial context to help us to understand the basic under-pinning of behaviour and see to what extent they impinge upon problem solving, decision making and resource optimisation. The obsession with the national characteristics, of course, has to be kept within the bounds, because as David Hume writing in 1741 commented "the vulgar are apt to carry all national characteristic to extremes and having once established it as a principle that any people are knavish or cowardly or ignorant they will admit of no exception but comprehend every individual under the same censure. The men of sense condemn these indistinguishing judgments though at the same time, allow that each nation has a particular set of manners and that some particular qualities are more frequently to be met with among one people that among their neighbours."

Freud later in his writings dwelt at great length on the "burden of culture" and in the post Freudian-era of psychoanalytic thought there was a great deal of shift of focus away from the allegedly inherent opposition between the wishes, drives and impulses of individual personality on the one hand and the constraints of culture on the other to an exploration and exigencies of the complementarity of what was formerly opposed. It has now been accepted that a new born infant brings with him an innate capacity to adapt to the culture where he is received.

Writing on the Indian Childhood, Sudhir Kakkar emphasised that with the predeposition of Indian mother to follow rather to lead in dealing with the child inclinations and with his tempo of development, does not spring from some universal component of maternal pride. In part it reflects the facts of life in traditional India. Given the infant morality rate which could range above 20 per cent survival of a child especially a son was regarded by his mother with the most deferential care for he would become the parent's source of economic support in later life and through his participation in their ritual, death and mourning be their guarantee of religious merit and righteous passage into the next life. This ritual role has been for many a preserve exclusively meant for the male. Above all this quality of defence and indulgence in motherhood has its origins in the identity and the development of the Indian women which is strongly influenced by the cultural idealisation and emphasis on motherhood as the predominant constituent of feminine identity.

It is not a matter of coincidental correlation that in the folklore powers are seen as focused in the *Matrishakti* as against other forms of deity. An empirical study of various devotional systems through various regions of this country though not very carefully annotated has shown similar results (White-head *Village Gods of South India*, Calcutta Association Press, 1921). Here the male gods are always subordinate to the female one, if not positively survile. At this stage of the discussion it may be an easy temptation to attack the motherhood emphasis on feminity as a sublimation of sex symbolism of male chauvinists. It may not be necessary to enter to this debate here because any situation has two sides of the coin. To pursue with the logic of the narration, suffice it to emphasise that to one's knowledge this is one of the cores of the Indian value systems. In other words the emphasis on the "motherhood concept" leads to one of the key components of the Indian mind. This has so many ramifications, indeed forming a cosmology of its own exploration. The concept may be argued for and against tossed back-and-forth and debated, but to contend with it is an essential part of understanding the Indian identity.

It has been argued by various people, including Sudhir Kakkar, that one of the most conspicuous elements of child rearing in India is the close bond and a peculiar form of an intimacy between mother and the son during the first three to four years of his life. During the period of prolonged infancy the Indian mother is inclined towards the total indulgence of infant's wishes, demands elimination, sleep or being kept company. Since it has been argued earlier that to understand child rearing practices it is essential to understand issues of Indian feminity I would like to mention here my association with the work done by the committee on Status of Women and a subsequent paper which I wrote on Managing Change in non-Change prone environment—A case of

Dowry. I pointed out in this paper that in the colonial context the outgoing flanks of emergence of capitalism, which gradually converted itself to industrial capitalism, affected not-inconsiderably the concept of Indian feminity, (for further discussion on this please, see Vinayshil Gautam "*Decision Making and Development*", National Publishing Co., 1983, Delhi, p. 54).

Being deprived and being a sojourner in her own family when the girl gets married she becomes less of a wife than a daughter-in-law. It is motherhood alone that gives to her a clear personality profile. The early deprivation and submissiveness which she as a young girl and a daughter-in-law had to observe would become less or gradually disappear all together as she bore a son. The women's deep need to overcome her frustrating position would thus also be helped by her becoming the mother of a male child. This would change her tragic position, and her narassistic desire for reperation and her age old demand that her son be virile, both seek satisfaction. Her unconscious ambivalence towards male practices would come through. She would have the need to establish her superiority. Her son becoming a highly esteemed extension of herself, a narassistic tool of retribution against society.

At this stage to revert to Anthropology may be useful because one very soon sees that family relations as stated by Anthropologist (such as D.N. Narain, Growing up in India, *Family Process*, 3, 1965, J.W. Elder Industrialisation in Hindu Society: A case study of Social Change, unpublished Ph.D. Thesis, Havard University) confirm the existence of a very close mother-son relationship of the "good mother" variety, followed in different regions and social classes throughout India. Besides, this idealistic image of the "good-mother", there is a strong evidence from clinical sources which is not without support in the major projective system of local culture, such as mythology, legends folk tales etc. that there is deep ambivalence in the mother-son relationships. In the deeper recesses of the psyche "bad mother" coexists, more less unintegrated and as a focus of sexual and aggressive passions, besides the protective and benign "good mother". The theoretical explanation of this ambivalence can be viewed differently but Spratt has stressed a fixation at the stage of "primary naracissism". This theory rests on an uncritical acceptance of Freud's contention that an excess of parental love serves to magnity for the child the danger of losing his love and renders him in later life incapable of either temporarily doing without love or accepting small amount of it. Similarly, it can be argued about the extent of power which he can operate. All this shows in an organisational frame when he grows up and it is ones understanding of the situation that lot of what happens in Indian work organisations can be understood in terms of deprivations and experiences of sex and power in the formative years of ones life.

The Indian hierarchical system of family pattern is well known. Most decisions are taken by elders and not by those whom the decisions affect.

Because of such a situation the individual from his early stage in the life cycle grows up with a sense of power deprivation, wishing to yield power and for ever being denied access to it. He tends to seek fulfilment through unbridled exercise of power on a later point in life. More likely than not he would not have known its use in a collective form. It is ones perception that along with sex frustration, power frustration is amongst the two of the more permanent hallmarks in Indian work organisations. Unfortunately however this has been confused with the Indian tradition. Scientifically a distinction has to be drawn between the tradition and traditionalism. Edward Shils followed by Hoselitz and Spengler has defined traditionalism as a more extremist negative reaction to the impingement of forces of modernity, and tradition as a society's reservoir of behaviour and symbols. The perceived resistance of strong traditions in modern or modernizing societies, binding ways of behaviour rooted in the past and to some degree referring to the past has been recognised as characteristics of the Indian Society. Conversely, several scholars, Singer and Rudolph particularly have demonstrated that traditional forces or groups—be they castes or tribal units would tend to reorganize themselves in a new modern setting in effective ways. Management is itself a symbolic activity. It means that the manager influences other persons through wielding symbol that have meaning for these persons and motivate them towards desired actions. An example of such a symbol is the memorandum written by the manager to announce a change in procedure. Its effect depends on complex set of pre-programmed interpretations by the receivers whether they can read; whether they understand language used; whether there is a respect, the legitimacy of the decision by this manager; whether they consider the style of the memorandum appropriate to the status, whether they are accustomed to react on written messages, whether they consider themselves as competent to take the requisite steps etc., are all embedded in the value frame.

Taking into account the cultural set of management presupposes an understanding of the way people can be programmed differently by their different life experiences. Pattern models of behaviour between the subordinates and superiors, among colleagues and towards clients in the work situation have been set outside the work situation: between children and parents in the family (from conception and birth onwards) among friends; between students and teachers, citizens and authorities. It should be important to note that an understanding of the people's minds does not mean that everybody in a society is programmed in an exactly the same way. It should be seen as a collective component shared in the minds of otherwise different individuals and absent in the minds of individuals belonging to a different society.

Take for example, planning, an important component of management, it is also a symbolic activity; which may or may not have an impact on what happens afterwards. Even if it has not, it will in some cultures, still be functional, because it allows management to feel secure.

Understandably, the cultures of complex nation like ours cannot be prescribed in simple terms. Select aspects have to be identified for interpretation and years of exploration alone can yield meaningful conclusions. Among the categories which have been variously used by scholars, in some of the paragraphs which follow, I will explore a few selectively.

One such aspect is individualism *versus* collectivism. Individualism stands for a preference for a loosely knit social framework in a society in which individuals are supposed to take care of themselves and their immediate families only. Its opposite collectivism stands for a preference for a tightly knit social framework in which individuals can expect their relatives, client and other in groups to look after them in an exchange for unquestioning loyalty. In a country like India inter-dependences are very high and collectivism determines behaviour as few things would.

Power distances concept is also important because it relates to the extent to which members of a society expect to wield power in institutions and organisations. This may be distributed unequally and it effects the behaviour of the less powerful as well as of the more powerful members of the society. People in large power distances society expect hierarchical order in which everybody has his/her place and which needs no further justification. Nevertheless, pent-up emotions of self-realisation remain and it creates contradictions.

Indian organisations of the traditional order had developed a certain coping mechanism for meeting such contradictions. When embedded in a modern frame it becomes a very difficult exercise and a correlation between traditional ethos and modern sophistication do create problems of functioning. It is around this value system that institutions and organisations build. One must also pay attention to what in creativity movement is termed allergy to ambiguity or what some other people term as an uncertainty avoidance mechanism. Uncertainty avoidance is the degree to which members of the society feel uncomfortable when faced with uncertainty and ambiguity. This feeling leads them to supporting beliefs promising certainty and to maintaining institutions practising conformity. Strong uncertainty avoidance societies maintain rigid codes of belief and behaviour and are intolerant towards defiant persons and ideas. Weak uncertainty avoidance societies maintain a more relaxed atmosphere in which practice counts more than principles and defiance is more easily tolerated. Examples of this can be cited one way or the other in the Indian ethos.

Historical roots of modern capitalist economics were laid in the late eighteenth century with David Hume and Adams Smith. Both their followers and critics have rarely disputed the assumption made explicit by Smith that each individual is motivated by self-interest. How this self-interest is passive in different cultures is however another matter altogether. Modern managerial psychology, especially, as enunciated by Abraham H. Maslow when he talks of self-actualisation falls into a very interesting debate in a society where self-denial is recommended to one and all as the ideal. In the Indian Society filial piety, maintenance of harmony with others, perhaps encapsuled in folk tales such as of *Shravankumar* hardly confirm Maslows favourite hypothesis. In individualistic cultures, relationship between the employees and employing organisation is a business relationship based on assurance of mutual advantages. In a more collectivist cultures relationship between employees and his employing organisation has a moral component. It is felt to be similar to the relationship of a child to his extended family and there are mutual traditional obligations: on the subject of the employer protection of the employee, almost regardless of the latters performance; on the side of the employees loyalty towards employer almost at times in an unthinking fashion. The movement of labour in these cultures would hardly follow market mechanism not only because of a moral component, but also because of economic inevitability. That, parts of the corporate sector in this country have tended to have certain degree of mobility for the individual, as such, underscores the creative potential available for development in multiplicity of directions.

In the individualist cultures, it is felt to be right that in business all people should be treated alike, friendship and enmity should not effect business deals. Business considerations should have precedence over 'personal friendships and preferences. In collectivist cultures, even in business people think in terms of "We" (or family type organisations and others), relations, tribesmen get better deals than strangers because it is perceived to be normal and right. "Modern" educated individual throwing himself in a tantraum over this is neither here nor there so far as the local ethos is concerned.

In individualistic cultures when a person wants to work from a collectivist point of view, he will have to learn that he will have to invest in personal relationship of trust before a task can be completed. This can be a matter of a few minutes or a few years depending upon personal alchemy in collectivist culture and an integration is necessary between business life and private life, the latter playing the role of developing relationship which is essential in business life. Usually if proper time is spent a relationship is successfully established, the business partner is adopted in ones circle of friends and relatives, Thus a lasting tie on the basis of which from then onwards business can be done much more quickly and effectively, mistakes could well be easily tolerated. In a country such as ours, personal relationships involve giving presents and rendering services. Such practices in an individualistic culture would be considered as bribes. In the course of one of my writings in *Enterprise and Society* (Concept Publishing Company, 1979, Delhi) I had referred to various types of give and take which have an accepted place in traditional Indian ethos and which would include activities such as *Nazarana, Sukharana, Dasturi, Bakshish,* etc., to name just a few. Alas (!!) English language has one equivalent for all this and that is "bribe". Whereas this remark itself may be made in light-hearted fashion, the implication of such an observation is not to be taken lightly.

In an individualistic society, nepotism and favouritism shown to relatives is clearly objectionable. Ones consulting experience indicates that in a collectivist society, domain of work and the domain of family interests cannot so easily be separated. I have known family concerns with a turn-over of three or four crores of rupees, having a situation where the Managing Director was stampeded by his father to accept one of his brothers into a managerial positions. This may be something which the Managing Director may not approve but in not so doing he was being a bad brother and therefore likely to fall out from the family kinship associations. One feels fairly certain that many others familiar with the Indian world of work would also vouchsafe this experience.

Employing members of family therefore is seen as something as 'proper' because it fits the pattern of employee loyalty which would then be the same as family loyalty. It is not for nothing that in the Indian ethos there are set expectations on how people should behave towards each other and violating these expectations would threaten the so important social framework. This would include getting up from ones seat when an elderly man enters the room, show the necessary deference to his opinion and beyond a point not indulging in argumentation. Harmony has the emphasis and though frank speech is constrainted a bit, it does not really matter. In the Indian environment words like *ezzat* (prestige) become critical. They are symbols of value system.

"Face" would be the English translation, of the Indian expression which in Hindustani shall be *chehere-ki-lalli* (glow of the face or prestige) which indicates both the front parts of the head and the dignity based on a correct relationship between a person and the collectivities to which he or she belongs. More collectivist cultures are very face conscious and loss of face can be felt to be more painful than physical maltreatment. Consider the ways in which the marriage of the young is negotiated in this country. To convert, adapting from Geert Hofstede, these considerations in management terms would mean following: (i) need for subordinate consultation; (ii) acceptability of paternalistic management; (iii) the meaning of status difference; (iv) respect for old-age; (v) manners of getting redressal for grievances; (vi) feasibility of certain leadership packages such as management by objectives; (vii) feasibility of appraisal systems in general.

To understand the need for subordinate consultation *versus* the need of acceptability of opportunistic management, it needs to be appreciated that models of behaviour are carried over from the culture off the job to the culture of the job. In culture such as ours, notwithstanding some notable exceptions of institutions manned by western education trained academics, in the larger value system of this country, formal dependence of children even adult children on parents carries forward into the relationships between teachers and students and superiors and subordinates. Students are expected to show respect to the teachers and to treat them as source of wisdom, never openly disputing their teachings. One way ex-catherda teaching is customary in such a cultural setting. If we, then, move to the work organisation, it is normal that subordinate relationships are modelled after the same pattern of subordinate dependence. This pattern is accepted and considered comfortable by superior and subordinate alike. A good superior is expected to behave like a god-father or mother towards subordinate. The norm is paternalism.

Similarly, whereas in low-power distance societies like the modern-west, status tends to be achieved, in large power distance societies like ours status is ascribed. Indeed, often, an individual's worth and endeavour in a particular direction is also seen in terms of furthering his movement in the direction of acquiring the trappings of an ascribed status.

Similarly, in large power distance societies paternal and maternal authority which subsists throughout life manifests the respect for older age both within organisations and fn social life In such cultures grievance channels are generally missing and very difficult to establish. The power of superior is more absolute and an act of complaint to a third party may expose the subordinate to the reprisal by the superior. There are, however, indirect ways of making grievances known when there is no way of redress for the individual. There may, however, still be collective redress: if many subordinates hold the same grievance and the superior is supposed to have the infringed collectvist norm of good behaviour, they can atleast in our culture collectively resist the superior but this is a very serious matter. It leads to considerable loss of face on the latter's part. It is unfortunate that while talking of Management by Objectives (Drucker), Theory X and Theory Y (McGregor), Achievement Motivation (McLelland), Managerial Grid (Blake-Mouton), System Y Management (Likert), Theory Z (Ouchi), almost without exception the cultural assumptions that went into these packages have not been explored. The status of research in this area in India, veering around to using the cultural argument, such as in this paper, have to be: sufficiently extended to analysing why our organisations are the way they are.

Obviously, in an "Indian" environment, the performance appraisal of a subordinate becomes a tricky one. If two way communication between superior subordinate is unlikely to grow, or get institutionalised, the entire appropriateness of this type of appraisal system as originated in industrial west becomes doubtful. Further work will have to be done for developing the local approaches, consistent with local cultural traditions to understand how best the subordinate can be appraised and developed.

Because of such factors prevalent in our society people may develop emotional need for formal and informal rules as guides of behaviour: formalisation, standardisation and ritualisation of organisational processes etc. Top planning and how it should be developed would become important subjects of consideration. In such an environment the meaning of time becomes significant. It may have, as is often realised, a circular concept rather than a linear one, especially in India. Time may not necessarily be a scarce commodity-culturally. Again in our context expression of emotions may be more easily tolerated than in less uncertainty avoiding cultures. Similarly the role and status of defiance in such a society has to be considered more carefully.

Models of our organisations and designs of jobs, in them, will have to account for such realities. Attempts at organising will have to take into consideration the concerned cultures sub-cultures, and symbolic structures available. This would raise the need of the symbolic structures being appropriately interpreted if these are to be effective. The people while inside or outside the organisation will naturally have some commonalities of perceptions and values and this will have implications for job effectiveness. In our cultural setting, where time very often assumes a framework for orientation rather than something to be mastered, life would clearly have some unique components in its underpinnings.

Regardless of the country's varying levels of economic development, it is plausible to argue that we are noisier and more emotional than many of our colleagues in the west. It is not for nothing that our daily lives are embedded in festivities that provide legitimate outlets to give vent to our emotions and intrinsic urges. Becoming emotional, pounding the table, raising one's voice can be perfectly acceptable for a manager in a more uncertainty avoiding culture but it is likely to lead to complete loss of respect from others in the organisation. We will further have to consider competitiveness *versus* solidarity, equity *versus* equality, sympathy for the strong or sympathy for weak as the need may be. We would need to look into achievement motivation *versus* relationship motivation. Concept of quality of work life, career expectations, acceptability of an ideal picture of a manager as a masculine aggressive hero with superhuman qualities taking fast important decisions, admired by his fellows and his women, crushing his adversaries, would have to be looked into carefully.

In a masculine culture such a behaviour may be acceptable to many and may be even functional, even if the manager in reality is not as much of a superman as the ideal as he tries to live up. The same behaviour in a feminine culture would disqualify the manager as a ridiculous loud talker that cannot be taken seriously. The evidence for and against this however has to be assessed carefully in the Indian context. Whereas we are a nation of hero worshippers and have always conferred godhood, atleast on some heroes and put them beyond the pale of human realities and ambit, I am not so sure if singly anyone of our organisations would be ready to have so many "gods" (super-men managers) in one frame. Effectiveness within a given culture and judging according to the values of the culture obviously needs management scholars and practitioners to integrate the global with the local.

Such a discussion as the one undertaken above on the Indian value system can definitionally never be exhaustive. The crucial issues remain of managing change, adapting it and developing systemic linkages both within the organisation and environment. It will be useful to emphasize, along with Eisenstadt, that in a situation of change there develops not just one possibility for restructuring resources and activities but rather a great variety of possibilities. Within each "type" of traditional or for that matter modern society different models of managerial order emerge which define their own parameters. It calls forth for an attempt to come to grips with a series of unanswered questions; who will be the carriers and what will be mechanism of identifying of such a managerial order? What would be the nature of relationship among the internal variables? What would be structural conditions that would facilitate development of different aspects of codes and the continuous maintenance of their major structural derivatives? Indeed, what would be conditions under which the relative importance of different codes within the society change? The questions are almost endless and possibilities of debate many. It is only in a creative pooling of our experiences and understanding that modes can be developed for truly identifying the unique paradigms of management in India. To work together in that direction may prove satisfying for all interested in dynamics of managerial effectiveness in this country.

10

Transfer of Technology from Lab to Land*

Devendra Kumar

The kind of technologies that are developed in the laboratories are not always in consonance with what are of priority to the masses or the people. This paper is addressing itself to technologies which fulfil the requirements of the people in our villages who basically depend on land.

Any new technology for greater production which is discovered for the people, is used mainly by the dominant group in the villages and not by the poorer people. Of this we have examples in the use of the technologies of the 'green revolution' or the 'white revolution'. These technologies are such which increase production by finding greater inputs of a new kind. However, as large number of people do not have the wherewithal's to be able to afford utilisation of such techniques, they are applied by comparatively affluent amongst them and so the production increases in pockets of prosperions.

There is no doubt that the total production significantly increases by this method but at the same time so also does disparity.

The technologies in the industrial field also have the same character of leading to greater production and create disparities consequently.

It is quite obvious that this mode of productivity lacks the basic component of social justice. We ought to be clear as to what kind of technology we want, which is to be transferred from lab to the land.

The characteristics which are necessary for the real good of the people of the land are: (a) that the technology should lead to the

* First published in IJTD in 1985.

diminution of disparities leading to a greater social justice, (b) its process should be such as consumes natural resources and affects the environment in a way that is ecologically sound. Once we have found such techniques which are socially just and ecologically appropriate, the mode of their transference for the good of the people has to be modelled. Another assessment that has to be kept in mind regarding the kind of technology is of assistance to a very large number of people and that its quotient of multipliability should be high *e.g.* the improvement in a tractor will help a smaller number of people whereas an improvement in the bullock-driven plough will have a high rnultipliability factor.

Transfer of Technologies

When a technology or process is evolved in a laboratory, it has got to be utilized in the field, but that does not necessarily happen at all times. Since by and large the kind of technologies developed are to fulfil the commercial interests of the industrialists and entrepreneurs and the users or technology are themselves in search of new processes by which they can increase their production and their profits, the laboratories have only to publicise their research through journals and papers and may be sometimes through exhibitions, to communicate with their prospective users. The users of technology being in a position to invest and take risks come forward and make use of it. This kind of technology transference has thus a set pattern. Even though in this model there are difficulties in the Indian scene because what is found out in the laboratories has yet to be optimised and proven on a large scale and the entrepreneurs find it difficult to take it up since it is not presented to him on a turnkey basis which is available in the other countries of the world.

Secondly, there are techniques which are of community benefit and which are not meant necessarily to be used by individual entrepreneurs. This is the case when the State takes up its application such as atomic energy research and the space and satellite programme etc. Here, ultimately, the community gets the benefit but the transfer pattern is of a different kind altogether.

In this discussion, however, we are not concerned with these two kinds of technologies but technologies which are meant for the rural masses. The above mentioned routes of transfer do not take place in regard to the technologies for the masses.

Technology for the Masses

The psychology of those for whom a technique is meant in this area, is quite depressing. They have seen many twists and turns in their environs and have seen that all the changes that take place have by and large benefited only the big at their expense. All efforts they made in the past to get out of the rut having failed, they suffer from a psychology of defeat and they cease to make further efforts. They lose confidence in themselves and look at askance to any new innovation. As application of any new technique involves an amount of risk and the poor of the land are devoid of any risk taking capacity, we have here a conundrum where we want to bring together two incompatibles. The transfer of technology for the masses from lab to land is therefore much more difficult than that in the case of the two sectors of private and public enterprise as explained in the previous para. We have to bring here an alchemy whereby the immissibles mentioned above become missible. Till we do that, technologies appropriate for the land having been found out will still remain in the labs like the mythological Ganga in the hair-locks of Shiva. It requires a 'Bhagirath' effort to transfer their knowledge from the heights of the labs to the people living below, who need it. For this the level of technology presently available with the masses will have to be fully understood and the new technology, we want to introduce, should not be very much higher from the current level. A low gradient is to be maintained for the inflow of a new technology. There will still be a certain risk in the adoption of the new technique. This risk will have to be got covered by the agency which transfers the technology and not leave it on the Users. Otherwise the users will fight shy of the innovation, more so because of their past experiences of techniques received being inimical to their interests.

To win over the confidence of the users, a low gradient technique be carefully introduced where the risk involved is covered This would bring a change from defeat to confidence in their mental make up. Small changes through introduction of appropriate technology will lead to the weaker sections getting confident of themselves and imbibing further innovations and thus strengthening their position. Big structural changes in the power equation as well will ensue as the process of strengthening the weak continues. The utter dependence of the have-not on haves will be gradually reduced and ultimately a balanced interdependence could be achieved through this process of transference of technology. The new technology once adopted and imbibed by the masses gives them not only the confidence to search for other innovations but also arouses the latent talents of innovativeness amongst them.

The psychological change is so very important for the growth of the people that in the beginning, the techniques to be taken to them need not necessarily be of income generating nature but could be simple as to help in improving their environment or reduce the "drudgery" of the family members. Income generating processes are essential but their seeds can be sown after the soil has been ploughed and is ready to receive them. This psychological receptivity is to be brought about first through techniques of the kind mentioned above.

Transfer Methodology

The appropriate techniques which are beneficial to the masses are not easy to be found out as in their evolution and optimisation, close, communication with the users is necessary. Actually the participation of the people while the technique is being evolved becomes necessary. This not only brings the right results but also commits them to accept it. Technology for the people has to be evolved with the people. In cases where large laboratories have got the technique it has to be optimised and made assimilable for the target group.

In the final stage any technique which is good for the people will have to be converted into some sort of a trade by which one who transfers or multiplies it can make his living out of it. It is a patent fact that unless a 'process' becomes a 'profession' and a 'technique' is transferred into a trade, its transference is not easy. Take the example of *gobar* gas technology. We have a very good technique here which helps the growth of the village but it is not multiplying fast. This is because we have biogas technology but not 'biogas wallas'—artisans who have adopted this technology as their trade. Hence the transformation of technique into trade is also a very essential task. This step is as much, if not more, difficult than the generating of a new technology.

In transferring new technologies to the people another factor is—through whom do you take it to them? But let me repeat that here we are dealing with the sections of people who are reluctant to try new things. So the agency through which the unknown technique is to be taken should be known to them. Here, the role of voluntary agencies becomes very important because they are the ones who have established rapport with the people and gained their confidence. The new techniques should, therefore, be tried through voluntary agencies who have some commitment and are working for the poor in the villages.

To sum up, the transfer methodology which emerges is:

1. The low-gradient technique should be used in taking S & T inputs to the masses and in evolving/adopting it, the people should be involved.
2. Firstly, such kind of techniques should be chosen where risk is minimal and which improve the environment and/or reduce drudgery.
3. The income generating techniques be introduced when and where the people have been prepared to imbibe new techniques.
4. The technique to be introduced should become an occupation to give gainful employment to the people.
5. The new technique be introduced through old people, i e. those known to them and in this, voluntary agencies working amongst them should be used.
6. Infrastructure support being absent in many villages the planning should be to involve a group of small, middle and big villages in the productive process. These need to be net-worked and a proper system evolved by which a technique could be broken into processes which could be suitably divided in the various types of villages having different kinds of infrastructural support.

Thus it will be seen that the methodology of transfer is more intricate when we need to take the products of the lab to the land to assist the large mass of people living below the line of subsistence. These steps are to be well worked out and may require much research. If a proper transfer mechanism is available, generation of technology in this sector will also be augmented. When off-take is less the generation is also small.

Success Stories

In transfer of techniques, the above mentioned mechanism has been tried out in some places and here are a few success stories which illustrate the points made out. The pulley in the village well fitted with ball bearing made the drawing of water easy and increased, the life of the pulley. This brought a smile on the face of the poorest woman, of the village since for the first time she saw something which brought concrete assistance to her. Even though it was a non-monetary change, it brought her hope. Similarly, technologies like the soakage pit keeping the well surrounding dry and clean gave the villagers further confidence. The mudwall of the poor man's hut gets eroded with rain; given a cladding of red clay tiles made by the village potter makes it non-erodable. The smokeless cookstove made in the village itself can give better working condition and greater thermal efficiency. The pot-chlorination-method for well water and filter-candle fitted in the drinking water mud pots, kept one over the other, can make the water safe for drinking even in remote villages. The biogas plants giving both manure and cooking fuel can change the entire complexion of the village. The lavatory attached to the gas plants will make the environment clean by right disposal of nightsoil. The double mud pot with an outer jacket where water evaporates and keeps it cool is a cheap mode for preserving foods. The wind mill for drawing water from the well or river, in areas where wind is regular, can help the village economy. The improved techniques in low cost housing mainly using mud as the building material bring new occupations and better dwellings. Herbs and plants in the household for medicinal and economic utility can be introduced for economic gain and better health. The solar cooker saves fuel wood and the drudgery of women in collecting the fire wood. Better yet cheap modes of storage of agricultural produce need to be introduced from available models. Tree plantation and orchards in community land can bring employment to the landless. The utilisation of the various agro-wastes for economic products like pulp products and boards from stalks of cotton, stem of plantain etc., open a new field of economic gain to the poor. Essential oils from aromatic material available in the village is another field which needs to be explored.

These are only examples to show how low-gredient technology can reach the poorest in the land and the labs get connected with the needs of the last and the least. Many of the above examples have been tried out and their potentialities made evident.

Conclusions

The generation of technology for the benefit of the masses must be of such nature which will bring hope, faith and confidence amongst the largest number of people and the weakest to begin with. This needs a close liaison between the field conditions and the labs. The scientists should directly get in touch with the villages, through voluntary agencies working there. The voluntary agencies having established rapport with the villagers are the best media through which new technology can be tried. The voluntary agency will also be in a position to communicate to the labs what the felt needs are—'where the shoe pinches to those who wear no shoes'. It is in this area that the new techniques are to be evolved. Identification of right problems having been done, the labs will find a technological solution of the same. They will be able to see its applicability in the field conditions through the help of voluntary agencies The voluntary agencies have a greater manoeuvrability and commitment to enable them to tryout such experimentations better. This two-way commemoration has to be constant to arrive at the right results.

Thus proven technologies have to be tried out in a larger area with the help of the government. Many lacunae will again be found and the model will need to be adjusted accordingly. Here again voluntary agency linkage should not be left out. Assisted by government agencies the motivating work be done by voluntary agencies which is close to the people. When a new technique has been well tried out by a number of voluntary agencies in various geo-physical regions and the mode of converting the technique into a pattern whereby people themselves can manage it with the necessary support has been evolved. Then and then alone, the technique can be sought to be universalised by having training programmes, subsidy schemes, sales management, quality control etc., formulated.

If a large base for an innovative optimistic atmosphere is to be created, the technological inputs must touch the life of the last and the least. This will create a healthy and robust ethos in the country leading to a tremendous outburst of creativity and confidence which the present day developmental structure keeps restricted to a small minority. The small drops of rain are able to keep the whole earth green because their spread is immense whereas the impressive looking, rushing and gushing waters of the canal can command only a small portion of land into prosperity at a level much higher than the rest. We may need, both, but in priorities the small yet multiplied infinitely will always be more potent.

11

Training Functions in India*

Mirza S. Saiyadain

Introduction

Training as an independent function is supposed to have started as easily as the beginning of stone age, when man started amassing knowledge and transferring it through signs and deeds to others. Subsequently, the skill and knowledge of the crafts were transmitted by direct instructions through the apprenticeship system. The advent of Industrial Revolution (1750 AD) could perhaps be taken as the beginning of vocational training (Steinmetz, 1967). Today, training is not only an essential prerequisite for all kinds of jobs, but a large numbèr of studies are also carried out regularly to develop methods and systems to make training as effective as possible.

Research on Training in India

India trainers and researches have been able to generate a systematic body of knowledge on various aspects of training in India. We have, in India, a reasonably good understanding of the various facets of training and a meaningful grip on them for human exploitation. Such studies can broadly be classified into three different categories dealing with identification of training needs, training methodology, and training effectiveness. A brief review of some of these studies is presented below:

* First published in IJTD in 1987.

Studies on Need Identification

A number of studies on the identification of training needs are available. Some of them deal with the general framework while others are specific company based studies.

For training activity to be meaningful, Dayal (1970) suggests that a detailed study of jobs and skill analysis is absolutely necessary. The training thus imparted would help the employee to adjust to their job requirements. As far as the supervisory category is concerned, Sundaram (1970) points out that the training needs for supervisors can be identified through careful observation of their work which is indicative of poor performance, low production, high cost, poor product quality, high scrap, spoilage, wastage, accidents, absenteeism, and turnover. The day-to-day complaints and grievances also form a useful source for identifying their training needs. Given that supervisors are the first contact point for the workers, Ghosh (1984) stresses the need for behavioural inputs in any training programme organized for supervisors. Using the Delhi technique for assessing the training needs for Managers, Srinivasan (1977) recommends that their training programmes should focus on corporate planning, organisational development and personnel management.

As far as identifying the training needs by the company is concerned, Glaxo Laboratories consider the following factors:

1. Level and rapidity of technological and administrative changes;
2. Level of individual and group performance;
3. Changing organisational structure; and
4. Perceived organisational imbalances.

At the individual level, the person himself identifies the need for training and records it or the appraisee discusses, the individual's training needs in view of his deficiencies on the job. Since Glaxo uses MbO system this process helps a great deal in making training useful to both the employees and the organisation (Lawande, 1980).

Bhatia (1981) sees a shift from knowledge to attitude as the main objective of training. He identifies three areas of training—technical skills and knowledge, knowledge of organisation and external systems and conceptual and interpersonal skills. He suggests that the emphasis on these three must vary according to the level of the employee. The workers' training should focus on technical skills and knowledge followed by conceptual and interpersonal skills, and knowledge of organisation and external system. In the case of supervisors, conceptual and interpersonal skills should be emphasized followed by technical skills and knowledge, and knowledge of organization and external environment. As far as managers are concerned, the sequence is the same as that of supervisors except that the order of knowledge of organisation and external environment and technical skills and knowledge is interchanged.

Seth (1984) administered a 72-item questionnaire on 119 personnel managers. The cluster analysis revealed personnel managers to be more employee oriented, able to recognise the utility of group processes, and having faith in workers' ability to take initiative and handle responsibility. On the basis of results, Seth suggested that training for personnel managers should be directed towards attitudes and beliefs underlying managerial philosophy and their inter-relatedness.

The studies on the identification of training thus emphasize not only the organisational analysis but job and individual role analysis as well.

Studies on Training Methodology

There is some debate on the feasibility of certain training methods used in the Indian context. Basha (1971) takes the stand that multinationals operating in India find that their home tested training techniques do not have the same impact here. Due to differences in culture and background, business games, T-groups, case methods and workshops are not as effective in India as perhaps in Europe or America. He concluded that given the Indian context, the lecture-cum-discussion method would be most useful. Much in the same sprit, Prahlad and Thiagarajan (1971) suggest that structured exercises seem to offer greater scope in India. Such techniques as T-group, management games, and MITRA exercises assume a minimum level of intellectual competence in the participants. The trainer, therefore, has the additional responsibility of assessing the relevance of the method before using it.

Saxena (1973) suggests that the OD technique can be most useful for training employees in government. The training programmes of the government are designed to inculcate capabilities to introduce change and review the environment. OD can help in improving organisational design, introducing organisational flexibility, reducing impersonality, improving interpersonal relations and differentiating operational decision making from policy decision making.

In order to create a realistic atmosphere in training, Srinivasan (1980) used experimental learning techniques in training a group of postal employees in the Post Staff College, New Delhi. The technique consisted of requesting the participants to bring real life data to classrooms. A detailed analysis of this data helped the participants to understand problem areas and take well informed decisions.

Agarwal (1982) in his study on graduate engineering trainees in three large public sector organisations found that both the method and the contents of the training were perceived by the trainees as demotivating and dissatisfying.

Studies on Training Effectiveness

The basic question of effectiveness of training deals with the issues whether formal training programmes contribute to the development of job related skills eventually leading to greater effectiveness. Mehta (1970) points out the training effectiveness is dependent on two considerations—(1) trainers are fully responsible for training. If the employees do not show results the trainer should be held accountable for it; (2) training *per se* is not the answer to the problems. Training effectiveness depends on the kind of atmosphere and culture that is prevalent back home.

Accepting these constraints as contributory, many studies have shown that training does make a difference. Jain (1985) collected data on 119 managers in the steel industry who had attended in-company or external training programmes. A questionnaire was administered and their responses were tallied. A majority of the respondents were found to be satisfied with the instructors, the size of training group, the training duration, the reading material and the training equipment. Except for one respondent, all felt that training contributed substantially in developing their knowledge skills, and attitudes. They also felt that the environment did help in implementing some of the learning that took place during training.

Yet two studies suggest some opposite findings. Benerji (1981) collected data on supervisors who had undergone training in an Indian engineering company. They were administered a check list. The responses indicated that the inputs in industrial relations had little or no impact on their effectiveness. However, most of them felt that training did improve their self-confidence, motivation, identification with management goals, and communication ability. In another, Mahaeshwari (1981) collected data on 999 respondents from banking institutions. Though these managers found training programmes less effective with respect to their contribution to job performance, they did endorse the usefulness of formal training.

Sikka (1985) suggests two models to evaluate training effectiveness. First is the expectation-achievement model consisting of matching post-training achievements with pre-training expectations of the boss, peers, the subordinates and trainee himself. The second is the experimental control group model, wherein a group of employees who have gone through training is compared in terms of their performance with those who have not. The models are useful in generating comparative data to judge if training has really made a dent.

While the studies reviewed here and many others in the area of training have contributed extensively in developing a body knowledge, each one of them has dealt with one specific aspect of training. None of the studies has dealt with the state-of-art as it exists in India today.

The Present Survey*

The present survey was undertaken to examine the nature of training functions in India. Specifically, through this survey, we wanted to understand:

1. The significance attached to training in terms of the overall functions of the organisations—the level and/or the structural location of training departments, their management; nature and size of infrastructure and cost.
2. The systems and methods used in identifying training needs.
3. The nature, duration, and frequency of training programmes mounted by organisations and sponsorship to the external programmes including those organized abroad.
4. The attempts made to assess training effectiveness; preparedness in making adjustments in packages for better results.

Methodology

Data were collected through a questionnaire (*See* Exhibit 1) which

* The cooperation of participating organisations is gratefully acknowledged.

was mailed along with a self-addressed unstamped envelope to 761 organisations randomly chosen to represent a variety of industries, technologies, sectors, geographic locations, products, services, size and age. Two months were given for their return and hence end of July 1986 was prefixed as the last day for accepting questionnaires to be included in the sample. Unfortunately the rate of return did not turn out to be as encouraging as originally envisaged. Most of the completed questionnaires that came back were received within a month of the dispatch. In all, 49 completed questionnaires were received which represented 6.4 per cent of the total sample to which questionnaires were mailed. A list of these organisations is given in Exhibit 2. The participating organisations are fairly representative of the variety of industries in India.

Sample Characteristics

The sample organisations represented 17 different kinds of industries. (*See* Exhibit 3). In terms of their age, there were some that were more than 36 years old while others were recently established (5 years or less). The sample distribution by age of the organisations is given below:

5 Years or less	8
6-10 years	3
11-15 years	6
16-20 years	5
21-25 years	4
26-30 years	8
31-35 years	1
36 and above	14
Total	49

Of the 49 organisations, 17 have their head office/corporate offices located in the Western region, 6 in the East, 13 in the North and 13 in the South. The percentage of public sector undertakings in the sample* was 22.91, private sector 66.66, and joint sector 4.16. There were

* All 49 organisations have not always responded to all the items in the questionnaire. The percentages quoted in this report are based on the number of organisations that have responded to various questions. These numbers are indicated in the parentheses immediately after the percentages wherever the total is less than 49.

three organisations in the sample which were either a partnership firm or a cooperative society 18 of them had foreign collaborations with parent companies in the USA, Japan, UK, France, West Germany, Canada, Holland, Belgium, Switzerland, Italy and East Germany.

As of last accounting year the average employee strength of the sample organisations and the standard deviations are given below:

Employees	*X*	*S.D.*
Managers	132	182.60
Supervisors	341	428.24
Workers	1570	1703.37

As can be seen from the data above the standard deviations for all three categories are large because of the wide range of employees in these categories across organisations. In terms of the span of control, on an average, 4.76 workers are controlled by one supervisor and 2.64 supervisors report to one manager.

The average annual turnover over the last five years was found to be 60.90 crores (range = 0.25 to 535.00 crores) and the average annual turnover in the last accounting year was found to be 72.31 crores (range 0.26 to 711.00 crores). These organisations varied from .05 per cent to 41.0 per cent in their cost of human resources over the total turnover in the last accounting year (average = 10.32%). Of the total of 45 organisations that answered this question, 86.66 per cent organisations made profit in the last accounting year. Of the 49 organisations, 4 are reported to be totally self-financed while the rest acquired funds from the following sources. (The percentages) do not add to 100 because many organisations have acquired funds from more than one source):

	Per cent
Shares	48.98
Debentures	24.48
Fixed deposits	46.93
Banks	81.63
Other financial institutions	67.34
Other sources	16.32

Manning of Training Departments

Of the 49 sample organisations, 16 (32.65%) have their separate training departments, while for the rest, training function is a part of the general personnel and administration activities.

On an average, the separate training departments of 16 organisations have been functioning as separate entities for the last 9 years (range = 1-24). In 68.7 per cent of the sample, the incharge of the department is designated as Manager (Training) while in the remaining, they are designated as principal, general manager, superintendent (training) etc. in 75 per cent of the cases they report directly to the General Manager/Director/Corporate Vice President (Personnel). In one case, however, the incharge of training reports directly to the Chairman. The manpower for these departments usually consists of officers and ministerial staff. The average staff strength was found to be 3.1 employees. There were faculty and instructors on the payroll of three of these organisations. Fifty-seven per cent of the incharge of departments have bachelor's degree while 43 percent have a master's degree. Surprisingly, while a large majority of them have their first degree either in engineering or in science, they have acquired their post-graduate education in fields relevant to training functions. They have been in their respective organisations for an average period of 8 years and 6 months and in training departments for 5 years and 7 months.

For the 33 organisations which do not have separate training departments, the training functions are looked after by managers who are also incharge of industrial relations, recruitment, manpower planning, appraisal, etc. However what is more interesting to note is that as many as 27.27 per cent of the managers whose prime concern is with materials management, production, maintenance, finance and marketing are also looking after training functions in their organisations. In both cases they report to the general managers (64%), the executive directors (20%), the president (4%), the chairman (8%) and the production engineer (4%). They have been in the organisation for 8 years and 6 months and have been looking after the training functions, for almost 5 years on an average. While everyone of them has a minimum bachelor's degree, except for 4 out of 33, none has formal professional degree relevant to manage training functions.

A subsequent analysis of the characteristics of the organisations that do not have separate training departments suggest is that majority of them:

1. employ hundred or less managers (54.5%)
2. employ five hundred or less workers (43.2%)
3. have shown an average turnover of 10 crores or less in the last five years (45.4%)
4. had an average annual turnover of 10 crores or less in the last accounting year (36.4%)

The above observations are based on the analysis of the distributions of organisations on various characteristics and the existence of training departments in these organisations. The above profile includes only those characteristics where values of Chi-square are significant beyond the conventional levels of significances (*See* Exhibit 4).

Of the 38 organisations which responded to the question "have you sent your training incharge to external training programmes", 25(65.79%) have replied that they were doing so. These programmes varied in duration from 1 day to 5 months and 55 per cent of them focused fully or partially on packages relating to training functions. Such organisations as Indian Institute of Management (IIM) Ahmedabad, Administrative Staff College of India (ASCI), Indian Society of Training and Development, Board of Apprentice Training, NITIE Bank Staff Training College and Indian Institute of Technology, Madras have been pointed out as training organisations where the managers were sponsored for courses on training.

Training Facilities

In order to impart effective training, adequate infrastructure facilities are important. It is unfortunate to note that only 12.2 per cent of the organisations have full-fledged training college/institutions of their own, indicating the inadequacy of necessary infrastructure to mount training programmes. The facilities includes class-rooms, library, audio-visual equipment, faculty on permanent payroll, residential facilities, and a training secretariat. While other organisations are not as fully equipped as these, they have limited facilities of their own. For example, 48.9 per cent of the organisations have their own modest libraries containing more than 100 books on management and allied fields; 38.7

per cent has audio-visual equipment; and 20.4 per cent has permanent faculty on the payroll. Other than these, infrastructural facilities for training are almost non-existent.

Training Cost

The significance of the training function can be estimated in terms of the cost incurred on training programmes. Often the needs are clear ant the employees who need training and the training programmes that would be most beneficial to them are well known. However, because of financial constraints, they are not sent to appropriate programmes and compromises are made on both the contents and the agency offering the programmes. The organisations were asked to indicate how much they spent on training in the last accounting year. Twenty-three organisations responded to this item. While the organisation-wise cost varied from Rs. 8,000 to Rs. 10 lakh, the average cost works out to be Rs. 2.19 lakh per organisation.

The organisation were asked to indicate total turnover, percentage cost of human resources and the total cost of training during the last accounting year. 20 organisations provided all three kinds of data. The total turnover for these 20 organisations varied from 1 crore to 1000 crores (X = 104.2 crores), the percentage cost of human resources varied from 2 to 25 (average percentage = 9.86) and the training cost varied from 8 to 100 thousands ($\bar{X}$ = 1,93,983). While the average cost of human resour es was as 986 per cent of the total turnover, the average cost of training works out to .017 per cent of the total cost of human resources. The rank order coefficients between the cost of human resources and total turnover as well as cost of training work out to be –.097 and –.109 respectively. Both coefficients are statistically insignificant but their direction suggests that the higher the turnover the lesser the percentage cost of human resources and the higher the percentage cost of human resources the less the expenses on training.

Identification of Training Needs

In order to be able to sponsor and/or mount relevant training programmes for the employees, it is necessary that organisations establish the training needs as realistically as possible. One major opportunity for need assessment comes at the time of annual performance evaluation. Organisations were asked to indicate if they have formal mechanisms of appraisal available to them and if yes whether they use them for identifying training needs.

The results suggest that 65.3 per cent and 67.3 per cent of the organisations do have formal appraisal systems for managers and supervisors respectively. Of these, 60 per cent and 58 per cent seek appraisers recommendations specifically on the training needs for managers and supervisors respectively. Generally the training needs indicated managers cover such areas as interpersonal skills, communication, leadership competence, attitudinal training, and functional competence in that order. As far as supervisors are concerned, the training needs indicated follow the order of updating functional knowledge, social skills, leadership, effectiveness, motivation, industrial relations and overall development.

In addition to identifying training needs through appraisal reports, the following mechanisms are also used by organisations to assess the needs. These mechanisms for managers, supervisors and workers along with the percentages of organisations endorsing them are discussed below:

Managers	*Per cent*
Growth and diversification in business	59.2
Managers themselves indicate	42.8
Through performance review meetings	34.6
Changes in specific roles	34.6
Overall performance of their units	34.6
Surveys of training needs	30.6
Through potential appraisal	28.5
Through external consultant	12.2

Growth and diversification of business provides the next best indicator of training needs after formal appraisal for managers. What is interesting to note is that in 42.8 per cent of the organisation managers themselves come forward to indicate the nature of training they would like to have. In a small percentage of cases, the organisations would like to seek the assistance of external consultants in identifying their training needs. The data for supervisors are given below:

Supervisors	*Per cent*
Feedback in appraisal	53.0
In consultation with concerned supervisor	40.8
Survey of training needs	34.6
Overall performance of the unit	34.6
Feedback from workers	18.3
Through external consultant	16.3

As far as supervisors are concerned, besides specific information in appraisal reports, general feedback by the reporting authority is used by 53 per cent of the organisations to identify the training needs. This is further confirmed by consulting the immediate supervisors by 40.8 per cent of the organisations. Once again like managers external consultant's assistant is also sought but that is only done by 16.3 per cent of the organisations. The training needs for workers are identified through following mechanisms.

Workers	*Per cent*
Recommendations of immediate supervisor	55.1
At the time of transfers	26.5
At the time of promotion	24.4
Analysis of work behaviour	24.4
Through workers' suggestions	18.3
In consultation with unions	14.2

More than fifty per cent of the organisations go by supervisors recommendations in deciding for the training programme for workers. However the times for transfer and promotion also provide occasions for sponsoring workers for training. In 14.2 per cent of organisations, unions seem to play a role in deciding the training needs of the workers.

In the last changing world of today, the nature of jobs and the skills required to perform these jobs are also undergoing changes. Organisations that are not conscious of this and are not willing to examine today's realities afresh may have to pay a high price for their ignorance and/or unwillingness. The participating organisations were asked to indicate how often they reviewed job description in the organisations. Twenty-five organisations had responded to this question of which 10 said that they reviewed their job description every year, 9 every fifth year or more, 4 once in three years and one each for every alternate year and once in four years. In the case of 20 organisations, this exercise had led to training/retraining of the employees.

Perhaps another source for identifying training needs is the occasion provided by the mobility pattern, particularly transfer of the employees. About 65 percent of the participating organisations are multiunit, multiproduct companies and they do have the policy of transferring their managerial/supervisory personnel from one unit/ product to another unit/product. The results suggest that 61.2 per cent and 59.1 per cent of the organisations transfer their managers and supervisors respectively to other units and products. However, before the new postings take place, these managers and supervisors are equipped for new responsibilities by trianign provided through a variety of mechanisms. These mechanisms with the percentage of managers and supervisors trained by them are given below:

Mechanisms	*Managers*	*Supervisors*
In-house internal faculty	34.6	32.6
In-house external faculty	14.2	14.2
External agencies	16.3	10.2
On-the-job training	53.0	44.8
Training abroad	20.4	12.2

A majority of the transferred employees are trained on-the-job. The percentages in case of managers and supervisors are 53.0 and 44.8. This is followed by in-house training using faculty on the payroll of the organisations. 34.6 per cent and 32.6 per cent of the organisations equip their managers and supervisors respectively through this mechanism. Few organisations (10.2%) use external agencies for supervisors. Similarly least percentage of organisations (14.2%) use in-house programmes with external faculty to train their managers for new positions accruing because of transfers.

Training Programmes

In this section we would examine both in-company as well as external programmes (national and foreign) along with orientation/induction training programmes.

1. *Induction Training*

It seems that a large percentage of organisations has formal induction training programmes for managers, supervisors, and workers. The percentage of such organisations for three categories are given below:

	Yes (Per cent)	*No (Per cent)*	*N*
Managers	74.4	25.6	43
Supervisors	86.1	13.9	37
Workers	73.8	26.2	42

The last column in the data above represents the number of organisations that responded to this item. Of these organisations that arrange formal induction training for their employees, the average duration of such programmes are given below:

	Average Duration
Managers	36.6 days
Supervisors	31.8 days
Workers	28.8 days

It seems that as we go down the hierarchical levels, the number of days required to complete the induction training also decreases showing a positive relationship between level and duration of induction training.

The induction training programmes for managers emphasize such aspects as organisational philosophy, culture and value systems, plans, policies and procedures, working of the total system, business environment, structure and processes of the organisation, familiarisation with company's products and services; and authority, responsibility, and accountability in the organisation. In the case of supervisors while the orientation is given on the company policy, culture, product, environment, rules and regulations, reporting relationship, etc., the focus seems to be more on job training, safety, entitlements working of relevant departments, shop floor responsibilities, leadership orientation and an understanding of the profile of workforce. They are also familiarized with the company's products or services. However, when it comes to the induction training of workers, majority of the organisations seem to focus on such issues as motivation, work attitudes, safety, discipline, welfare schemes, productivity and efficiency, first aid, technical knowledge of the work, immediate supervision and company rules and regulations. The differential focuses in the induction training suggest that as the level goes down the items relating to productivity welfare and safety become more predominant contents in the induction training.

While a majority of the organisations offer induction training programmes for all levels of the employees, only a small percentage of organisations (28.6%) has undertaken follow-up study of the effectiveness of such training programmes. The follow-up studies have helped them in improving advance planning, adjusting the duration, shifting emphasis selecting faculty, improving methodology of training, relooking at the job descriptions of various levels, and modifying training technology.

2. *In-company Programmes*

During the last accounting year, as many as 118 programmes for managers, 206 for supervisors and 168 in-company programmes for workers for organized, averaging 2.4 for manages 4.2 for supervisors and 3.4 programmes for workers per organisation per year. The emphasis generally seems to be on supervisory development followed by the development of workers and then managers. However, in terms of sheer numbers, on an average, 98.1 workers, 82.2 supervisors and 60.9 managers per organisation per year were trained by the in-company training programmes. The distribution of programmes and employees trained over the year using internal, external, or both faculty resources are given below:

	Managers	*Supervisors*	*Workers*
Internal faculty only	35(1107)	116(2733)	121(3589)
External faculty only	54(934)	67(406)	24(685)
A combination of both	29(855)	23(889)	23(542)
	118(2896)	206(4028)	168(4806)

The number in brackets indicate the number of employees trained. We can draw the following conclusions from the data given above.

1. A large number of in-company programmes where internal faculty is used are organized for workers (72%) followed by supervisors (56%) and managers (30%).

2. The trend in 1 above is reversed when it comes to calling the external faculty for in-company programmes. Here the largest percentage is that for managers (45.7%) followed by supervisors (32.5%) and workers (14.2%).
3. However, when there is a combination of both internal and external faculty more managers (24.5%) as compared to supervisors (11.1%) and workers (13.6%) are exposed to such in-company training programmes.
4. While larger percentage of in-company training programmes were organized for managers using external faculty (45.7%) the average number of managers trained per programmes was lowest ($\bar{X}$= 17.29) as compared to programmes where internal faculty ($\bar{X}$= 31.62) or both ($\bar{X}$= 29.48) were utilized.
5. While for managers more in-company programmes with external faculty are organized, for supervisors and workers most of these programmes are handled by internal faculty. As far as workers are concerned on an average, more workers per programme are trained by internal faculty.

The decision to offer are in-company training programme is a function of a variety of factors. The sample organisations seem to use a mix of these factors.

	Factors	*Percentage*
1.	Specific need based programmes identified at the planning stage	77.5
2.	Availability of sufficient participants	24.5
3.	Availability of external consultants	20.4
4.	Cost considerations	18.3
5.	Pressure from certain departments	6.1
6.	Pressure from employees	2.0
7.	Pressure from unions/associations	2.0

The results suggest that in more than three-fourth of the cases, the organisations offer such programmes based on the specific needs identified at the time of the annual planning exercise. While the availability of the external consultant, sufficient participants and funds are also factors to reckon with, they do not play as significant a role as the specific need for such programmes.

The organisations were requested to provide the titles of in-company training programmes organized by them during the last accounting year. The objective was to get an indication of the themes on which such programmes were mounted. The results indicate that for managers they mounted programmes on such themes as management development, electronic data processing, management information systems, appraisal and counselling, training techniques, transactional analysis, and worker's particapaiton. Transactional analysis, quality circles, productivity, computers, industrial relations, human relations, communications, technical know-how and merit ratings were the themes on which programmes were organized for the supervisors. For workers the majority of the programmes were on safety, accident prevention, motivation, and technical know-how.

A number of teaching technologies are available to the trainers. As far as the in-company training programmes are concerned, the information was sought on the use of these training methods for various categories of employees. The methods along with the percentage of organisation using them for employees during in-company training programmes are given in Table 11.1.

Table 11.1: Percentage of methods used for various categories of employees (in-company training)

Methods	*Managers*	*Supervisors*	*Workers*
Straight lecture	20.4	38.7	34.6
Lecture-cum-discussion	59.1	65.3	46.9
Role play	24.4	26.5	12.2
Close circuit video recording	16.3	14.2	6.1
Educational films	36.7	44.8	28.5
Case method	40.8	40.8	24.4
Simulation techniques	16.3	18.3	2.0
Computer games	6.1	6.1	–
Group exercises	36.7	36.7	18.3
Sensitivity training	10.2	2.0	6.1
Seminars	32.6	20.4	6.1
Syndicate methods	24.4	18.3	6.1
Presentations	14.2	18.3	12.2
Location visits	16.3	26.5	22.4

The percentages in Table 11.1 suggest that lecture-cum-discussion continues to be the most predominant method of training for all three classes of employees followed by case method for managers and straight lectures for supervisors and workers. Although the use of computer games is nominal for managers and supervisors, this methodology is non-existent as far as workers the concerned.

3. *External Training Programmes*

61 per cent of the sample organisations sponsored their employees in the last accounting year to training programmes organized by external agencies. The names of these agencies and the number of organisations that sponsored their employees to such training programmes are given in Table 11.2. The following conclusions can be drawn from data in Table 11.2.

Table 11.2: Sponsorship to External Programmes

Agencies	*No. of Organisations*	*Managers*	*Supervisors*	*Workers*
Administrative Staff College, Hyderabad	12	15	–	–
All Indian Management Association*	28	113	59	18
External programmes organized for companies**	8	18	4	5
Indian Institute of Management, Ahmedabad	13	32	–	–
Indian Institute of Management, Bangalore	4	9	–	–
Indian Institute of Management, Calcutta	2	2	–	–
Indo-American Society	3	7	2	–
National Productivity Council*	19	36	71	109
Xavier Labour Relations Institute	5	5	–	–
National Institute of Training of Industrial Engineers	10	55	8	–
Professional Associations (*See* Exhibit 5)	28	80	98	206
Private Consultants	16	48	–	4
Others***	7	11	2	15
Total	155	431	244	357

* Includes local chapters.

** Like Computer Maintenance Corpn., BHEL, Tata Steel Training Centre etc.

*** Include Indian Society of Training and Development, Central Labour Institute, Gandhi Labour Institute, Indian Institute of Foreign Trade, National Institute of Banking Management, IIT (Kharagpur), IIT Madras.

1. Indian organisations seem to have a very wide choice of external agencies offering different kinds of training programmes. In one year, the sample organisations have sponsored their employees to approximately 50 agencies (including those in Exhibit 5).
2. Agencies vary in terms of the mix of programmes for various segments of employees. Some offer programmes for managers

only (ASCI, IIMS, Xavier Labour, Relations Institute) while others offer programmes for supervisors as well (Indo-American Society), and yet other mount training programmes for all classes of employees.

3. Most organisations seem to sponsor a large number of their employees to the All India Management Association and its local chapters, and the National Productivity Council and its local chapters and professional associations. Of the three institutes of management, IIM, Ahmedabad seems to attract a large number of organisations. Surprisingly, private consultants also attract a sizeable number of organisations to sponsor their employees for training programmes organized by them.
4. On the basis of data given in Table 11.2, it seems that on an average 2.7 managers, 2.3 supervisors and 3.3 workers are sponsored per programme. Subsequent analysis isolating organisation specific programmes reveals that on an average the pattern of sponsorship of 2 mangers, 1 supervisor and about 0.3 worker per programmes is followed. The results, suggest that more managers are sponsored to external programmes than supervisors and workers. In fact as far as workers' category is concerned the sponsorship to external problems is very nominal: just about 1 worker per three programmes is sponsored.

Based on the data provided by 24 organisations on the nature and duration of the external programmes to which managers were sponsored, the number of programmes by areas and duration for the last accounting year were worked out (See Table 11.3).

Table 11.3: Training Programmes and their Duration

Area	*No. of Programmes*	*Total duration (in days)*	*Average Duration*
Computer and information systems	10	73	7.3
General Management	24	171	7.1
Finance and Accounting	15	47	3.1
Marketing	10	80	8.0
Organisational Behaviour	11	32	2.9
Personnel & Industrial Relations	18	46	2.5
Production	35	159	4.5
Total	123	608	4.9

The results suggest that of the total number of external programmes to which managers were sponsored, the largest number went to programmes in production field. This was followed by general management programmes. Though the least number was sponsored to programmes in marketing, the average duration per programme in marketing was 8 days. It seems that the programmes offered in personnel and industrial relation areas were comparatively for short duration followed by organisational behaviour and finance and accounting programme. Overall it could be said that the duration of the programmes varied between 2 days and 10 days. Unfortunately, not enough data on external programmes for supervisors were made available to draw meaningful conclusions.

Regarding sponsorship to foreign programmes, during the last accounting year, 14 sample organisations had sent their employees abroad. Most of them sent their managers to the training programmes organized by collaborators. These programmes varied in duration from 2 weeks to 4 months and were organised in the USA, Japan, and West Germany.

Training Evaluation

Perhaps as a feedback mechanism, it is necessary to evaluate the effectiveness of training in bringing about the desired results and/or changes. Such an evaluation presents an opportunity for the organisations to make adjustments in their choices of training courses or redesigning the existing training packages. Since this is a crucial stage in training activities several questions on the practices of evaluating training uses were asked to the organisations. The results indicate that as many as 57.1 per cent of the organisations asked the immediate supervisors to report on the improvement of performance of the visors to report on the improvement of performance of the employee sent for training. In 16.3 per cent of the cases such evaluations were made by involving external consultants.

In seeking this feedback from immediate supervisors, improvements in such aspects as general behaviour and attitude, job knowledge and skills, and overall work performance were used as indicators for both managers and supervisors by a majority of the organisations. This feedback was sought both formally as well as informally. In cases where employees were sent for specific skill development, a close watch was kept to see if training had made a difference.

Organisations insist on format feedback from employees who have attended the training programmes. As many as 69.3 per cent of the organisations asked their employees to provide formal reports of their assessment of training programmes as far as in-house programmes were concerned. For the programmes organized by external agencies the percentage was 65.3%. Such reports become a part of the overall training activity in the organisations and are used to bring about appropriate modifications in training activities.

As far as in-company training programmes are concerned, organisations use the participant feedback reports for following purposes. The percentages of the organisations endorsing these purposes are also provided along with.

Modify contents of the programme	67.3
Repeat the programme	65.3
Change duration of the programme	63.2
Change faculty	46.9
Drop the programme	44.8

A majority of the organisations take the participants' feedback seriously in modifying the contents, deciding to repeat the programme, adjusting the duration of the programme, and choice of faculty. In fact, if the feedback is not up to the mark, 44.8 per cent of the organisations discontinue the programme.

If the participants' feedback on the programme organized by external agencies are negative, 34.6 per cent of the organisations would not sponsor their employees to that specific agency and 44.8 per cent of the organisations would not send their employees to that programme. However, if the feedback reports are positive they would sponsor more of their employees to the programmes offered by that external agency (57.1%) and to the specific programme) (51.0%). It seems that organisations rely heavily on the participants' feedback. In fact our results suggest that only 4 organisations have taken the help of external consultants in the last five years in estimating the effectiveness of training programmes.

Concluding Remarks

This survey was undertaken to examine the state-of-art of the training function in India. It covered such areas as manning of training departments, training infrastructure and cost, methods used to identify training needs, nature and durations of training programmes and evaluation of training effectiveness. Some major findings are summarized below:

1. One-third of the organisations have separate training departments under manager (training) who reports directly to the highest position in the personnel department. Most of these managers are professionally trained. Training departments which are not separate units are unfortunately managed by those who do not seem to have basic professional qualifications though they are sent to short duration training programmes.
2. While one-third of the organisations have separate training department, only a few have fully equipped training infrastructure including teaching faculty of their own. Most seem to depend on others for training.
3. A very small portion (.017%) of the total budget of human resources is spent on training.
4. Training needs in majority of the cases are identified on the basis of annual appraisal, growth and diversification of business. In 42.8 per cent of the cases, managers themselves identify their training requirements. Very few organisations seek the help of external consultants in identifying training needs. In case of supervisors appraisal feedback and in case of workers, recommendations of immediate supervisor are major inputs for training requirements. Transfers and promotions also provide opportunities for training for managers and supervisors though mechanisms used for such training vary across organisations and levels.
5. More than two-third organisations, have the institution of induction training for managers, supervisors and workers. The focus of induction training varies according to the category of employee and duration of such training decreases with decreasing levels. With decreasing level the focus of induction training shifts to productivity, welfare and safety.
6. As far as in-company progı ammes are concerned more reliance is placed on internal faculty for the training of workers. While for managers external faculty is the major sources of training.

7. A large number of managers are sponsored to external programmes compared to supervisors and workers. Most managers participated in programmes on production followed by general management.
8. A large number of organisations take post-training feedback and evaluation seriously and make adjustments in their training plans accordingly.

While the survey results provide an overall picture of the training functions in India, a large sample would have helped in undertaking more comprehensive analysis of some of the aspects of training.

REFERENCES

Agarwal, M.C. (1982), Training of Graduate Engineer Trainees, *Indian Journal of Training and Development*, 12 (3 & 4) 17-18.

Banerji, K. (1981), Evaluation of Training—A study of Supervisory Development, *Indian Journal of Training and Development*, 11 (4), 150-155.

Basha, M.M.A. (1971), *Training Techniques in Varying Cultures: American Methods for India Integrated Management*, 59, 43-48.

Bhatia, S.K. (1981), Trends in Training and Development, *Indian Journal of Training and Development*, 11(4), 142-145.

Dayal, I. (1970), Conceptual Framework for Determining Training Needs in an Organisation, *Indian Manager*, 1(2), 21-28.

Ghosh, M.K. (1984), Balancing of Training Inputs for the First line Supervisors, *Indian Journal of Training and Development*, 14(4), 153-157.

Lawande, K.N. (1980), Identification of Training Needs and Designs of Training Programmes, *Indian Journal of Training and Development*, 10(1), 34-37.

Maheshwari, B.L. (1981), Formal Training, Skills Development and Job Performance, *ASCI Journal of Management*, 11(1), 28-38.

Mehta, K.K. (1970), Problems of Supervisory and Managerial Training, *Indian Management*, 9(11), 9-14.

Prahlad, C.K. & Thiagarajan, K.M. (1971), Human Relations Training in India, *ISTD Review*, 1(6), 19-23.

Saxena, A.P. (1973), OD Training in Government, *Management in Government*, 5(3), 209-217.

Seth, P. (1984), Impact of Training on Personnel Managers, *Productivity*, 25(2), 207-216.

Sikka, S.K. (1985), Management Training Evaluation, *Indian Journal of Industrial Relations*, 20(4), 491-497.

Srinivasan G. (1977), Executive Development in India, A Futuristic Profile, *ASCI Journal of Management*, 6(2), 136-146.

Steinmetz, C.S. (1967), The Evolution of Training, In Craig, R.L. & Bittel, L.R. (Eds.), *Training and Development Handbook*, New York: McGraw Hill.

Sundaram, S. (1970), Locating the Supervisory Training Needs in an Organisation, *Industrial India*, 21(6). 17-20.

Jain, K.K. (1985), *Training and Development in Public Enterprises—A Case Study of Indian Iron and Steel Industry, Lok Udyog*, 18(11), 21-27.

EXHIBIT 1

Part I

1. What is the nature of your industry? (Tick as many as applicable)

   ☐ Automotive ☐ Banking & Insurance ☐ Coal
   ☐ Electrical Products ☐ Electronics ☐ General Engineering
   ☐ Steel ☐ Textile ☐ Paper
   ☐ Printing & Publishing ☐ Leather ☐ Mining
   ☐ Trading ☐ Service (specify).
   ☐ Any other (specify)

2. How old is your organisation?

   ☐ 5 years or less ☐ 6-10 years
   ☐ 11-15 years ☐ 16-20 years
   ☐ 21-25 years ☐ 26-30 years
   ☐ 31-35 years ☐ 36 or more

3. What is your product(s)/service(s)?..

4. As of last accounting year what was your employees strength?
   1. Managers ....
   2. Supervisors ....
   3. Workers ....

5. What has been your average annual turnover over the last five years? Rs.........................

6. What was your turnover in the last accounting year? Rs................

7. What was your percentage cost of the human resources over the total turnover in the last accounting year?.....................................

8. Did you make profit after tax last year? ☐ Yes ☐ No

9. Where is your head office? (Name of the city)...............................

10. Are you collaborating with any foreign organisation? ☐ Yes ☐ No

11. If yes, give its name and country
    Name..................................... Country...

12. Are you
    ☐ A public sector undertaking
    ☐ A private sector undertaking
    ☐ A joint venture
    ☐ Any other (specify)...

13. Have you acquired funds from (tick as many as applicable)
    ☐ Public issues ☐ Financial Institutions
    ☐ Shares ☐ Banks
    ☐ Debentures ☐ Any other (specify)...............................
    ☐ Fixed deposits ☐ None of the above

Part II

1. Do you have a separate Training Department? ☐ Yes ☐ No
   If Yes, please indicate
2. When was the separate training department established? (Year).............
3. The designation of person incharge of separate training department...
4. Staff strength in training department

Positions	Numbers
....	....
....	....
....	....

5. The incharge of training department reports to..............................
6. His qualifications
   First formal degree
   ☐ High School ☐ Bachelors ☐ Ph.D
   ☐ Intermediate (10+2) ☐ Masters
7. His first formal degree is in
   ☐ Arts ☐ Pharmacy
   ☐ Agriculture ☐ Medical
   ☐ Commerce ☐ Law
   ☐ Engineering ☐ Social Work
   ☐ Science ☐ Labour Welfare
   ☐ Management ☐ Any other (Specify).......................
8. Professional qualifications, if any (please specify).........................
9. How long has the been with you.........................years
10. How long has been incharge of Training Department ....years
    If No please indicate...
11. Who is incharge of training in your organisation? Designation:
    ....
12. What other functions does he perform:..
13. Whom does he report to:...
14. How long has he been in the organisation?..................................Years
15. How long has he been looking after training functions...............years
16. His qualifications:
    First formal degree?
    ☐ High School ☐ Bachelors degree ☐ Ph.D.
    ☐ Intermediate (10+2) ☐ Masters degree

17. His first formal degree is in

☐ Arts	☐ Pharmacy
☐ Commerce	☐ Medical
☐ Engineering	☐ Law
☐ Science	☐ Social Work
☐ Management	☐ Labour Welfare
☐ Agriculture	

☐ Any other (specify)..

18. Professional qualifications, if any (please specify)..........................

19. Have you ever sent your training incharge to external training programme? ☐ Yes ☐ No

20. If Yes, indicate the

Name(s) of training organisation ....

Title(s) of training programme ....

Duration(s) of training programme...

Was this an Indian or foreign training programme(s)? ☐ Indian ☐ Foreign

21. During the last accounting year how many in-company training programmes were organized by you.

	Programmes for		
	Managers	**Supervisors**	**Workers**
Using internal faculty only	....	....	....
Using external consultants only	....	....	....
Involving both	....	....	....

22. How many employees were trained in the last accounting year? (in Company Programmes)

	Programmes for		
	Managers	**Supervisors**	**Workers**
Using internal faculty only	....	....	....
Using external consultants only	....	....	....
When both were involved	....	....	....

23. How do you decide to offer in-company training programme? (Tick as many as applicable)

☐ availability of external consultant	☐ specific need based programmes identified at planning stage
☐ availability of sufficient participants	☐ pressure from Unions/ Associations
☐ pressure from certain department(s)	☐ Cost consideration
☐ pressure from employees	☐ Any other (specify)

24. Please give titles of in-company training programmes organized during the last accounting year

	Titles
For Managers	....
	....
For Supervisors	....
	....
For Workers	....
	....

25. Listed below are a number of training techniques. Please indicate those which were used for in-company training programmes during the last year for the three groups of employees (tick as many as applicable)

	Managers	**Supervisors**	**Workers**
Straight lectures	....	....	....
Lectures-cum-discussion	....	....	....
Role play	....	....	....
Close Video Recording circuit	....	....	....
Educational Films	....	....	....
Case method	....	....	....
Simulation techniques	....	....	....
Computer games	....	....	....
Group exercises	....	....	....
Sensitivity training	....	....	....
Seminars	....	....	....
Syndicate method	....	....	....
Presentations only	....	....	....
Plant visits	....	....	....
Any other (specify)	....	....	....

26. What kind of training facilities do you have? (tick as many as applicable)

- ☐ Full-fledged training college
- ☐ Library (more than 100 books)
- ☐ Just a class room
- ☐ Residential facilities
- ☐ Audio-visual equipment
- ☐ Trainers on the permanent payroll
- ☐ Training Secretariat
- ☐ Any other specify.........................

27. During the last accounting year how many employees were sponsored to external programme (excluding incharge of training activity) Please indicate numbers relevant columns and rows.

External Agency	**Managers**	**Supervisors**	**Workers**
IIM, Ahmedabad	....	....	....
IIM, Calcutta	....	....	....
IIM, Bangalore	....	....	....

National Productivity Council	....	....	....
Local Management Associations	....	....	....
All India Management Association	....	....	....
Administrative Staff College	....	....	....
Xavier Labour Institute	....	....	....
International or Management Institute	....	....	....
NITIE	....	....	....
IITs	....	....	....
Other (specify)	....	....	....

28. Please list the titles and duration of the training programmes offered by external agencies where your managers and supervisors were sponsored (For last accounting year). Attach extra sheet, it necessary.

Managers	*Titles*	*Duration*
1	....	....
2	....	....
3	....	....
4	....	....
5	....	....
6	....	....

Supervisors	*Programmes*	*Duration*
1	....	....
2	....	....
3	....	....
4	....	....
5	....	....
6	....	....

29. During the last accounting year did you sponsor employees to training programmes abroad? ☐ Yes ☐ No

30. If yes, please indicate:

For Managers
Name(s) of the training organisation ....
Title(s) of the training programme ....
Duration(s) of the training programme ....
Total cost in Indian Rupees ....
For Supervisors ....
Name(s) of the training organisation ....
Title(s) of the training programme ....
Duration(s) of the training programme ....
Total cost in the Indian Rupees ....

31. If No, have you ever sponsored your employees to foreign training programmes? ☐ Yes ☐ No

32. How much did you spent on training during the *last accounting Year*? Rs..

33. How was the volume of training budget decided?

☐ by chief executive | ☐ by training incharge in consultation with chief executive
☐ by a team of top managers
☐ by training incharge alone | ☐ Any other (specify)...................

34. Is the training budget allocated by department? ☐ Yes ☐ No

35. Is the training budget allocated by positions? ☐ Yes ☐ No

36. Is the training budget allocated by training organisations/agencies? ☐ Yes ☐ No

37. After a suitable time period do you ask the supervisors to report on improvement, if any, of the employees sent for training? ☐ Yes ☐ No

38. What indicators are generally used to see if training has made a difference?

For Managers ....
....

For Supervisors ....
....

For Workers ....
....

39. Have you ever involved external consultants in evaluating training effectiveness? ☐ Yes ☐ No

40. Do you ask employees to formally report their assessment of training programme?

For in-company training ☐ Yes ☐ No
For training by external agencies ☐ Yes ☐ No
For training abroad ☐ Yes ☐ No

41. Are the formal feedback reports by employees used (for in-company programmes only)

☐ In deciding whether to repeat the programme
☐ To change the duration of the programme
☐ To modify contents
☐ To change faculty
☐ To drop the programme

42. If the employee feedback reports are negative do you stop sponsoring employees to that

specific external agency ☐ Yes ☐ No
specific training programme ☐ Yes ☐ No

43. If the feedback reports are positive do you sponsor more employees to that

    specific external agency ☐ Yes ☐ No

    specific training programme ☐ Yes ☐ No

44. How do you identify training needs of your Managers? (tick as many as applicable)

    ☐ From performance appraisal reports
    ☐ Through potential appraisal
    ☐ During performance review meetings
    ☐ Managers themselves indicate the nature of training needed
    ☐ Subject to larger changes in the organisation (growth/diversification)
    ☐ Subject to changes in the task because of larger changes elsewhere
    ☐ By doing frequent surveys of the training needs
    ☐ Involving the external consultants
    ☐ Overall performance of their units
    ☐ Any other (specify)..

45. How do you identify training needs of your supervisors? (tick as many as applicable)

    ☐ Through feedback in appraisal reports
    ☐ Through feedback from workers
    ☐ In consultation with the concerned supervisor
    ☐ By doing frequent surveys of the training needs
    ☐ Involving an external consultant
    ☐ Overall performance of their units
    ☐ Any other (specify)..

46. How do you identify the training needs of your Workers? (tick as many as applicable)

    ☐ Recommendation of immediate supervisor
    ☐ In consultation with unions
    ☐ Through workers suggestions
    ☐ Analysing actual work behaviour
    ☐ At times of transfers
    ☐ At time of promotions
    ☐ Any other (specify)..

47. Do you offer formal/informal induction training to new entrants?

    For Managers ☐ Yes ☐ No

    For Supervisors ☐ Yes ☐ No

    For Workers ☐ Yes ☐ No

48. What is duration of such training programmes?

    For Managers ☐ Yes ☐ No

    For Supervisors ☐ Yes ☐ No

    For Workers ☐ Yes ☐ No

49. What aspects are emphasized in such *induction* Programmes?

    For Managers ....
    ....

    For Supervisors ....
    ....

    For Workers ....
    ....

50. Have you done any follow up study to measure the effectiveness of induction training? ☐ Yes ☐ No

51. What changes, if any, are incorporated in the induction as a result of follow up study? ....
    ....
    ....
    ....

52. In the last five years has your organisation undertaken a survey of estimating the effectiveness of training activity. ☐ Yes ☐ No

53. If yes, please give some broad conclusions.
    ....
    ....
    ....
    ....

54. If yes, when was such a study undertaken (Please give the year)...........

55. Was this study undertaken by external consultant or the organisation.

    ☐ External Consultant ☐ Employees of the Organisation

56. How often do you review job descriptions in your organisation?

    ☐ Once in a year ☐ Once in 4 years
    ☐ Every alternate year ☐ Every fifth year or more
    ☐ Once in 3 years

57. Do changes in job descriptions lead to training/retraining of the employees? ☐ Yes ☐ No

58. In last ten years how many times review of job descriptions had lead to training/retraining of the employees.

    ☐ Never ☐ 1-2 times ☐ 3-4 times
    ☐ 5-6 times ☐ 7-8 times ☐ 9 or more

59. Do you have a formal appraisal system?

    For Managers ☐ Yes ☐ No
    For Supervisors ☐ Yes ☐ No

60. If yes, do you seek appraisers' recommendations on the training needs in the appraisal forms.

For Managers ☐ Yes ☐ No
For Supervisors ☐ Yes ☐ No

61. What kinds of Training needs are generally indicated in performance reports

For Managers ....
....
....
....

For Supervisors ....
....
....
....

62. How often training need data (see question 61) is utilized in deciding the training requirements of the managers/supervisors?

	Managers	**Supervisors**
Always	....	....
Often	....	....
Seldom	....	....
Never	....	....

63. Please tick those statements which *truly* represent the practices in your organisation (tick as many as applicable)

☐ Performance evaluation is followed by performance counselling meeting wherein training needs are jointly identified by employee and his/her superior.

☐ There is no counselling session, but training needs are identified by a committee consisting of the employee's superior, the departmental head and the training manager.

☐ Performance appraisal and subsequent identification of training needs is entirely confidential.

☐ On the basis of the performance appraisal, employee is allowed to suggest his own training needs.

☐ After individual performance in appraisal group meeting within department decide training needs of individual employee.

☐ The concerned department head alone determines training needs of each individual employee in his department.

☐ After a particular training the employee is *usually* appropriately placed.

☐ After a particular training the employee is *always* appropriately placed.

64. Are you a multi-unit/multi-product organisation. ☐ Yes ☐ No

65. If yes, do you have a policy to transfer your managerial/supervisory personnel from one unit/product to another unit/product.

Managers	☐ Yes	☐ No
Supervisors	☐ Yes	☐ No

66. If yes in 65 above, how do you prepare them for new responsibilities (tick as many as applicable)

	Managers	**Supervisors**
☐ In-house training	....	....
☐ In-house training with external consultants	....	....
☐ Training by external agencies	....	....
☐ On the job training	....	....
☐ Send abroad for training	....	....
☐ Any other (specify)	....	....

EXHIBIT 2

List of Participating Companies

Sl. No.	*Name of the Company*	*City*
1.	Ahmedabad Electricity Co. Ltd	Ahmedabad
2.	Aurangabad Asbestos	Aurangabad
3.	Bagalkot Udyog Ltd.	Bijapur
4.	Bank of Madura Ltd.	Madras
5.	Berger Paints India Ltd.	Calcutta
6.	Bharat Pipers & Fitting Ltd.	Bombay
7.	Bhilwara Processors Ltd.	Bhilwara
8.	Comfortaire Imex Pvt. Ltd.	Secundrabad
9.	Escorts Ltd.	Delhi
10.	ESKAYEF	Bangalore
11.	Excel Industries Ltd.	Bhavnagar
12.	Guest Keen Williams Ltd.	Howrah
13.	Gujarat Steel Tubes	Ahmedabad
14.	Gujarat Tractor Corpn.	Baroda
15.	Hindustan Zinc Ltd.	Udaipur
16.	Hoechst India Ltd.	Bombay
17.	IFFCO	Kalol
18.	Indian Seemless Metal Tubes Ltd.	Poona
19.	Jalawahini Pipes	Mysore
20.	Kirloskar Electric Co. Ltd.	Poona
21.	Krishak Bharati Coop. Ltd.	Surat
22.	Malabar Cements Ltd.	Palghat
23.	Maruti Udyog Ltd.	Delhi
24.	MM Publications Ltd.	Kottayam
25.	Narbheram & Co. Ltd.	Jamshedpur
26.	OEN India Ltd.	Cochin
27.	Reliance	Ahmedbad
28.	Richardson Hindustan Ltd.	Bombay
29.	Roche Products Ltd.	Bombay
30.	Salem Steel Plant	Salem
31.	Sanvick Asia Ltd.	Poona
32.	Sanghi Engineers	Jaipur
33.	Servo Electronics	Delhi
34.	Srinam Foods & Fertilizers Industries	Delhi
35.	Standard Woven & Wires	Bombay
36.	Steelworths	Assam
37.	Stovec Screens India Ltd.	Ahmedabad
38.	Steel Light Electric Company	Faridabad

(*Contd.*)

(*Contd.*)

Sl. No.	*Name of the Company*	*City*
39.	Superphone India	Bombay
40.	Tamil Nadu Magnesite Ltd.	Madras
41.	The Cotton Corpn. of India Ltd.	Bombay
42.	Tobacco Products Ltd.	Jaina
43.	Transport Corporation	Secunderabad
44.	Trimurtee Fertilizers	Lucknow
45.	TTK Pharma Ltd.	Madras
46.	UP State Cement Corporation Ltd.	Mirzapur
47.	Vijaya Bank	Bangalore
48.	Walchandnagar Industries Ltd.	Poona
49.	Windsor Food Ltd.	Baroda

EXHIBIT 3

Sl. No.	*Nature of Industry*	*No. of Organisations*
1.	Automotive	5
2.	Bank & Insurance	2
3.	Chemicals	3
4.	Cement	4
5.	Electrical Products	1
6.	Electronies	4
7.	Fertilizer	3
8.	Food	1
9.	General Engineering	9
10.	Mining	2
11.	Pharmaceuticals	5
12.	Publishing	1
13.	Plastic	2
14.	Steel	1
15.	Textile	4
16.	Tobacco	1
17.	Transport	1
	Total	49

EXHIBIT 4

Distribution of Organisations (Existence of Separate Training Department by Other Characteristics)

Sl. No.	*Characteristics*	*Existence of Separate Training Department*		*Value Chi-square*
		Yes	*No*	
1.	**Age**			
	0-15 years	7	10	
	16-30 years	8	9	
	31 and above	3	12	2.59
2.	**Managers Employed**			
	100 or less	4	24	
	More than 100	11	5	13.45**
3.	**Workers Employed**			
	500 or less	3	19	
	More than 500	11	11	6.72**
4.	**5 Year Turnover**			
	10 crores or less	4	20	
	More than 10 crores	9	11	4.23*
5.	**Turnover Last Accounting Year**			
	10 crores or less	3	16	
	More than 10 crores	12	12	5.43*
6.	**Sector**			
	Private	10	22	
	Public	4	7	0.10
7.	**Collaboration**			
	Yes	10	9	
	No	8	21	3.06
8.	**Zone**			
	West	5	12	
	East	2	4	
	North	5	8	
	South	5	8	0.37
9.	**Cost of Human Resources**			
	Less than 8 per cent	7	11	
	8 per cent or more	5	12	0.35

EXHIBIT 5

Professional Associations

1. Ahmedabad Industrial Employers Union, Ahmedabad.
2. Central Mechanical Engineers Institute, Durgapur.
3. Computer Association of India, Bombay.
4. Deccan Sugar Technologists Association, Pune.
5. Electrical Research & Development Association, Bombay.
6. Environmental Protection and Research Foundation, Sangli.
7. Indian Gear Manufacturing Association, Bombay.
8. Indian Institute of Industrial Engineers, Hyderbad.
9. Indian Institute of Materials Management.
10. Indian Institute of Meals.
11. Indian Paint Association.
12. Indian Society of Advertisers.
13. Institute of Cost and W/AC's of India.
14. Institute of Electricals & Electronics Engineers, Delhi.
15. Institute of Engineers, New Delhi.
16. Institute of Marine Engineers, New Delhi.
17. Loss Prevention Association of India, Bombay.
18. Maharashtra Industrial & Technical Organisations.
19. National Institute of Personnel Management.
20. Oil Technologists of India.
21. Petroleum Conservation Research Association, Bombay.
22. Press Club of India.
23. Quality Circle Forum of India.
24. Society for Advancement of Electro Chemical Techniques.
25. Sugar Technologists Association of India, Kanpur.

12

HRD Needs for Employment Oriented Education*

T.V. Rao

One of the goals of education is to prepare people for productive work life. The linkage between education and economic development is well established. While in the developed countries education has become a means for productive work life in the developing and less developed economies, education continues to be a means of generating unemployment and underemployment. This is because education is seen by the planners and policy-makers as an end in itself. It is considered as the duty of the government, policy-makers and planners to provide educational opportunity for as many as possible in the country. In their eagerness to provide such educational opportunities to as many as possible the plaÿp-1Xnners and policy-makers get less concerned about w happens to those who get educated. Employment generation and economic development activities are not generated at the same pace at which the education opportunities are generated. As a result many of those who get educated remain unemployed or underemployed. An ideal situation will be when a country plans first its economic activities, assesses the skill needs for these economic activities and moulds its education system for that purpose. A perfect match between education and employment is never possible. However the gap can be reduced substantially by planning the economic and other development activities properly on one hand and orienting education towards productive work and employment on the other hand. In this paper I am making an attempt to trace some of the steps that are required to make education more

* First published in IJTD in 1989.

employment-oriented. I would first like to highlight the efforts made by some countries in this direction and draw lessons from these. I will focus subsequently on the HRD needs of education systems and other development agencies in order to promote employment-oriented education.

Country Experiences

In the last decade the education ministries of various countries have shown increased awareness of the need to promote entrepreneurship, self-employment and employment-oriented education. This is reflected in the efforts made in several countries to undertake entrepreneurship development programmes. In the Commonwealth countries alone almost every country has shown interest in promoting self-employment and entrepreneurship in some form or the other. At the Tenth Commonwealth Conference of Education Ministers held at Nairobi, Kenya in 1987 major concern was expressed on issues relating to youth education, training and employment. It was felt that with diminishing opportunities for formal employment, educational institutes need to provide relevant forms of education designed to promote self-reliance and responsible entrepreneurial capacity for self-employment. The examples given below from some of the countries indicate the emphasis on employment-oriented education and the experiments being conducted towards this goal.

In Australia in the last few years employers/unionists, and politicians have been voicing their demand that education should be more closely linked to economy. The government has been emphasizing the need to develop a 'productive culture' and education is seen as a means to it. A lot of curricular changes have been made in this direction. For example, various Australian schools offer programmes where the students learn about the enterprise, for the enterprise or through the enterprise. The Senior Secondary Assessment Board of South Australia provides accredited subjects like Accounting, Business Mathematics, Business Studies, Small Business Management etc. The Young Achievement Australia programme initiated in 1977 under the auspices of American Chamber of Commerce and operated by a Board of Trustees is a novel programme for developing business skills in youth. In this programme students establish a commercial venture, offer products and services, take responsibilities and function as directors, raise capital by selling shares, open bank accounts, establish registers and records, conduct board meetings, produce, promote and sell their products and distribute profits. At the end of the exercise they liquidate the company. Local business people provide physical and human resources.

In Gambia, the Gambian Technical Training Institute has introduced a self-employment component in the general studies curriculum of that institute to encourage self-employment among its students. A Rural Vocational Training Programme was designed to provide the rural artisans with alternative sources of income and job creation. This programme aims at school dropouts, illiterate artisans and other rural poor. The programme attempts to make the best use of human resources by providing a trained and motivated cadre of development workers who will enable people to help themselves. Major elements of this programme include: in-village training programmes conducted in villages, rural artisan skill upgrading courses carried out in Mixed Farming Centres, a skill upgrading activities, and a material supply service to support in-village programmes. A 'Key-village' is one selected from a cluster of villages chosen as the base from which training activities are carried on for about 16 villages surrounding it. A mixed farming centre is a base for the Agricultural Extension workers and a centre for Blacksmith's training programme. The in-village programmes are non-formal, on-the-job training courses carried out on a self-help basis by multi-disciplinary training teams composed of one Community Development Assistant and four instructors for various skills. The in-village teams supported by extension services for Agriculture, Animal Husbandry, Health and Hygiene and Functional Literacy. The courses include special programmes for women in Home Economics, Home Handicrafts, Poultry, Bookkeeping, Vegetable Gardening and Fruit Growing.

In India a large number of agencies not associated with the Education Ministry have been promoting educational and training interventions leading to employment generation. Banks and other financial institutions, industrial and other development agencies are heavily involved in conducting training programmes ranging from one week to three months duration. In the last five years educational institutions involved in technical skill development have started entrepreneurial development programmes. Recently even the Ministry of Education has shown a good degree of concern about changing School Curricula to generate self-employment and entrepreneurial activities. A few experiments have been initiated in this direction.

In Jamaica, the Jamaica Chamber of Commerce sponsors a Junior Achievement Award (JAA) for entrepreneurship among secondary students. This project operates similar to that of Young Achievement Australia in which the student form themselves into a mini corporation, run business projects for about 25 weeks and learn about it. A new agency called HEART (Human Employment and Resource Training) established in 1982 by the government offers programmes to train school leavers for employment in private firms, government and voluntary agencies.

In Malawi, the Malawian Entrepreneurs Development Institute offers a variety of programmes including a 10 month on-campus Seminars for those who possess neither technical nor entrepreneurial skills.

In Papua New Guinea, with increasing number of educated unemployed the attention of policymakers has turned to ways of fostering employment-oriented education. The failure of specialist vocational programmes during 1970s and the widespread criticism of the formal education system, led to a reconsideration of the role of School Curriculum in the process of preparation for employment and entrepreneurship. A Secondary School Curriculum Extension Project was initiated as a way of providing secondary education that would be relevant both for those who did not find paid employment as well as for those who went on for further study and careers in modern sector. Several curricular changes have been made as a result of this project. For example core subjects of English, Mathematics, Science and Social Science were revised; core projects with a business orientation and of local relevance were introduced (*e.g.* boat building, trade, store management etc.); a component called "outstations" were introduced where students are required to live in a village-like environment and take responsibility for their own affairs; and community extension activities requiring the student to work directly in the community were incorporated in the learning model. These changes were introduced in Grades 9 and 10 and appropriate instructional changes and support systems were prepared.

In Malaysia following the New Economic Policy formulated in the second five year plan focusing on eradication of poverty and increasing employment opportunities a large number of agencies and ministries started taking interest in employment generation activities. There are about 13 ministries and 30 government/private/ commercial agencies involved in promoting entrepreneurship development.

In Sierra Leone where unemployment figures range from 9.5 per cent to 15.5 per cent in different provinces the focus has been on technical and vocational skills development. Programmes were established for students to study technology and related science and acquire skills for industrial, agricultural and commercial sectors of the economy. Technical institutes and trade centres were established to train technicians and craftmen for employment in government service, commerce and industry. As part of the educational reforms, in one of the experiments conducted at Bunumbu Teachers College teachers are being prepared to promote community education that emphasizes productive employment among school dropouts, primary students and illiterates in the community. The teacher training programmes include in their curricula leadership training of teachers for rural areas, education for productive work and emphasis on practical subject areas of agriculture, home economics, practical arts, and community development studies.

Very similar trends can be observed in countries like Swaziland, Uganda, Sri Lanka and Zimbabwe. In all these countries there is concern for increasing employment opportunities for youth. This is being attempted through: (i) changes in the existing curricula at school levels to make then, more skill-oriented, relevant to local needs and rural-community based; (ii) establishment of new institutions/centres and/or employment generation activities, (iii) starting of short-term or long-term courses outside the existing education system to provide technical/vocational/entrepreneurial skills, (iv) training of teachers to cope with new challenges, and (v) involvement of other agencies interested in development. For example, in Sri Lanka the National Youth Services Council (NYSC) has been doing a lot to promote employment and entrepreneurship among youth through youth cooperatives and community based training. In Swaziland a number of experimental projects are being tried out to develop self-employment. In Uganda projects have been undertaken to integrate Basic Education into Rural Development in which teacher training colleges and secondary schools are involved and other agencies are assisting them. In Zimbabwe where unemployment among youth is a serious problem, small beginnings have been made through the establishment of centres to develop self-employment.

Lessons from the Select Experiences

The experiences of a few countries outlined above indicate the following:

1. Unemployment among youth appears to be a concern of most countries.
2. Self-employment generation and entrepreneurship development activities are seen as potential mechanisms of reducing the burden of unemployment among the youth.
3. Education systems play a vital role in training participants for employment-oriented activities. They could facilitate employment generation in the following ways:
   (i) By redesigning the existing curriculum at the primary and secondary school levels and making them oriented to help students use local employment opportunities.
   (ii) By developing entrepreneurial attitudes.
   (iii) Skills in students—By emphasising technical and vocational courses in institutions.
   (iv) By starting short-term education and training programmes for school participants, school levers, out-of-school youth, unemployed, etc.
   (v) By re-orienting and developing teachers to change the curricula and train students for employment.
   (vi) By actively collaborating with various other development agencies involved in entrepreneurial skill development and employment generation.
4. Although it is a very important activity of the education ministries and educational institutions, other ministries and development agencies seem to have taken lead and played leadership role in employment generation.
5. Parallel and alternative education systems will start if education systems are not responsive to this pressing need of various economics.
6. Employment-generation programmes cannot be sustained by the efforts of education systems alone and a large number of other development agencies need to support them.

Activities and Steps

Therefore, there is an urgent need for making education employment-oriented. In order to do this the policy-makers, education-planners, educational administrators, curriculum specialists etc. need to orient themselves properly. The following activities/steps need to be undertaken for this purpose.

1. Preparing an appropriate policy of education that promotes employment-oriented education. Such a policy needs to provide enough flexibility to schools and higher level education institutions to design their own curricula and learning activities depending on the local needs. The policy also should emphasize skill development and sensitivity to local community needs. The policy should also envisage close working between the educational institutions and other employment promotion agencies.
2. Allocation of budgets for educational institutions to undertake employment generation activities on an experimental basis in order to generate learning opportunities for their students.
3. Encouraging educational institutions to go beyond long term education programmes and initiate short-term employment-oriented training programmes. Such short term programmes will enable faculty to enrich themselves through their inter-actions with adult learners and eventually may be able to transfer the learning experiences into the long-term education programmes. For example, an educational institution offering a 12 week entrepreneurship development programme may be able to change its curriculum of the school eventually to incorporate the inputs on entrepreneurship.
4. Encouraging educational institutions to use practitioners from the field (*e.g.* as those in the financial institutions, industry, agricultural, trade and other potential employment providing occupations) as faculty in their training programmes. Budgetary provisions may need to be made for this purpose. Educational institutions should open their doors and be willing to involve others to teach in their programmes.
5. Undertaking field experiments involving close working with other institutions, fieldwork, skill development and such other employment-oriented activities.

Agents and Agencies Involved in Making Education Employment-oriented

For undertaking the activities mentioned above a number of agents and agencies are involved who need to be oriented. These include:

1. *Educational Institutions*: Schools, Colleges, Universities, Professional Institutions, Non-formal education centres etc. Heads of these institutions, faculty and support staff are three major constituents of these institutions that need to be re-oriented.
2. *Regional or Provincial Level Development Agencies*: These include the regional level educational administrative set up, various development agencies dealing with business, agriculture and other economic activities. The agents involved may be the chief executives of these agencies at regional level and development agents employed by these agencies.
3. *Financial Institutions*: Commercial and development banks and other agencies that finance entrepreneurs. The staff of these agencies dealing with entrepreneurs.
4. *National Level Policy Making Agencies*: These include those in the Ministry of education, industry, commerce, youth, cooperatives etc. Those who make policies, civil servants who execute them, educational planners, ministers, parliamentarians etc.
5. *Others*: Community leaders, parents of potential employment seekers, local leaders where the institutions are located and potential employers.

If education has to become employment-oriented, all these categories of staff and institutions need to be prepared for the change. Mere curricular changes may not be able to achieve much unless accompanied by changes in a number of other support systems and link systems for promoting employment. In the last section of this paper, the HRD needs of those directly involved in the education systems are highlighted.

HRD Needs of Those in Education for Making it Employment-oriented

In order to make education more employment-oriented than what it is today, all the above identified agencies and agents need to be oriented or re-oriented. Such reorientation may be done at the cognitive, attitudinal and skill levels.

Four categories of those involved in education play a critical role. These are planners and policy makers, Apex Level Education Administrators, Institutional Heads and Faculty. The HRD needs of these four groups are different. The following is a highlight of the directions in which their competencies and orientations need to be developed.

Planners and Policy-Makers

There are a number of countries that have successfully introduced employment generation activities. For example, the Youth Cooperatives Movement in Sri Lanka, the Entrepreneurship Development Programmes in Malaysia and India, the Secondary School Curriculum Extension Project of Papua New Guinea, the Young Achievement Australia Programme of Australia etc. provide reasonably success stories. Several innovations have taken place outside the school systems and in the non-formal sector. International agencies like the Commonwealth Secretariat, ILO, World Bank etc. have documented such experiences. The policy makers and planners need to study these experiences. While formulating educational plans and policies, they should not be satisfied with making marginal improvements in the education system but take risks and go all the way out to facilitate entrepreneurship and employment generation. A lot of attitudinal and skill development is taking place outside the schools and education systems. Policy makers and planners need to learn from these and incorporate these into their systems.

Apex Level Administrators

In administering the entrepreneurship and employment generation programmes, a lot of support is needed by the institutions undertaking them. Apex level administrators need to train themselves first to know the needs of educational institutions and to understand the employment generation work being done by other agencies like the financial institutions, industrial development agencies, business associations and other professional bodies and agricultural departments. They need to be trained through specially designed programmes to appreciate the amount of good education and training work being done outside the education system. They need to be exposed to concepts and skills of entrepreneurship, achievement motivation, business development, creativity and problem solving, project planning, market survey, taxation, enterprise-building etc. They also need to be familiarised with the employment opportunities in their region and should undertake surveys to identify the skills required for employment in their regions. The Apex level administrators may undertake experimental employment generation project in select institutions of their region.

Heads of Institutions

Heads of institutions play a very critical role in undertaking employment generation activities. No education policy or plan can specify exactly the kind of activities that should be undertaken by every institution. The head of the institutions plays the leadership role in terms of translating the educational policies and plans into action.

In order to promote employment-oriented education the educational institution itself should be enterprising. An entrepreneurial culture characterised by high initiative, risk-taking, hard work, perseverance, creativity and action-orientation needs to be developed. The Heads of Institutions themselves need to be trained in entrepreneurship and institution-building skills. They should be able to promote and encourage faculty initiative, should be able to mobilise resources for undertaking employment generation activities and should be able to work in a collaborative way with other agents and agencies be able to provide support to the faculty by being flexible in his approach, initiative-taking and development-oriented.

Faculty

Faculty are the ultimate implementers of all programmes. Teachers of educational institutions tend to be rigid, conventional and conformistic with passage of time. This is because in most educational institutions the teachers are expected to keep on teaching the same subject year after year. Teachers may develop their pet ways of teaching over a period of time. Teachers also tend to limit their roles to classroom teaching. Employment generation activities require a very active, outgoing and entrepreneurial roles to be performed by teachers. This change requires a very intensive training of the faculty. Thus the HRD needs of faculty may start with a re-definition of the role of a teacher and enabling them to accept a new role as a "facilitator". Teachers themselves need to be trained in entrepreneurial skills. They need to know about employment opportunities in the region where the school is located, methods of using these, skills required to be developed, ways of developing them and so on. Faculty should become aware of the local institutions that are interested in employment generation, their functions, activities and the help they are likely to render to the educational institution in their efforts to generate employment opportunities. The Faculty should be able to learn and specialise in one or more areas that facilitate employment for students (*e.g.* one or more technical skills that could be passed on to students or business skills like enterprise building, taxation, project planning etc.). The Faculty also may acquire general management skills to be passed on to students.

Summary and Conclusions

It is difficult to make an exhaustive list of the HRD needs of all agents and agencies in education for making it employment-oriented. The inputs listed above are only illustrative. Those in-charge of managing education should be able to prepare an exhaustive list of HRD needs of their constituents depending on their own situation and local conditions.

Agencies like the Commonwealth Secretariat, UNESCO and ILO have brought out documents that are likely to be of use in planning for employment generation. What is most important for educational planners, administrators, heads of institutions and faculty is to recognise the fact that they have an important role to play in employment generation and sticking to the age-old curricula is not going to get the education system far. They need to bring change in curricula to promote employment and entrepreneurship. In order to do this they themselves have to become entrepreneurial and enterprising. They should re-define their roles; learn to be less bureaucratic and more flexible; learn to take risks; be willing to go into the world outside and learn from the experiences of other agencies; collaboration with other agencies; be willing to put in hard work; be ready to work outside the classroom in the field; undertake experimentation and make the culture of the education systems more dynamic and action-oriented.

13

Management Training Development

*An Evaluation Approach**

B.R. Virmani

During the last two decades, there has been greater awareness regarding management training and development in all the sectors of the Indian economy. As a result of this awareness, there has been a growing need to find ways and means to determine the efficiency and effectiveness of management training and development activity from the point of view of organisation improvements. However, in spite of the increasing need for assessing the impact of management training and development efforts, there has been very little systematic emphasis on avaluation available which can help enhance the process of management development. To fill this gap, a longitudinal study of management training and development and its evaluation was undertaken. The research study was divided into two phases. The first phase dealt with transfer of learning in the training institution; and the second phase relates to the transfer of learning to the job. The first phase of the study was completed in 1984 (see, Virmani, B.R. Evaluating and Measuring Management Training and Development, *Indian Journal of Training & Development,* April-June 1984). This paper deals with some of the findings of the second phase of the study which has, as its major focus, training and its impact with special reference to transfer of learning to the job.

* First published in IJTD in 1989.

The Study aimed at:

1. Analysing the impact of management training and development programmes, if any;
2. Evolving suitable; criteria for checking the application of training inputs for equipping the trainee for the specific needs of their sponsoring organisations;
3. Exploring and correlating various organisational factors and help/hinder transfer of training to the job; and finally
4. To study, given the adequacy and applicability of training inputs directed towards the development of the manager, the tangible benefits to the sponsoring organisation, if any.

The selection of the trainees was confined to selected programmes conducted by the Administrative Staff College of India (ASCI). In addition, for case studies, the data was collected through questionnaire from trainees representing over 30 organisations, while 5 organisations were chosen for in-depth study. In case of training in the Government training institutions, the data was collected from 30 Heads/Faculty of major government training institutions. In addition, trainees from various government departments were interviewed separately which included Ministers and Secretaries to the Government of India level who had come to attend training programmes at the ASCI. The initial data was collected through questionnaire which was followed-up with in-depth interviews. During the interviews, it was found that there was difference in responses based on the mailed questionnaire and the interviews. Therefore, subsequently, major emphasis was shifted to interviews and filling up of the questionnaires by the researchers.

A multi-pronged data collection methodology was adopted which included, apart from interviews, questionnaire, observations, in-depth case study of selected organisations; case studies of individual trainees; group discussions among trainees, follow up of the job improvement plans prepared by the trainees. All the tools used for measuring the transfer of learning were administered at least 6-12 months after training. For the purpose of analysis of data both quantitative and qualitative approaches were adopted.

The Training Function

In most organisations, of late, there has been a greater awareness to have a full-fledged, separate, training set-up, called either training or human resource development or organisation development department, though the functions of all these are similar. The major function of the training department is either to organise in-company training programmes or sponsor executives for external training programmes.

In a majority of the organisations, there was a feeling that the persons manning the training departments have been transferred from various other line functions and in a few, from the staff functions, because they were not considered very competent in their own areas, However, of late this trend is gradually changing in some of the organisations. It was also found that the trainers were not happy in the training department and barring a few exceptions, a majority of them were looking forward to being posted to their original or line functions with the result that very little effort was made to develop the skill of the trainers in the training function. The trainers perceived their role more in terms of the administrative aspects of training, rather than developing themselves as trainers. For example, in in-company management development programmes, they perceive their role as limited to arranging the faculty (external or internal) outside their departments, preparing the time table and making the administrative arrangements. In the case of external training programmes, they play very little role in training needs identification; instead, they confined their role to getting nominations from various departments and sponsoring executives for various external programmes, corresponding with the training institutions, etc. Most of the executives interviewed also, do not have much regard for the training department and perceive the role more in terms of administrative aspects of training.

The Status of the Training Department

This differs from organisation to organisation. In some cases, the head was equivalent to the level of a Deputy General Manager, which, in most organisations, ranks lower than the head of the personnel function; while in other case, the position was still lower, to the level of middle or lower-middle management.

Training Needs Identification

It was interesting to find that though the budget for training has been increasing and there is greater awareness about training, in most organisation very little efforts have gone into at systematic identification of training needs.

In a large number of case, training need identification was perceived as *ad hoc*, especially in the government departments where neither the trainee nor his boss were consulted. For example, in one large organisation, just two or three days before the training programme, the executives were ordered to attend a particular programme. In spite of their reluctance to go, they were forced to go under threat of disciplinary action. In the government set-up, a major complaint was that may of the courses selected were not relevant to their job. In some cases a person was nominated twice for the similar programme, on the same subject within a span of two years and the theme of the training programme was either connected to the person's current job nor was it likely to be helpful in his immediate future job. This resulted in a lot of hostility toward training, especially in the government and contributed to the development of cynicism about training. The result is that the trainees started perceiving training more as a paid holiday or as a free trip than as a means to learn or implement something new.

Coming to the tools for identification of training needs, in most organisations there is a column in their annual appraisal report with regard to the training needs. However, in reality, we found that in most cases, while taking training decisions, the appraisal reports were rarely consulted and even if they were consulted, not much weightage was given to them. Part of the problem was also with regard to the column in the appraisal format as to what kind of training the executive should be given. In most cases, they mentioned the names of the courses, or at times the institutes or places of training which had very little relevance to their area of weakness and strengths as substantiated in the first part of the appraisal about result achievement, or work performance.

In other organisations, both government departments and a few public sector organisations, the personnel/training department would arbitrarily decide on the training programmes needed, without consulting the appraisal report, the trainee or his boss. For example, one person in the government, dealing with tourism, was sent for a programme on urban development twice. In another case a person dealing with development administration was sent for training relating to marketing aspects. The assumption here was that in their future postings, as job rotation they may get posted to some of these areas, in which they were trained. However, the executives interviewed, felt that the chances of such postings were very remote and if at all they materialised, it was not in the foreseeable future. They would have certainly appreciated at least part of the training to be linked to their present job or to the immediate job to which they were likely to be posted in the foreseeable future.

There were also case where training needs identification exercise was done, when there was necessity for grooming people to shoulder higher responsibilities, *i.e.*, training was linked to promotion. However, in such cases also, there were instances where the trainee found the training not relevant to their future jobs and they perceived it more as an additional reward before promotion.

Where the training need.identification and appraisal for promotion were combined, there was always an apprehension in the minds of the executives as well as their bosses, that any deficiencies expressed under training need identification may be perceived as areas of weakness and would hamper the individual executive's promotional prospects. Therefore, in most cases, the executives were well guarded in giving their remarks about the deficiencies of the executives for training purposes.

In public sector and government organisations, sponsoring of executives for training is linked to the budget and since the budget has increased considerably, in many situations there are pressures, particularly towards the end of the financial year, to send more personnel for training and the executives were sent for training without really considering the specific training requirements of the executives concerned. This has a two-fold effect: one, that in many cases, it was perceived as a waste of money and in other cases it developed a totally negative attitude towards training and change. In some cases where training and organisational philosophy were at variance and the executives after training found themselves helpless in bringing about any change due to lack of organisation support, the training resulted in greater frustration with their own job or the organisation. This also brought in the attitude of cynicism towards any change.

Selection of Trainees

In the course of our study, various reasons/criteria for selection came to our notice. For example, in one organisation, certain courses were earmarked for every executive who completed a minimum period of service and then, based on their seniority and budget availability, the executives were sponsored for further training mechanically, irrespective of their training need, the usefulness of the programmes or the relevance of the programme to their respective areas of work. This process was amplified by a typical statement of one of the trained managers who said that, although a systematic selection procedure was chalked out on paper, it was limited to paper alone and not put into practice. Neither the trainee, nor his boss were consulted on the training needs and the ultimate selection was done by the personnel department or by the various heads of departments in the organisations arbitrarily.

Where the training was linked to promotion, it was perceived more as an encouragement of good work and additional reward rather than for strengthening the trainees potential and supplementing their knowledge. In such instances, the training needs of the organisations were not clear and in any case, it did not matter much to the trainees, as training only mechanically perceived promotion.

In another kind of organisation, the selection procedure, specially for external courses, was considered as an incentive to do better on the job after training; while in another case, it was considered a paid holiday and relief from the regular work routine. There were also instances where there were systematic selection procedures but the executives selected were considered indispensable at work with the result that others who could be spared during that period were sent to the training course. There was also instance of an organisation, where only the younger managers were preferred to be sent for training, which created disharmony and ill-feeling among the executives.

One of the common methods of training needs identification and selection of trainees, is based on notification and circulation of the training brochure (for internal as well as external training programmes) to various departments inviting nominations. The departmental heads, normally based on their own judgement or in many cases on the initiative of the executives themselves, make the nominations for different training programmes and then, the training department, based on the budget allocation sends the nominations for training. In certain cases, if all the aspiring executives could not be accommodated, then a priority list was prepared and as soon as funds were available, the nominations were sent. In such cases, very little effort was made to link training with the needs of the particular individual, the department or the organisation.

In one organisation, an interesting case was brought to our notice when, one of the top executives of the organisation was invited by a training institution as a guest faculty. The training institution also sent a few brochures to the executive concerned, with a request to send 2/3 nominations for the programme. The top executive, in turn, sent the brochures to the training department to send 2/3 executives for that particular training programme. When it was pointed out that none of the executives were available and those who were available may not be suitable for that particular programme, they were pressurised to send any three executives irrespective of their suitability. In another organisation also, similar instances were quoted. In all such cases, the selection of participants for training had absolutely no relevance to the training needs identification.

There were a few organisations where a systematic procedure was adopted. For example, in one organisation, there was a systematic identification of potential and based on that, the training programmes were selected and executives were sent. However, in one case this was applicable only in the case of a multinational organisation before it was nationalised. After nationalisation, the procedure was given up.

Budget for Training

Most of the organisations studied, especially in the public sector, had a formal training budget. Recently, there was trend of increasing budget allocation. However, in many organisations, the budget was decided first and then the selection of trainees was done while in reality it should have been the other way round, *i.e.*, the training needs should have been identified first, based on which the budget could be prepared.

In some of the government organisations, there was a dear directive from the government that every executive must undergo a training programme once a year and that the budget for training must be utilised. Therefore, there is always a pressure at the end of the year to send as many persons as possible for training with the sole idea of exhausting the training budget. An interesting case came to our notice where a particular executive was sponsored for an external programme and his name was rejected for the course by the training institution. There was an immediate telex message sent to the training institution, that as per the directions of the Prime Minister every government executive concerned had to be accepted for that particular training programme or for any other training programme in the institution and that, in any case the executive would be reaching the training institution irrespective of whether he is accepted or not!

In some organisations, the budget was strictly adhered to, while in a few cases, the budget was not only flexible but also inflationary factors were built into it. In a few cases, though the budget was meant for training, there was an understanding that the training would be used as a reward or paid holiday and there were no expectations from training. In some cases, the training budget could not be utilised for training at all because training always took a second place compared to the exigencies of work.

Selection of Courses

The selection process for the external training programmes was normally based on the reputation of the training institution; reputation of its faculty; physical facilities available at the training institution; the feedback of the earlier training and at times, the relevance of the course to the organisational needs. In certain situations, the physical location of the training institution also counted. For example, when there was adequate budget, the other weighty consideration was the surroundings, like hill stations which were preferred even if the course was not fully relevant.

The most common methodology adopted in choosing a training programme was by circulation of the brochures and recommendations of the departmental head. In certain cases, especially in government, the executive was given 2-3 options of courses to choose from, and accordingly nominated for one of the courses. So far as training abroad was concerned, it was always treated as a reward. It was interesting to find that the persons selected for a particular training programme were not aware of the reason for their selection, about the course objectives, content and in most cases, they did not even see the course brochure, or the brochures were sent to them after they were nominated for the course. This was largely applicable in government departments and a few public sector undertakings.

Pre-Course Preparation

In most organisations studied by us, there was hardly any pre-course preparation. In many cases, the trainees were neither aware of the training programme nor of their selection for training, nor about the content or objectives of the training programme. In some cases, the training material was sent in advance by the training institutions but the trainees hardly got the time to read the same. In some cases where selection for training was without prior notice, it invited the wrath and distrust of the trainee/participants against the training programme as well as their organisation. There was hardly any time to even think of pre-course preparation.

However, in one private sector organisation, we found that there was a systematic pre-course preparation. The executive was released from his normal work at least one week in advance so that he could visit the various departments of the organisation, understand their functioning and problems. The trainees were also given certain books related to the training programme by the training department to read so that they got familiarity with the background of the subjects. Of course, one of the objectives of such an elaborate procedure, as stated by the organisation, was to ensure that their executives projected a good image of the organisation during training. In the process, it was found that there was greater receptivity of the training inputs as well as commitment to transfer of learning to the job later on.[1]

Learning and Transfer of Learning

Any training activity has two aspects: one is learning in the training institution and the other is the transfer of learning to the job. So far as learning in the training context is concerned, the most common tool used is that perception of the participants as to how much they would learn from specific inputs. However, in our earlier studies, we found that the participants' immediate perception was not a reliable tool and other methods for measuring the transfer of learning like pre and post-course questionnaire, job improvement plan, feedback after a time gap were devised.' In the course of our case studies, although immediately after the course, a positive feedback was given, over a period of time it was revealed that a substantial number of inputs during training especially in service industry, were irrelevant. For example, in the banking sector, it was revealed that many of the inputs of external programmes to which they were sent, did not relate to their kind of set-up and even if they did, they were like refresher courses rather than any addition to their knowledge. Yet, the executives were sponsored for such external training programmes on a regular basis. This possibly reflects that training was treated more as a reward or in some case, the executives were deliberately sent to such programmes to get an insight into the working of other industries. The training, though not directly relevant, had some indirect benefits like change of atmosphere from the regular work routine, getting to know people of other organisations, a free holiday which in the process added to their general knowledge and relieved their work tension.

Apart from the direct benefits of training in the form of additional knowledge and skills, most of the cases revealed that training helped to develop the confidence of the trainees. The training programmes which included course inputs which were not only directly related to the trainee's area of work but also generalist in nature helped the trainees to view their organisation's problems in totality, improved their attitude and enhanced their decision making skills.

It was found that some organisations did not make any deliberate effort to ensure that training resulted in learning. Very rarely there was any discussion between the trainee and his boss as to what was learnt and what could be transferred. In most cases, feedback about the training was sought by simply asking the executive how he liked the place and the course with no emphasis on any concrete action plan.

In certain instances, the training institution made an effort in asking the trainees to prepare job improvement plans at the end of the course, which was followed up later on. In such case, the training did result in some steps to improve the performance and also resulted in a positive perception towards the training by the trainee, his boss and the organisation. However, in some other instances, where the job improvement plan was prepared either there was no subsequent follow-up or the trainee was immediately transferred to some other function not related to the training.

Most of the benefits of transfer of learning were in the case of functional management programmes rather than in general management programmes. There were also instances where the transfer of learning was more after a time gap, when the participants had an opportunity to implement what they had learnt.

In organisation where a systematic job improvement plan was asked for by the organisation, discussed by the boss as well as with the chief executive, it did result in positive benefits to the organisation. Another phenomenon noticed in the study was that in organisations where there was no systematic effort for transfer of learning, there was a "relapse" of the original ideas. For example, during the training, the trainees did acquire new knowledge, skills and attitudes and after training they made sincere efforts to transfer their learning to the job, but due to lack of organisational support, they failed to implement any of the aspects. This either produced frustration with training or in many cases, frustration with the job and the organisation. They felt that no systems and procedures learnt were practicable, with the result that they lost faith in training and change, and relapsed back to their original ideas with much greater conviction. If this happens in a large number of cases, then in due course of time, organisations cease to change. This phenomenon could be partly due to the fault of the trainers, because when they discuss any organisational aspects and change, they must take into account the kind of resistance the trainees might face while implementing such changes in their respective organisations and prepare the trainees to overcome such resistance. Partly, the organisations were responsible, because they believed in training but not necessarily in change or implementation of what their executives had learnt during training.

It was also found that the transfer was greater in case of in-company programmes mainly because, in many cases the training inputs were geared to the needs of the organisation. In another case, because a large number of people in the organisation were put through similar training, they all understood and appreciated the implications of change and therefore, it became easier to implement changes in the organisation. While with external training programmes, as only a few executives could be trained at a time, there was always resistance from the other, to bring about changes.

Help and Hinder Factors in Transfer of Learning to the Job

It has been stated earlier that there could be various factors which could facilitate or hinder the transfer of learning to the job. Some of the factors could be: organisational climate, support received from the top management, colleagues and subordinates, attitude of the trainee and his boss towards training etc.

Organisational Factors

In one of the case studies, it was found that a total change in the organisational set-up led to a lot of disharmony and redundancy in the organisation, resulting in resistance to any change. However, after reorganisation, gradually there was streamlining of the distribution and delegation of authority and the trainees felt that they had greater freedom to put their learning into practice. Lack of proper communication between various levels in the organisational set up also was quoted as a hindrance factor.

Organisational climate played a major role in transfer of training to the job. The major organisation climate factors mentioned were indifference of the superiors, peers and subordinates towards the trained executives and deliberate efforts to abstruct any change.

Rigid Rules and Conservativeness of the Organisation

Other organisational climate factors which prevented transfer of learning as mentioned were, rigid rules and regulations, lack of freedom to introduce change, lack of encouragement for innovation etc. In actual practice, it was found that the transfer of training was possible where the trainee proceeded with deliberate efforts and was able to manipulate the situation to change, especially if the trainee had a good record, created a favourable impression about his work in the organisation and had favourable relationship with the management and colleagues. In other words, his own personal goodwill played a major role in different aspects of transfer of learning to the job.

Relevance of Training

In the service organisations studied, it was noticed that in many cases, the training was irrelevant, the selection of courses has no rational and no transfer of learning could be effected. There were also instances of the executives who had earlier reported that the training was irrelevant and useless, contradicting their statement after a time gap, stating that they were able to change their attitude and transfer some of the training to the job.

Managements Attitude to Changes

In one particular organisation, it was revealed that absence of rigid rules and regulations and a culture of giving freedom to introduce innovative changes had helped in the process of transfer of learning to the job. The proper identification of training needs; proper selection of courses did play a major role in transfer of learning. On the other hand, selection based on criteria such as influence with the management, meritorious work performance, sparability at the time of training, did affect the interest and motivation of the trainees to learn, with the result transfer of learning was minimised. Above all the attitude of the organisation, especially that of the boss towards the trainee played a major role in bringing about organisational changes after training.

Training of Critical Mass

Another aspect noticed about the transfer of learning was the training of the critical mass. Where a number of executives were sent for similar training, the transfer was greater than when only a selected few people were sent for training from various departments. Cases were even quoted where a number of people who attended a particular programme in the same institution, developed a fellow feeling, which resulted in an improvement in interpersonal relations, not only at personal level but even at the official level, which in turn greatly reduced inter-departmental clashes, led to better understanding of people and consequently, greater support to the transfer of learning to the job.

The other hindrances mentioned were: union resistance, government interference, over-centralisation of decision making etc.

Evaluation of Training and Development

Since organisations spend a lot of money, time and effort in training, they are naturally keen on evaluating the training to find out whether it resulted not only in the acquiring of learning in the training context, but also its subsequent transfer to the job situation. In most cases, the organisations did not have a proper evaluation system. At the most, a report was asked after a trainee attended a programme as to how useful the training was and if the participants gave a favourable report about the course then it was assumed that the training was useful. In some organisations, the intention of evaluation was mainly to determine the utility of the course in the perception of the executives to decide whether more executives should be sponsored to the same course or to the same institution in future. There were also cases where although the trainees found the courses irrelevant, they did not give a negative feedback to the organisation. This was attributed to the executives consideration for their colleagues in terms of spoiling their chances for a sort of paid holiday in one of the training institutions. In another case, there was also a fear that any un favourable report could reflect upon the executive's own non-responsiveness or capacity to learn; therefore, they always gave a positive feedback. In the case of government, it was revealed that in some cases a confidential report about each trainee was sought from the training institution and that in itself created a fear among the trainees that they may get a bad report from the training institution for giving an adverse feedback about training, which in turn could spoil their career prospects. Therefore, even if they felt that the training did not result in much learning, they tend to give a positive feedback.

There were also a few cases where the executives were asked to give a thorough feedback about the training programme including both the benefits and the drawbacks. The evaluation of the programme by the executives was given due weightage. The utility of training was also assessed in terms of the job improvement plan. Subsequently, if it was found necessary, the executives were made to undergo another training programme to reinforce their learning and to refresh their knowledge. In certain cases, the preparation of the job improvement plan also helped the training institution in terms of measuring the training effectiveness and based on this, the subsequent training programmes were rescheduled or modified.

In-Company Training Programmes

Normally, most of the organisations follow a two-pronged strategy of training their executives; one, through organising training programmes of their own, or in company training and the other, by sending executives to external training programmes. Both these methods of training have their own advantages and disadvantages. However, if used with discretion, they could supplement and complement each other.

The external training programmes are generally more helpful in cases where the trained executives are expected to act as change agents in the organisation, specially where attitudinal change is the major focus. There is an opportunity for interacting with diverse group of personnel and spontaneous exchange of ideas and feelings, giving the executives an insight into the functioning of other organisations. In the process, the trained executives develop confidence and also through group pressure they tend to accept different ideas and new systems for implementation in their own organisations.

So far as in company programmes are concerned, the main utility lies in training a critical mass or a large number of personnel in the similar philosophy or subject, concerning the organisation. The training programmes provide a common platform for the executives of the organisation to meet, exchange views and understand each other's role in the organisation leading to better and smooth functioning of the organisation the training helps to tackle the specific problems and issues of the organisation. But, there is hesitancy for open expression in in-company training either due to the hierarchical status of the executives or due to concern for the colleagues, feelings, which therefore, cannot result in concrete attitudinal or behavioural changes.

Considering the cost effectiveness of training programmes, in company training was reported to be more economical as compared to sending a large number of personnel for external training. But our observations regarding the various aspects of incompany training revealed that the training was considered cost effective only in terms of the number of executives trained at a time, rather than the qualitative impact of training, implying, the amount of knowledge acquired and transferred to the work environment.

The internal programmes are ideally intended to be more specific in nature, relating to particular functions and issues of the organisation, reinforcing the existing potential of the executives and strengthening their weak points. As a result the executives should be well equipped to tackle the specific problems of functioning in the organisation.

Whereas the content of the external programmes is more of a general kind, providing new knowledge and ideas and a wider perspective. Therefore, although not directly problem solving in nature, the external programmes help the executives to analyse a situation in its totality. Due to the confidence gained through training the risk taking ability of the executives is enhanced and at times, they are in a better position to visualise and also bring about, desirable changes in the organisation.

The one major disadvantage of an external programme as expressed, was that the course contents could not be planned taking into account each and every individual's organisational background. Moreover, the capacity of each participant to grasp the inputs differed because of their varied backgrounds whereas this problem was less in in-company training.

Most executives of organisations preferred external training to internal training, firstly, because of the prestige attached to selection for external training which may be linked to promotion and secondly, because the training gives them respite from their regular work routine. In some cases external training was preferred for the quality of the course content.

In the case studied we tried to elicit information regarding the objectives, process and impact of incompany training programmes as against the external training. Although incompany training could be most beneficial to organisations, resulting in optimum impact, there were major lapses in the functioning of in-company training which have been analysed as under:

In-company Training Department

In most of the large organisations studied, there were in-company training centres with reasonably good infrastructure facilities and training staff, but in reality, they assumed a purely administrative role. Their involvement was limited to selecting participants for training in consultation with the heads of departments, designing the curriculum, sometimes in consultation with external trainers, selecting the faculty (outside and training department) and making all other physical arrangements for the training programmes. The training centre personnel were rarely trainers themselves and there was no training scheme for improving the skills of the trainers.

In-company Training Faculty

In organisation's where the training department personnel were themselves involved in the actual process of imparting training it was found that most of the personnel posted in the training department were from line functions, who did not find much scope for advancement in the training centre and looked forward to being posted back to their respective areas of work. Some trainees who sincerely tried to contribute to training, were transferred back to their functions in no time and there were a few instances where some of them were not transferred mainly due to not being acceptable to most of the line functions. As a result, the training department personnel were in a constant state of instability and uncertainty and their role was perceived as a stop gap arrangement.

It was found that the incompany training programmes relied greatly on external faculty, who were selected on the basis of their qualification and individual reputation, rather than their competence to relate the training session to the organisation's problems or the specific training objective. The training, therefore, results in giving only a theoretical perspective. In most cases the external faculty was not even briefed about the training design, the training objectives and organisational problems.

Types of Internal Training

In all the cases studied, the incompany training consisted of various types of induction programmes for the new employees, with a view to exposing them to the organisational policies. In addition, there were functional programmes and some organisations also had general management programmes for their executives.

Selection of Participants for In-company Training

So far as the selection of trainees for internal programmes is concerned, normally the executive, his superior and the training department are involved. In some organisations training was compulsory for all the executives, irrespective of their training need, which resulted in resentment towards training. When selection for training was based on the merit of the individuals, the training was considered as a matter of prestige whereas in some organisations selection for training was considered as a pointer to the executive's inefficiency at work.

In internal training also as in external training, some executives who were selected for training were indispensable at work and hence not released by the heads of department. Instead, 'separable' alternative executives were sent for training.

Incompany Training Design

By the very fact of being an incompany training programme, it is assumed that the organisation's goals and problems are taken into consideration to ensure that the training is effectively utilised in the company's progress. But in reality it was found that the curriculum design was not effectively geared towards organisational problems. The course material did not have much bearing to the issues concerning the organisation and the topics to be covered were left to the discretion of the faculty and the respective areas of their specialisation, as already pointed out.

Impact of Incompany Training

By virtue of being an incompany training programme with internal involvement, it is imperative that the organisation's goals and issues are taken into consideration, for the specific programme design and selection of participants to result in greater impact of training. Since in-company training exposes large number of executives in the organisation to similar kind of training simultaneously, the executives tend to think alike, and cooperate in transferring learning to the job effectively, to achieve common organisational goals. Therefore ideally, in-company training can ensure that training is effectively utilised in the company's progress.

Our observations regarding incompany training revealed a different picture. The lacunae in curriculum design and selection of faculty as already discussed, did not really have the purpose of incompany training. The courses neither reinforce the existing potential of the executives nor strengthened their weak points, as was intended through incompany training.

Help/Hinder Factors in Transfer of Incompany Training

By being a company organised programme, directed towards company's progress, the participants can neither be disinterested nor irresponsible during the training programme. Due to the internal involvement in training, factors like rigid organisational policies, resistance and apathy for superiors, colleagues and subordinates were minimised whereas the same factors were a hindrance for the transfer of external training to the company.

The lack of proper incompany training design with suitable faculty, was itself a major hindrance factor firstly in terms of acquiring knowledge and secondly, since the inputs were not really geared to the organisational issues, there could not be much transfer of learning to the job.

Evaluation and Follow-up of In-company Training

Perhaps due to the lacunae in the effective conduct of incompany training, it was noticed that most organisations did not resort to any kind of evaluation of the training. In very rare cases, an evaluation system was reported, though it was limited to a feedback about the training at the end of the course, about whether they liked the sessions or not. No information was sought regarding the actual learning, its relevance and applicability to the job. No Job Improvement Plans were prepared and most often, the training is forgotten after conclusion and never followed up again.

Although massive amounts are invested in in-company training, there is no cost benefit analysis (evaluation) of the programmes to ensure that the investment was fruitfully utilised. Evaluation of a training programme therefore should be built into the training policy especially in an incompany training which is claimed to be more company oriented and cost effective.

Transfer of Learning—Some Suggestions

In the study it was found that learning and its transfer were linked to various organisational and personal variables of the trainees. Where there was a positive attitude towards training, then there was greater learning and its transfer to the job. Learning and its transfer were also linked to the selection procedure of the trainees. Where the trainee was involved in his selection and was sent in preparation for taking up higher responsibilities, then there was greater commitment to transfer. However, in a substantive number of cases, the trainees were sent for training as a general policy; as per the turn without any thought process going into the identification of their training needs.

In most of the cases the learning was mentioned in generic terms like they developed better understanding of managerial role or requirements or they got an opportunity to compare the managerial styles and experiences of others from different organisations. Where the training was based on proper training needs identification, then they did mention that they got new knowledge and specific managerial skills for solving their managerial problems faced in their day to day work situation. However, such responses were minimal.

A substantive number of trainees felt that they could not transfer their learning to the job as immediately after training they were given a new job assignment unconnected with the training or the training did not relate to the organisational conditions in which the trainee works. Another interesting finding of this study was that the bosses reported greater change in the trainees after training as compared to the trainees themselves. The trainees felt that what was covered in the training was already known to them; however, it was revealed during the interviews of the bosses that though the trainees had the knowledge, a greater consciousness developed during training which prompted them to bring about changes after training. Therefore, the development of awareness in itself was perceived by the bosses as an advantage of the training. Similarly, the bosses portrayed favourable organisational climate to bring about changes as compared to the trainees themselves. This again indicates some sort of a lack of communication between the bosses and the subordinates about training and its transfer. Where there was a discussion between the bosses and the subordinates about an action plan for changes, then there was a greater transfer of learning and also greater support from the superiors while implementing changes.

Some of the following suggestions could be help of improving the effectiveness of training:

1. It may be desirablé to have congruency of objectives among all the invōlved parties, *i.e.*, sponsoring organisation; the trainee; his superiors and the training institution. This could possibly be achieved by: (i) the concerned parties meeting at periodic intervals; (ii) the organisations should have a clear 3-5 year growth plan and pattern giving details of anticipated movements—vertical or lateral. This would facilitate setting up of specific objectives for the training programme; the specific standards for validation and also to plan the training strategies, identification of training needs etc. This will also prompt the trainees and the trainers to undertake programmes for self-growth and thereby ensure effectiveness. No doubt, there are difficulties in developing congruency of objectives of all the involved parties. However, an attempt could be made to unite their efforts at maximising the areas of agreement.
2. The objectives could be qualitative as well as quantitative—organisations might have targeted number to be trained during a period. However, the trend of giving exclusive importance to quantitative aspects could result in forgetting the qualitative objective. The study also revealed that in may cases, the mangers, themselves are not clear about the objectives of their jobs. Given such situations, understanding the objectives of training could be a far-fetched expectation what is required in such situations is first to make job objective charts. However, where the training is based on the availability of people, then one cannot expect meaningful objectives for training.
3. Objectives can be clear and specific for skill-oriented programmes. However, for general management programmes,

"aimed at improvements in attitude, motivation, confidence, leadership and other behavioural dimensions", objectives will be mainly of generic nature; or at times they could be a combination of specific and generic.

4. Matching of training content to objectives could be obtained by informing the training institutions about all details of the trainees; biographical details, organisational background, level of maturity, expectations out of training (of the organisation as well as trainees) well in time so that adequate lead time is available to the trainers to make suitable changes in the training inputs. This matching of objectives to training content would be more difficult for external training programmes. In fact, the major focus of training should be on internal training programmes and the external training should supplement the internal efforts. At times, effort could also be made to internalise some of the external training programmes when a set of externally trained personnel are available.
5. It is imperative that the trainee is involved in the identification of his own training needs. Even the training aspects could be linked with the annual appraisal report. However, enough care should be taken so that such reporting should not be perceived as a weakness and come in the way of professional growth of the trainee. If this assured, a lot of sincere reporting could be expected. This, in turn, will help ensure the basic objective of training for improvement and growth. It may even be advisable to have a separate appraisal for developmental purposes which should not be made available to those responsible for promotion decisions.
6. Attitude of top management plays a pivotal role in making training more effective. The commitment of the higher administrative echelons to training and development is very necessary. With this, training can smoothly merge with other functions, in the organisation. The top level decision-makers' involvement in training will ensure that training is purposive.

The training (training institutions) have a vital role to play in obtaining this commitment. This commitment of top level can be obtained through various ways: (i) to form advisory hoards which meet and discuss issues pertaining to training and development regularly; (ii) formal/ informal sessions to bring out clearly the role of top level in functionaries in training activity; (iii) involving the top level in inaugural, valedictory, and experience-sharing sessions; (iv) trainers should build up rapport with top management. This will be possible if the training section is headed by a really senior person and training as an activity is given more prestige; (v) regularly inform the top decision-makers about training programmes, their contents, evaluation studies, and how training had lead to improved performance; (vi) there should be training coordinators in each large department of the organisation. These persons would be able to appraise the top level of training activities, assist in proper and adequate nominations and also facilitate evaluations.

The basic idea behind training is to improve the overall effectiveness and thereby reduce waste in the use of manpower, money, materials etc. The measurement of this improved effectiveness is the major crux of any evaluation of training. Learning from training programmes should be transferred to the job. There are various factors which help or hinder this transfer. The basic requirements to facilitate this transfer are:

1. Supportive organisational climate (systems have to be evolved for measuring such a climate);
2. Top level administrative/managerial commitment (barriers of hierarchy hinder actual transfer of learning and also make training difficult);
3. High level of motivation among trainees;
4. Trainer's attitude—if this is improper, it might build in the trainees, a resistance to the task of learning; and
5. Consistency of views on the fundamental objectives among trainers.

In the ultimate analysis, it is the performance on the job which is the best available measure of effectiveness of training. Hence a coordinated effort to the user organisations and the training institutions/ trainers is very necessary in the evaluation of training in terms of its transfer to the job.

NOTES

1. For details on Pre-course preparation, see, B.R. Virmani, Premile Seth, *Evaluating Management Training and Development*, New Delhi, Vision Book, 1985.
2. *Ibid.*

14

Beyond Skills

*Training for Values**

M.B. Athreya

This paper offers a Model for Value Training. It is hoped that the model would help trainers and top managements to deal with perhaps the most important aspect of management; namely, enhancing corporate beliefs and culture, as a step towards excellence. It is an experiential model derived from the author's learning in working with culture change in several client organisations. Each of these experiences is described briefly in order to illustrate the model.

Beyond Skills Training

Training for skills is probably the oldest form of training in industry. Even this more on the job, by observation and apprenticeship, rather than formal training. In the last few decades, there has been an explosion in skills training. Initially, it was primarily at the point of entry into the organisation. The idea of career long training has now been gaining ground. The lopsided emphasis on only executive skills training is now being partly corrected, through greater efforts at workmen training.

Skill training is necessary but not sufficient. It can take an individual, the group and organisation upto a point, but not beyond. It has several limitations, such as the following:

- Skills may be learned by the trainers, but they may not be able to use them on the job due to the discouraging attitudes and styles of the boss, colleagues, subordinates or even themselves.

* First published in IJTD in 1989.

- Skills may be misused, not for the departmental and organisational goals, but for substitute personal or group goals of one or more members of the role set.
- Skills learned may not be sustained and even less updated.
- Skills may not be passed on and multiplied.

These limitations can be overcome to some extent by knowledge, but not fully. The acquisition of additional knowledge and its appropriate use will have to become a habit. But we know the human dilemma that "bad" habits are easier to form, and "good" habits easier to break in the context of managerial and organisational effectiveness, "bad" habits are those which are easier, more convenient, path of least resistance shortcuts, which appear to produce short term results, but at much higher long term costs.

So we need a kind of training, going beyond skill training, which can help to overcome the above limitations. In particular, such a different kind of training should contribute to the following:

- Lead to the appropriate utilisation of skill, its sustenance by the trainee.
- Encourage him to share and multiply the skills, by disseminating it to his role set.
- Enable him to break certain habits, which inhabit full use of the skill, and form/strengthen those habits, which facilitate full use of the skill.

The kind of new training, in addition to skill training, that we are looking for is "Value Training" which in my view is most appropriate for effective growth of the managers and workers of today.

Issues in Value Training

When we consider Value Training, several questions arise in practice—its feasibility, range and effectiveness.

A frequent doubt expressed by executives is whether we can really "train" people in values. Externally, we see the manifested behaviour. Behind it are certain "attitude", or patterned ways of responding to people; situations and problems. These attitudes themselves spring from deeper systems of values and beliefs held by the individual. This issue gives rise to two action needs.

- 'We cannot change another person's attitudes and values by authority. But persuasion and dialogue would help. Even more effective would be personal examples.
- Training can help a person to voluntarily change his attitudes and values if he can be helped to reexamine his present predispositions and postures from even an "enlightened self-interest" point of view.

The second issue is which ones out of a wide range of possible value dimensions should be chosen for training. Here, the need for Value Training, can be and should be identified more specifically. For example, it is possible to think of the following subsets of values:

1. Values for Leadership.
2. Values for Team Membership.
3. Values for Quality.
4. Values for Productivity.
5. Values for Long Range Planning.
6. Values for HRD.
7. Values for Systematic Management.
8. Values for Industrial Harmony.

One can identify certain specific values for each of the above dimensions of management, quite apart from the more general, universal, humanistic values.

The third issue is about effectiveness of Value Training. At the beginning itself, it ¿p-6Xmay be useful for trainers and managements to accept the following:

(a) Value Training will take longer to be effective compared to skill training. Its effects are less easily quantified and measured.
(b) But Value Training, once effective, will be effective for a much longer period than skill training; may be even for a lifetime.
(c) A smaller success in Value Training is, in the long run, more beneficial to the team and the organisation compared to a bigger success in skill training.
(d) At middle and senior levels, Value Training is more crucial than Skill Training.

Some Experiences

We have been involved in Value Training on different Value dimensions such as the following:

1. Values for Team Work.
2. Values for Industrial Harmony.
3. Values for Planning Leadership.
4. Values for Systematic Management.
5. Values for Institution Building.

We give below a brief account of each, as the data base for the experiential model for value training.

(i) Team Work Values

In a large tyre manufacturing plant, the capacity utilisation was stagnating at around 60 per cent, despite relatively more modern technology and newer equipment compared to competition. The key problem was identified as gaps in values and attitudes, hindering teamwork. Eight batches at executives were exposed to the same basic Value Training programme. The management has perceived improvement in the following areas of team work:

1. Between three successive stages of production—Tyre Components, Tyre Building and Curing.
2. Between Production and Maintenance in each of these three divisions within the plant.
3. Between Production and Quality Assurance.
4. Between the three wings of Maintenance—Mechanical, Electrical and Instrumentation.

The design involved in different kinds of group tasks—functional and mixed groups and problem-solving in mini-groups. They were invited to look at existing patterns of behaviour, the underlying values, the resulting problems for each other, and collective failure experiences. They were then led on to look at an alternative set of values, and behaviours and skills required for collective success experiences.

(ii) Industrial Harmony Values

The programme of human resource development in a large Oil Refining and Marketing Company, included an attempt at moving from traditional patterns of industrial harmony. The start was made with senior executives. They were heads of departments and members of the top management teams of their respective locations—either a refinery or a marketing region. Two batches of senior executives were given inputs in values for industrial harmony. The design involved examination of existing and desired values for senior line and staff executives and how they can influence employee, and even union values in a constructive direction.

(iii) Planning Leadership Values

In the same Oil Company a formal Corporate Planning System had been initiated four years ago. A ten year Perspective Plan and a five year Long Range Plan formed part of the system. While the system was found useful, it was felt to be not as well rooted as the company's HRD system. It was decided to make planning more participative, decentralise the structure for planning and strengthen leadership support.

The top management group, just one level below the Board, was exposed to a programme on those values required in role occupants at Executive Director/General Manager level, so as to provide the supportive climate and foster long term thinking and action.

(iv) Systematic Management Values

A multi-unit, core sector public enterprise has used the concept of an Annual Performance Plan as an important ingredient of its turn around strategy, along with other interventions in restructuring, HRD and technology. One of the major problems identified was unsystematic undisciplined, chaotic patterns of working, resulting in waste of capacity, materials, manpower, energy and funds. A vigorous three-year campaign was carried out for training executives at all manufacturing plants and marketing regions of the values required for methodical planning, scheduling, implementation, re-planning. The whole organisation has perceived the following benefits:

1. More balanced planning of production, despatches, stocks and deliveries.

2. More integrated scheduling of production, capital repairs and regular maintenance and adherence to those schedules.
3. Better dovetailing of schedules between Works and Non-Works departments.
4. Higher delegation by seniors of routine matters, and support to those at shop floor level.
5. Smoother production throughout the year, reducing the big gap between the first and last quarter outputs.
6. Significant improvements in capacity utilisation, cost, quality and profitability.

(*v*) *Institution Building Values*

A large Indian subsidiary of a multinational, with a sensitive leadership wanted to reexamine its position and plans in the Indian society and ethos. The Chairman and Directors of the parent company, as well as the Directors of the associated group companies were exposed to workshops on Institution Building and the role of values in guiding the leadership and membership. These inputs and events have acted as a fountainhead in initiating the following strategic directions.

1. Import-substitution oriented major diversification move into the broad vector of Agri-Business, including edible oils and hybrid seeds.
2. Export oriented diversification into vendor-based products.
3. Diversification into Financial Services, to help fund India's anticipated massive growth in the coming decades.
4. Opening international offices, as a step towards globalising the business.
5. Enhancing inter-divisionsal boundary respect, as well as transparency.
6. More towards a climate of candour, meritocracy and excellence.

The above six accounts Value Training are illustrative, and by no means exhaustive.

Model for Value Training

We present the model in four phases—through Figure 1-4, namely,

(i) Starting Value.
(ii) Desired value.
(iii) Value Gap.
(iv) Value Learning.

The fourth phase consists of two parts:

(a) Attitude Change, and
(b) Behavioural Skill Improvement.

These are shown in Figures 14.5 and 14.6. The total model is integrated in Fig. 14.7. The logic of the model flows as follows:

(i) Starting Value

One of the traps in Value Training is to assume that the target group of trainees know the existing value on the concerned dimensions. In fact, there are only "perceptions" of values. The training challenge is to get the group to reflect on two sets of perceptions. The first set is their own, in which certain defensiveness is likely. The second set is that of "significant others", in their role set, both within and outside the organization. Here, the problem is likely to be insentivity. (Fig. 14.1).

Phase 1 - STARTING VALUE

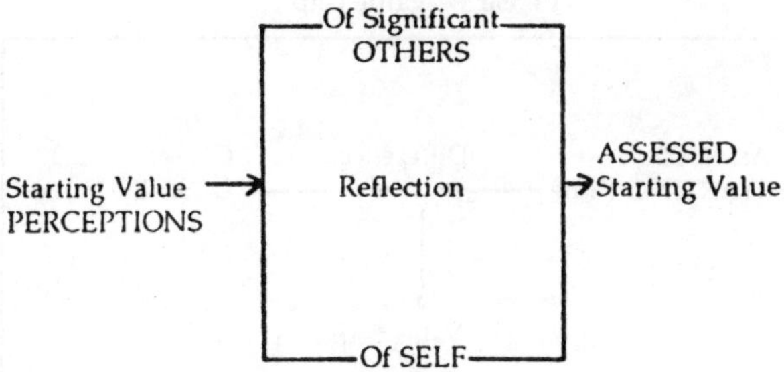

Fig. 14.1

(ii) Desired Value

Here again, two sets of preferences need to be balanced—their own and that of significant others. The challenges to get them to benefit from externally desired values, and enrich the chosen values. (Fig. 14.2).

Phase 2 – DESIRED VALUE

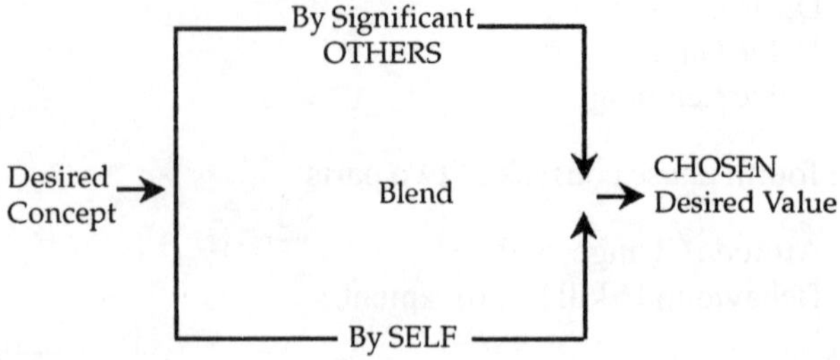

Fig. 14.2

(*iii*) *Value Gap*

The next step is to get the group to juxtapose two values and carry out a simple, arithme along.

> Chosen Desired Value – (Minus) Assessed 'Starting Value' = (Equals) Value Gap.

By now, we have reached approximately by way: Identifying the value "gap" is the equivalent diagnosis. The second-rule half is solving the problem (Fig. 14.3)

Phase 3 – Value Gap

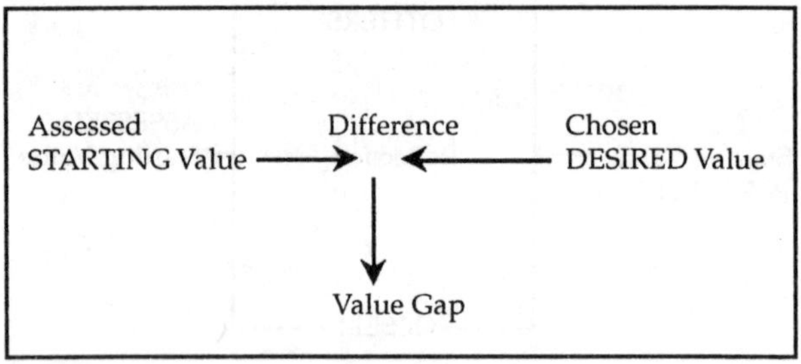

Fig. 14.3

(*iv*) *Value Learning*

The ultimate test of value learning is its effect of manifestation in practice. For this, it is not enough to bring attitudinal change. It is also necessary to provide skill inputs, so as to be able to translate the attitude change into practice. Here the, said dimension is recognised, but is subordinate to supportive to the value dimension.

Through discussion of the underlying values, the training seeks to bring about attitudinal change. These should reflect in more positive habits. On the other side, the skills learning should lead to more "refined" skills, building on the base strength already with the participants. These two, better habits are skills combined together should lead to perceptible impact of the desired value in "practice" (Fig. 14.4) These two components need to examined in more depth.

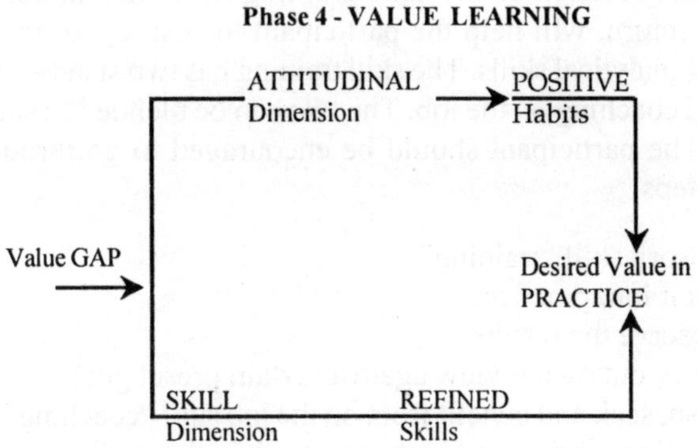

Fig. 14.4

(*a*) *Attitude Change*

Behavioural learning comes partly from attitudinal "training" inputs. Additional, valuable inputs can come from introspection, feedback, and reinforcement. The link may be seen as follows (Fig. 14.5).

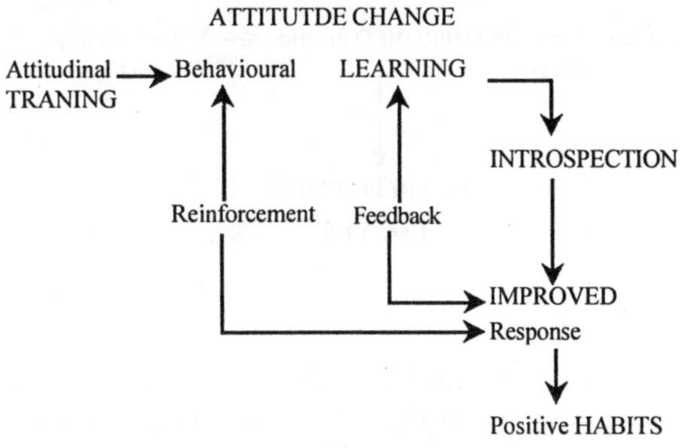

Fig. 14.5

- Introspection on the formal learning necessary, before the trainee can deliver, improved response.
- Behavioural learning can be further stimulated by feedback—both received by the individual, and perceived by him.
- Appreciation of improved responses will help to reinforce behavioural learning.

(*b*) *Skill Improvement*

We are initially concerned in Value Training with behavioural skills.

These, inturn, will help the participant to seek opportunities to improve his analytical skills. The skill training has two stands—formal training and coaching on the job. The two can be blended as shown in Fig. 14.6. The participant should be encouraged to go through the following steps:

- Absorb skill "training".
- Put it into practice.
- Observe the results.
- Carry out own review against certain preset goals.
- Also, seek and benefit from on the job skill "coaching" by his dyadic superior, and perhaps even by other seniors.

BEHAVIOURAL SKILL IMPROVEMENT

Fig. 14.6

Integrated Model

The comprehensive model for Value Training, incorporating all the above elements, is shown in Fig. 14.7. The logical sequence is as follows:

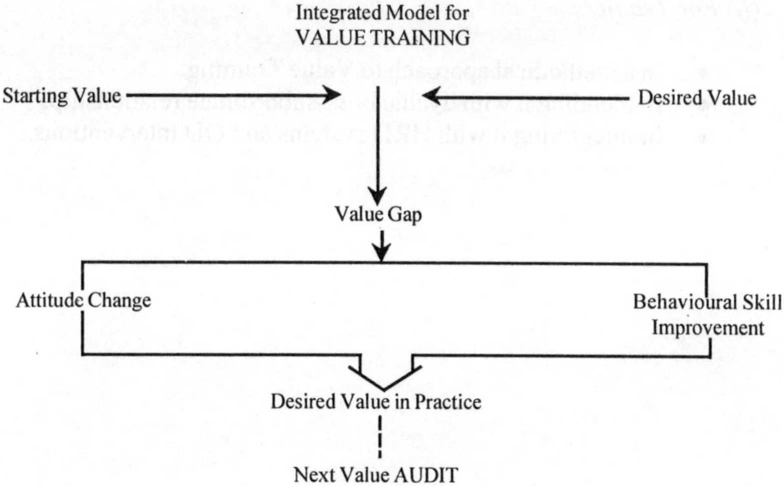

Fig. 14.7

1. Group to correctly understand the starting position in terms of the existing values.
2. Get them to choose the appropriate desired values.
3. Derive the value gap between existing and desired values.
4. Provide training for attitudinal change and behavioural skill improvement.
5. Support with feedback, coaching and reinforcement.
6. Observe practice and carry out periodical value audit.

The model enumerated above will be useful in the following ways.

(*i*) *For Top Managements*

- In identifying Value Training needs for themselves, senior manager, line and staff executives, workmen, union activists, dealers, suppliers and other relevant shareholders.
- In taking a longer term perspective and allow for value learning, action, review and improvement.
- In comissioning periodic value audits in the organisation.

(ii) For Trainers

- In a methodical approach to Value Training.
- In blending it with dyadic boss-subordinate relationship.
- In integrating it with HRD systems and OD interventions.

15

Training Perspectives
*Newer Concepts and Methodologies**

R.P. Billimoria

The rate of technology and managerial obsolescence is growing at an exponential rate. It is no longer considered valid to discuss if training is necessary. The debates, are more on how to conduct training and how to make it more effective and enduring.

Whereas obsolescene in avaition skills and the practice of medicine become easily apparent, the situation is not the same in human resources development area. This is partly so because of the subtle nature of the requirements and partly because the effect of obsolescene long in showing.

Training needs have two dimensions. One is the exposure to the Guru or mentor for conceptual inputs and the other is the exposure to the training market for meeting itemised needs. Some work has been done on the methods of identifying training needs and the methods of re-training and updating of knowledge. However, techniques used for these purposes are very often borrowings essentially from inputs from different academic disciplines. There is really no need to argue against these borrowings as they have proved helpful. However, what is required is for training and development activity to evolve as an area in its own right, more fully and in a more complete fashion.

Various discussions on training technology including workshops and recording of cases have made it apparent that the contours of this area were growing firmly. But then there is need for a continuous normative upgradation of the sophistication of these technologies. One

* First published in IJTD in 1991.

such way of normatively raising sophistication of training technologies would be by way of arranging training exchanges.

If individuals and institutions with experience in conducting training activities could get together to conduct what could be called training experience exchanges sessions, it would lead to cross-fertilisation of ideas and make the whole process of imparting training rich.

A close loop approach such as used in personnel management systems to provide a feedback to the management could be replicated for the training systems. Not only could individuals and institutions with training experience meet together to exchange their impressions and results, but one could be brought back after a given period of time to meet as a group and provide inputs to the training sponsoring agencies and trainers themselves on the real effectiveness of the training which was initially received by the participants. Thus a review of the objectives, training design and training technologies could be made to make the whole training process more effective.

It will be useful to remind ourselves that training effort is not complete with mere determination of training needs or selection of trainer, or holding of training programmes. But one has to go beyond this. The training objective is only attained if the skilled knowledge/ know-how reaches the lowest possible level and this results in application of the perceived advantage of the organisation and to the trainee. This is the primacy of the feedback.

It is unfortunate that there is currently prevailing a situation which could be called the label syndrome. High sounding titles and high flown training missions loudly stated are not good enough. What one requires is a sound academic base in research related to communication skills and the ability to relate to the participants. And yet something more needs to be done to make trainee an instrument in enhancing organisational effectiveness.

One way this could be achieved is by job rotation from training jobs and *vice versa*. That some organisations are doing so in India is a matter of satisfaction to all who have faith in training and development as an area worth investing in. When one talks of newer training methodologies, approaches which come to mind are of the use of the programmed instructions, teaching machines like simulators. They may indeed be useful. But high pressure and high cost training does not necessarily add to the effectiveness, the example of training in computer application in middle-sized industry readily comes to mind. The survey of the Government sector and the Public and Private sectors of the industry will bring out the layout of the land very clearly.

In the Central Government, excluding the Defence Services we employ 3.5 million in the civil service.

Till 1985, an officer in the Indian Administrative Service recruited in his early 20s did not go through any formal training programme after he has crossed the portals of the Lal Bahadur Shastri Academy. The learning renewal programmes launched with the blessings of the Government have marked a valid beginning. They have, however, a long way to catch up. The more disturbing aspect is that the public sector has absorbed enormous amounts of the civil service culture and its personnel, particularly in the early years. This pattern obviously needs correction through effective training.

Foundation for Organisational Research Study in 1984-85 on Training in Public Sector Enterprises showed that in 50 units covered by the study, 30 did not have training facilities or programmes, 24 had minimal inadequate and unsatisfactory training programmes. The position is much worse with State public sector units for which information is not available.

Barring exception in a few large units, there is a lack of information and the position is far from satisfactory. Many entrepreneurs, borrowing from the thinking of very many established institutions, also believe that investments in training are really of little use. They feel this way not because they believe truly that training is irrelevant but because they feel that it is better to do "executive pinching" of a trained employee with them. Obviously, if you can get an executive to move to your organisation after he has been trained in another, there is little rationale to the thinking of such people, in the investment of training of their own employees.

Such misconceptions can be removed if only a nexus between training and performance of all employees of an organisation is perceived rightly. There is also a nexus between training and job descriptions, not to mention of course the nexus between training and workers' participation.

It may be indeed valid to argue that training is a tool for survival and growth requiring a multi-sectoral approach on behalf of institutions organising, sponsoring and proclaiming to be guardians of training. This is so because they have to cater to the requirements of the government the public and the private sector as well as the teaching institutions.

Training efforts have a long way to go, especially to respond to the requirements of the public sector in the States and the needs of small and medium size units in all sectors.

What is required is far quicker and speedier correction and updating perceptions on the part of the trainers. A renewal of the thinking on training methodologies is also in order, so that they continually keep borrowing with the changing national and international environment.

In a research study conducted on some public sector undertaking by the Foundation for Organisational Research (many of whose findings could find application in the private sector no less than the public sector) a detailed study has been made for a large number of representative companies. Without going into unnecessary details, what it has to say on the organisations that it studied is worth reproducing for wider dissemination. 25 per cent of the 50 organisations studied did not, have any specialised training set up. They had to depend on outside agencies, even for availing bare infrastructural facilities. Even where there were operating training set-ups, a majority felt that they were inadequate.

Amongst the pedagogical techniques, lecture method was the most widely used. Other modern techniques and methodologies were lacking. On an average, 31 programmes were annually conducted. Percentage of in-house training programmes was as low as 37 per cent showing trends of heavy reliance on outside agencies. No correlation between internal faculty and number of training programmes conducted by them was apparent. Why this should have been so is not very clear. The budgetary allocations to the total budget was 0.1 per cent to 0.15 per cent. 85 per cent of the organisations did training needs analysis but most of them only on an *ad hoc* basis. Some used group meetings, others used perceptions or job analysis to identify training needs. 84 per cent of the organisations evaluated their training programmes through traditional participants feedback system and only 24 used pre and post-training feedback system. This itself is an index of the state-of-the-art.

Of course, general picture varies from total dependence on internal faculty to total dependence on external faculty. Internal faculty strengths were largely in functional areas; only 28 per cent were in the area of general management. Whether this indicated a deliberate choice or displayed a situation based on availability trends, one was not in a position to comment. A further interesting dimension of the study was that the selection of about 25 per cent of the faculty was through self-nomination.

It would hold to reason to argue that improvement in any system can be derived directly from quality of research in that area, but precious little seems to have been done by various organisations in this direction. Only 29 per cent "stated" they had done training needs analysis based on research, 25 per cent reported having done studies in developing training materials. The rest gleefully depended on outside agencies. The study further went into the problem of perceptions and considerations of the visions of the future.

At a later stage, the findings of the FORE research study were discussed at a national seminar and an action plan was evolved. The details of this are available with the concerned organisation. The important message is to remember that there is a natural weakness in drawing general conclusions based on study of larger units, be it in the public or in the private sector.

Never should we forget that the future growth and prosperity of this great country depends largely on the productivity of small and medium sized units in all sectors of the economy and not on the select few Brobingangians in training, as in all other functions of management. We ignore them at our own peril.

As we peer in hope at the next century, not far away, these observations and findings of the FORE research study on training should make the public sector, the private sector and the government ponder upon and at least think of alternatives which would improve upon the effectiveness of the training functions. For this purpose, specific action is required in the area of providing professional assistance to medium sized and small sized units. Similarly, some organisations, possibly ISTD can take on the role of a National Institute of Trainers. Similarly, there would be need for establishing a continuing research base for all aspects of training and re-training. In order to do this, however, any organisation, ISTD or otherwise, would need a continuity of high level, high technique effort through full-time well qualified and well paid professionals under the policy guidelines provided by an accredited group of professionals. In matters pertaining on training—technical and managerial, fulltime services of accepted experts is needed no less than in any other area.

Not withstanding what has been said above, in the ultimate analysis the end product of all training effort is the trainee himself. He must be encouraged to learn, and training must be conducted in a way which helps him to listen and retain learning. It is regrettable that comparatively little literature is available in this area. I would like, before concluding to make my personal contribution in recording some perceptions from my experience, which raise certain relevant considerations in the learning process of the trainee. I am conscious that this is a sensitive area, a relatively unexplored one, unchanted and unarticulated by Pundits of training technology. One must tread wearily but tread we must, because treading makes the path which becomes the highway of future progress.

The doubts started in the mind while researching on the "Co-ordination of the Personnel and Production Function in British Industry" for the Nuffield Fellowship at Birmingham University during 1951-53. While studying evaluation of training programmes in a select group of industries, a few observations on impediments in learning by line managers, personnel officers and trainers, seemed obtuse.

> "Trainers find it difficult to hold the attention of quite a few trainees. This affects effectiveness of Programmes". (Line Manager).
>
> "May be the trainees are stressed extraneous factor affecting their career and future growth". (Personnel Manager/Industrial Psychologist).
>
> "As a trainee, I want to learn, the trainers are good but my mind wanders. I fantacise. Mostly it is negative—death of a dear one, unemployment or loss of a limb. The more the mentors and trainers tell me not to day dream, the more I do so. I cannot forget the War and what it did to me." (Trainee).
>
> "The packet of remedies suggested by the same Group hardly seemed helpful."
>
> "Ask the Government to remove the stresses!"
>
> "Everytime your mind wanders pay a voluntary fine in the charity box."
>
> "Back to religion. Go to church and let God take care of your problems. I have tried it and it works."
>
> "Repeat again and yet again, 'I would not think of anything but what the teacher says'. (A trainee who followed this advice assiduously, promptly fell asleep!).

It seemed that the reasons and the remedies suggested were such that one would be wary of commiting them to paper in an erudite Post-Graduate thesis!"

All the same, the following four points scenario persisted:

1. Young trainees who had been through enemy bombings and loss of near and dear ones during Second World War, were highly stressed.
2. Conditions of stress adversely affected the efficacy of training.
3. Stress could not be removed by asking trainees to forget about it.
4. Some trainees reported some relief by going to church.

Let us analyse these one by one, in today's context.

Stress and Training

It is accepted that the training process in its broadest sense conditioning behaviour or transferring knowledge or skill is a womb to tomb affair.

Also, that conditions of stress retard the training effort.

The expression womb to tomb is not mere alliteration. Pre-natal suggestions and exposure to Western classical music have proven to make the child absorb training in music more quickly and perform significantly better than children not so exposed before birth. There are any number of authenticated cases of men and women—some of them invalids—being trained in skills like computer programming or learning a new language.

So too has the adverse effect of stress been chronicled and studies over years. The stress of wartime, it is found, is no more lethal than the stress created by the industrial and social environment of the setting years of the 20th Century. The pioneering efforts of Hans Selye in the study of stress have been followed up by others praticing Psychologists, Industrial Psychologists and Sociologists.

Law of Reversed Effort

This brings us to the third point in the scenario that some trainees refused to accept the reasonable suggestion to forget about the stressful conditions. Were they obtuse, non-conformist, unusual in their behaviour? I remember as a child, being scared of being in the dark. Admonitions and ridicule had no effect. One night, some wise elders made me repeat "I am not afraid of the dark" 15 times, and pitched me into a dark room for 10 minutes. Things became worse. The more I denied the fear, the more I was frightened. I had nightmares for a week.

Then came a wild uncle who said he was writing a book on Ghosts in the Dark. "But" he confessed "I have not seen one, you are afraid of the dark aren't you? So, you are bound to see one and describe it to me". Ha! Ha! none on your life, I said. He offered me five rupees for every description of the spook. I was to go into my bed-room, pitch dark, while he stood outside with a stick to rush in and protect, in case the ghost was an aggressive type. Every 10 minutes or so, 1 was to come out and describe my meeting with the spirits. If I had a conversation with them, it would mean an extra two rupees.

The fear was intense but five rupees in those days was a lot of much needed money. Incentive to see and describe a ghost intensified by an advance of three rupees, in anticipation. The first few efforts were abject failures—no ghost, no spook.

Uncle felt our home was too noisy and the ghosts here were more scared than scary. He took me to a 'haunted house' in the nighbouring town. Again there was failure. So uncle, a lawyer and not a psychologist by profession, had cured me of my phobia, not by negative suggestion but by a positive carrot based confrontation.

You try an experiment. Right now. Select a number from 1 to 10. Any number—say number 4. For the next 60 seconds—time yourself—YOU ARE NOT TO THINK OF NUMBER 4—You can think of anything else under the Sun but not number 4. Go!

The result, is obvious. Unless you are a highly evolved Yogi, never in your life have you thought of number 4, so often as in the last 60 seconds, in spite of the negative admonition. This is the Law of Reversed Effort. Psychologists recognise it, but our up-bringing and training system, right from childhood onwards is based on Do not do this and Do not do that.

We must replace this by positive assertion in order to reduce failure and reduce stress.

Stress — a possible antidote:

So, now we *know* that

Stress dampens the training effort and denying its existence or wishing it away makes it worse.

Psychologists and other medical specialists recommend 'including a relaxation response' in order to reduce stress. This is well backed up by research, particularly during the past three decades. The accepted indicators of an induced relation response are:

- decrease in oxygen consumption;
- decrease in respiratory rate,
- decrease in rate of heart beat;
- increase in Alpha wave activity in the brain as measured by EEC (electro-encephalogram);
- decrease in blood pressure; and
- decrease in muscle tension.

Given below is the table comprising methods for inducing the relaxation response:

COMPOSITION OF METHODS FOR INDUCING THE RELAXATION RESPONSE PHYSIOLOGICAL PARAMETERS						
	Oxygen Consump-tion	**Respira-tory Rate**	**Heart rate**	**Alpha waves**	**Blood pressure**	**Muscle tension**
Transcendental meditation	Decreases	Decreases	Decreases	Increases	Decreases	Not measured
Zen and Yog	Decreases	Decreases	Decreases	Increases	No Change	Not measured
Autogenic training	Not measured	Decreases	Decreases	Increases	Inconclu-sive	Decreases
Progressive relaxation	Not measured	Not measured	Not measured	Not measured	Inconclu-sive results	Decreases
Hypnosis with suggested deep relaxation	Decreases	Decreases	Decreases	Not measured	Inconclu-sive results	Not measured
Sentic cycles	Decreases	Decreases	Decreases	Not measured	Not measured	Not measured

The *Yoga Sutras* of Patanjali also give a comprehensive model, including cognitive structuring, effective or emotional stages and adaptive reactions. They also present the concept of Kriya Yoga, aimed at reducing the number of intensity of the stressors and to facilitate related conservation of mental energy devoid of tension through 'Samadhi—Bhavana'.

'Samadhi' through meditation can be either by the ritualistic or non-ritualistic path. But scientists have proved beyond doubt that non-ritualistic medication reduces stress. The above table proves the point.

There are other proven bonus fall-outs which help considerably in the learning process.

In a publication on 'How Meditation Can Reduce Stress', Harold H. Bloomfield MD, Michael Peter Cain, Dennis T. Jaffe and Robert B. Kory mention that in 1973 over 200 executives from the USA attended a symposium on a "Non-ritual Meditation Technique and its Contribution of Management Enrichment"; Hans Laue, senior management scientist at Stanford Research Institute, summarised the unique value of such meditation as follows:

"Six of the most significant problems facing management today are mounting grievances, job alienation, increasing absenteeism, reduced productivity, lower quality of output, and lack of innovation. In searching for solutions to these "people problems" management has investigated them in detail. But these problems are only symptoms of an underlying cause—the lack of full development of each individual working in an economic environment. To eliminate these problems we should attend to the cause, not merely the symptoms. The most effective treatment is to enable each individual to realise his dynamic potential, to maximise and make most intelligent use of his creative energies by practicing the methods of non-ritualistic meditation."

Another executive of a successful manufacturing firm states that some of the immediately applicable changes he felt after starting non-ritualistic meditation were:

"*Increased organisation ability*—capacity to take in ever larger amounts of data and carry more in the memory store".

"*Ease of concentration*—my mind is developing more and more to its full capacity, one aspect being the ability to focus, or return to the rhythms of the present".

"*Speed of thought*—the ability to draw quickly from accumulated knowledge, and piece connections in the rapid-fire order benefits greatly and adds to the development of confidence".

Diminishing of the sense of working to get a shiny new set of wheels—watching this fade has its own brand of nostelgia, but, the pleasure derived from work as its own reward supplants any desire to turn back. It is a pleasure to watch the business expand and provide a real service".

Prospect and Retrospect

It is not my recommendation that the reader wend his nearby mountains and plan a saffron-robe-sabbatical, meditating and returning stress free and training prone, to his managerial suite. Nor is it sought that he spend hours each day at home, in difficult poses, chanting, meditating and awaiting enlightenment. Be the reader of these lines an atheist, he has available to him a number of non-ritualistic or ritualistic, if he so, desires—techniques of meditation. They do not ask for any difficult regimen of life nor are they restricted to members of a cult.

He may take his choice and select or reject as he pleases.

16

Rethinking HRD
*The Context of Strategic Environment**

Y.R.K. Reddy

The present times are being variously described, but two terms capture their nature most appropriately—"Turbulent", and "discontinuous". "Turbulent" by the intensity and spread of changes in all segments of society, economy, and polity, with a discernible impact on organisational positions. And, "Discontinuous" in view of the unrelatedness of many changes with the past. These changes are enormously influencing organisational orthodoxies, and several activities may have to convulse to create fresh rationale and new role for the traditional functions. HRD, both as a discipline and as a function, is one such area where the ruling orthodoxy may need recrafting, or sometimes re-vamping. There are two major planks for examination which would be fruitful in this context—the HRD interface with external environment, and internal strategic concerns.

External Interface—Need for Expansionism

The ideology (in the nature of a powerful idea) that human resources are important for efficiency and well-being, has taken a firmer root in the developed and developing countries. While in the developed world, human resources discernibly give corporations the competitive advantage and leadership, in the developing world, HRD is moving to the centre stage of socio-economic development. This shift, evident

---

* First Published in IJTD in 1993.

during the last decade and pursued vigorously during the current one, owes its origin to several factors—such as the intensity of competitiveness, and requirement of innovations in technology and management in the developed world. In the case of the developing world, the factors are related to failure of purely growth oriented strategies, the growing gap between growth and development, and the evident impact of direct investment in human capital and population, health and equity.[1] The shifts in macro-policy and the new emphasis on human resources, which are fairly complex in themselves, have several signals for the organisational pursuit of HRD in the 1990s, of which two are the foremost.

Responsiveness of the Education System

The first is the relationship of the nature of labour market with the internal HRD activities at the organisation level. For long, the level and quality of education and skill in the labour market have remained stagnant or tardy in growth, consequent to slow pace of change in the educational and vocational training systems. Contrary to this, the changes in technology, management systems, policies and communication requirements, coupled with the emerging competitive compulsions, demand increasingly higher as well as different/specialised types of educational and vocational base than evident now. Hence, the effort of the organisation cannot obviously be limited to mere induction or adaptation efforts, but must extend to reforming and rebuilding the foundation to suit the internal requirements. If the effort of the State and the private institutions are likely to change dynamically, consequent to the perceived necessity of investment in human resource for gaining broader corporate and national goals, the organisation's task would be that much less onerous. For instance, it is believed that the systems of education and vocational/technical training in Japan, West Germany or South Korea are far better matched to strategic requirements than those in the US or the UK, thus giving the former an advantage in the factor conditions?[2] The mismatch, evident and emerging in several countries, implies that the domain of HRD activities of the organisation must expand horizontally. This demands greater assumption of education by the organisations (See Fig. 16.1).

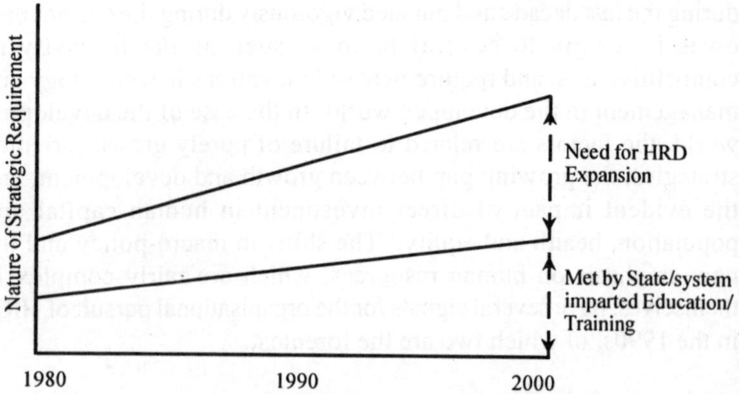

Fig. 16.1: Increasing Need for HRD Expansion

The cost-benefit ratios of such a measure are obviously different at the organisation and societal levels, after reckoning the external/ indirect costs and benefits. Despite the divergence, the costs and benefits even at the organisation level would probably demand better investment in education and training to bridge the mismatch. According to Porter, competitive firms had well developed internal training programmes, and leading companies in Japan, for example, had their own schools. The apprehension in the US regarding such extensive investment in education and training, arising out of high turnover of staff, could be misplaced.[3] Besides, the investment approach implicit in the above argument, there is a view that corporations must assume greater role in education and training, on the model of the churches, to improve commitment. The advocacy here is for a kind of parochialism (companyism?) to be developed for serving the share-holders of the company, in the best possible manner.[4]

Indirect Human Resource

The second area of examination in the external interface is the extent of attention to be bestowed by the organisation in relation to what may be termed as Indirect Human Resources (IHR). Attention to the quality of human resources in the indirect segments assumes importance not only in the context of competitiveness, in generic terms, but also in the light of differentiation/focus-related strategies, increasing contracting out, ancillarisation, and the growing adoption of Total Quality

Management (TQM). In the absence of sufficient attention to IHR, the results from the efforts at upgrading the human resources of the company would always be sub-optimal. IHR could be typically from three segments, which we will refer to as indirect segments—those engaged by the in-bound segments (suppliers of goods and services), those engaged by the out-bound segments (distribution, sales, product promotion, etc.), and the fringe ones engaged on a casual or temporary basis for the company's operations.

A portion of IHR may be falling under a separate corporate umbrella if the suppliers, distributors, etc., are corporate entities themselves. The quality of IHR should be of greater concern to the principal organisation, when the in-bound and out-bound linkages are mainly human resource driven—for instance, product promotion or maintenance work. On the other hand, if the linkages are products or material addition or value, the quality of human resource would be more indirect in relevance; however, this importance would increase should the organisation's requirements be varying/fast changing, needing faster responses and adaptations from the indirect segments. Apart from the nature of goods/services and the extent of human resource imbeddedness in these, (both qualitative as well as quantitative) the need for direct concern for the quality of IHR increases in situations where there is inadequate competition within the in-bound and out-bound segments.

From the foregoing, it evolves that the extent of HRD required depends upon three conditions: (a) the existing nature and level of IHR; (b) the level of human resource imbeddedness of the activities, and (c) the degree of competition. Fig. 16.2 presents the scale of HRD attention required under different conditions of the three interactive dimensions. The need for HRD concern would be least when the existing quality and nature of IHR is high, the human resource imbeddedness in the indirect activity is low (*i.e.* the activity is driven more by other factor conditions than human resource), and the level of competition in that segment is relatively high. The contrary situation demands a high level of concern from the organisation.

As there are obvious difficulties (legal as well as administrative) in undertaking directly the development of IHR, the principal organisation can only build human resource standards, and monitor indirectly by creating an information system. Such concern would send appropriate signals to the indirect segments which may respond positively. The additional costs, if any, in this process, would get in-built into the price of supply of goods and rendering of services. Obviously, the implicit escalation of costs (for the principal organisation) would be offset in other ways to result in net benefit.

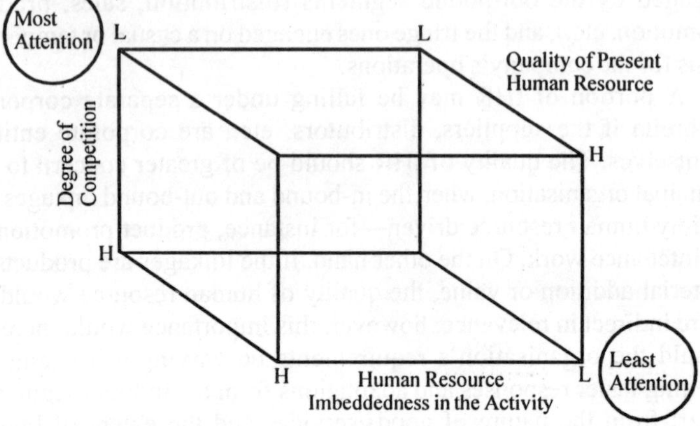

Fig. 16.2: Combination of Conditions in the Indirect Segment and Implications for HRD Attention

Stretching this still further, there is another segment of people which is remote from the organisation's operations, but has the potential to be supportive of the HRD activities. This segment is the community within which the company is operating, and the members of the family of the direct human resources. Several companies have launched upon community involvement schemes and family involvement programmes. While the former is primarily seen as a public relations strategy, its spin-off in attracting a field of good candidates, and possibly eliciting a few traditionally valued attributes as commitment, would be worthy. Additionally, the family involvement programmes (visits to the factory by the children and spouses, etc.) are believed to have similar reinforcing characteristics. However, the HRD function in most firms does not look upon these as having a linkage with its results. Presently, the linkage of HRD activity with universities, R&D establishments, and training institutes are the only acknowledged external interface. The future design of HRD activities must widen to recognise the linkages with other important supportive systems.

Strategy Concerns and IIRD

Having been practised more as an act of faith, HRD activities in several organisations have gathered momentum and direction of their own—they have become veritable rituals with questionable relevance to the organisational strategy. Strategy has been defined in several ways, and it is also the common understanding that there could be a hierarchy of strategies, from the grand corporate strategy to divisional, departmental or functional ones. The grand strategy may be seen as the combination of objectives, goals, and plans creating a vision of the organisation in the future dynamic environment. This assumes the dynamic nature of the external environment, internal conditions, and of the strategy itself. The extent of change would depend upon several forces, but it is evident that the rate and intensity of change would keep increasing in the coming years. In such an environment, the validity of several HRD practices would come under pressure, unless they are closely matched with the strategies of the organisation—both the grand strategy, as well as the connected lower order ones.

In this context, there are five issues that need review and an evaluative debate by management teams (See Fig. 16.3).

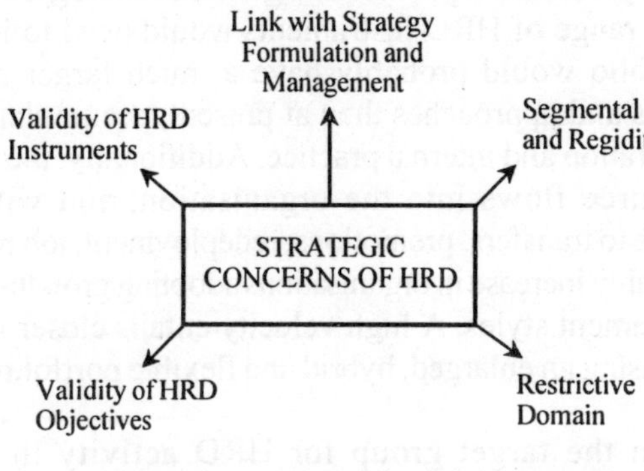

Fig. 16.3: Strategic Concerns of HRD

(i) IIRD and Strategic Management

The role of human resources in the grand strategy obviously differs from business to business, or portfolios of businesses. The higher the role of human resources (for instance, computer software, advertising, and high-tech manufacturing businesses), the closer should be the involvement of HRD in strategy formulation and implementation. It is naive, or even dogmatic, to claim that HRD could drive the corporate strategy, but to the extent that it can overcome an internal constraint or provide a strength, HRD would be shaping the strategy.[5] If the scope for product development, augmenting finances or improving production rates, are important in shaping the strategy, the same should be true of HRD as well. In implementation of strategy, an important step is, communication to all employees of the missions, opportunities, threats, internal weaknesses, strategies, values, goals and objectives, resource allocations and constraints. The most preferred mode of communication being a series of presentations/workshops to employees which obviously would be HRD.

(ii) Bias and Rigidities

In several organisations, HRD indicates bias and rigidities. The bias is in respect of—(a) the selection of instruments or methods; and (b) the target groups.

Consequent to closer study of jobs, increasing attention to the individual employee, and the pace of changes in technology, skills and job designs, the range of HRD instruments would need to increase. The ideal portfolio would probably have a much larger range of techniques, tools and approaches then at present, accumulated from theory, demonstration and internal practice. Additionally, the velocity of human resource flows into the organisation, and within the organisation (due to transfers, promotions, redeployment, job rotations, etc.) would probably increase in organisations adopting growth-oriented strategic management styles. A high velocity entails closer fit of the HRD activities using an enlarged, hybrid and flexible portfolio of tools and techniques.

The bias in the target group for HRD activity in several organisations is notably in respect of management development, forsaking skill adjustments/developments or communications. Since the pay-off from the target groups is diverse, depending upon the organisation's technology, range of products, nature of problems and envisaged strategy, it is essential to adopt a cost-benefit analysis frame of thinking.[6] Such an approach assures constant focus on prioritisation based on the strategic necessities of the organisation than mere "doing more better". HRD activities would need to look upon the investments in time, effort and money for different target groups, and the range of techniques and tools, as a matrix, out of which an optimal mix can be arrived at, for the given time period. Such an approach would ensure a cure for HRD sclerosis that seems to afflict many organisations. It would prod organisations to give up the mind-set in respect of the tools as well as the preferred target groups, bringing forth the essential ingredient of flexibility.

(iii) Validity of HRD Instruments

Relatively, the current practice of HRD, in several instances, betrays a lack of validity. This validity crisis arises at two planes—one, is the validity of the HRD instruments (techniques, tools, approaches) *vis-a-vis* the objectives; and the other, is the validity of the objectives *vis-a-vis* strategic performance. The promise of validity of HRD instruments with the objectives, originates primarily from the academic world, which often is the source for the instrument. In several instances, the objectives can be achieved by the instrument only under specified conditions (take the case of O.D., for illustration[7]). If the contingent conditions cannot be created, the instrument becomes invalid. Most organisations fail to reckon the assumed conditions of the instruments, and their match with the organisational realities. This problem is not peculiar to behavioural-oriented activities, as it could be true of skill development ones as well. (For example, the condition of "motivation to learn" as the corner stone of skill development training.) To avoid lack in HRD impact, organisations would need examine closely the promise of the instruments, the caveats which are often not too evident, and the results of their use in practice.

(iv) HRD and Strategic Performance

The other part of the validity crisis is relative to HRD objective and strategic performance. The term "strategic performance" may be seen as a result of a multitude of actions aimed at creating an advantageous posture for the organisation, in relation to its environment, also in line with its mission. Such performance is dependent on the creation of internal capabilities and their constant upgradation/modification. Thus, it is not mere profitability or increased performance in the year, but much more in content and longer in time perspective. Ideally, HRD objectives must be drawn from an understanding of the requirements of strategic performance, and the existing conditions, through close interaction in the process of strategy formulation. As this does not normally happen in practice, most of the objectives get invalidated. In negation of the ideal situation, several of the objectives often are a result of what may be termed "instrumentasis", where the existence and knowledge of the instruments dictates the objectives, thus entrapping the HRD functionary in a mind-set.

This obviously raises the related issue of what kind of behaviour, approaches, and activities best achieve strategic performance. Academicians have been at this for long at a high level, and have brought forth literature and instruments which go through cycles of exuberant emulation, and delayed disaffection, from the practising world.[8] In the 1990s, the analysis of what constitutes strategic performance, and what range of activities and behaviour are required to achieve it, have to be done at the individual firm level than accept the grand theories (such as Japanese management style). This implies that HRD specialists must adopt a research-orientation within the firm, and consciously test the grand theories regarding the desirable behaviour, style, performance criteria etc., in the organisational context, and seek to quickly redefine, refine and innovate. The compression of time does not give much scope or prosaic adoption of grand prescriptions and the interminable wait for the promised results; it calls for organisational insight and innovation, to define what kind of performance behaviour is strategic for its mission.

(*v*) *HRD Domain*

In the past, there has been little problem defining the domain of HRD. It was seen primarily as an enabling process for human resources to perform more effectively—it stopped where action began. This compartmental view is one of the main reasons for much dissipation of energies, and also the validity crisis. Rightly, HRD is not meant to be a substitute for good management, but a process that would help management. Nevertheless, in the context of strategic management which outstretches mere strategy formulation to its active implementation, monitoring and control, there is obviously a need for closer networking among functions, as also between analysis and action. In such a situation, HRD activities may have to get ingrained in all activities of the organisation, than maintain a constituency, assuming a well-spread ethos which is more visible in results than in organisation structure.[9] (Towards a kind of cubbyhole crash that Alvin Toffler talked of, in the context of third wave technologies[10].) This advice may conjure up visions of loss of identity for the HRD function, but this is an unnecessary nightmare—it is the nature of authority, control over resources, and exclusivity that may undergo a change, but the extent of responsibility to plan, advise, co-ordinate, monitor and evaluate would, in fact, increase. HRD specialists must draw the attention of all to ensure that every action and activity has a developmental dimension, continuously improving communications, knowledge, skills, actions, and feedback. The present times require greater disaggregation, decentralisation and action linkage for HRD activities than observed so far.

Conclusions

The emerging environment entails re-crafting corporate HRD activities and re-examining their role, to subserve objectives of competitive advantage and leadership of corporate businesses, as also the goals of socio-economic development of nations. There are two major planks of change that need to be brought into HRD activities. The first relates to the existing domain of its activities, *vis-a-vis* external publics. As the education and vocational training systems in several countries move at far slower pace than the strategic requirements of the firms in future, HRD may have to increasingly assume educational activities to fill the gap between the available quality of labour and the fast changing requirements of organisations. Further, the performance of the human resource in the firm is fairly dependent on the quality and performance of the human resources engaged in the indirect segments inter-linked with the firm, such as the suppliers, ancillaries, distributors, stockists, repacking units, product promoters, service agents etc. The increasing tendency of contracting out, the pressures of competitiveness, increasing differentiation and focus in markets and products, as also the requirement of faster responses from the indirect segments, imply that HRD function has to develop standards, information, and other methods of monitoring the human resources in these indirect segments. The degree of attention and concern to be bestowed on the indirect segments is contingent on the combinations of three major factors—the present nature and quality of these indirect human resources, the extent of human resource imbeddedness of the activities, and the degree of competition.

The second plank of review of HRD relates to aspects within the firm concerned primarily with strategy. In this context, there are five significant issues which are:

(a) the need to improve the involvement of IIRD function in strategy formulation and implementation, especially in the case of human resource driven firms.
(b) to recognise the bias in selection of target groups and HRD instruments, and strive to bring about flexibility and strategic orientation using a cost-benefit approach;
(c) to question the validity of HRD instruments, methods and approaches vis-a-vis the objectives/expected outcome;
(d) to examine the validity of HRD objectives vis-a-vis the strategic performance that enables the organisation to move in the direction of its mission; and lastly,
(e) to remove the HRD barriers, disaggregate, decentralise and spread the activities throughout, to make a way of organisational life, thus reducing its exclusivity.

REFERENCES

1. Rashid Amjad. (Ed), (1987) *Human Resource Planning—The Asian Experience*, ILO-ARTEP, New Delhi, p.1.
2. See, for example, Michael Porter, (1990) *The Competitive Advantage of Nations*, London, Macmillan Press,.
3. Michael Porter, *op cit.,* p. 593.
4. J.H. Foegen, (1991) 'Corporate Education: A New Parochialism,' *Business Horizons*, Vol. 34, No. 5, Sept.-Oct.,
5. The extent of HRM's role in board-level strategy, and the contradictory evidence, have been briefly presented in David Guest, "Personnel Management: The End of Orthodoxy?" *British Journal of Industrial Relations*, Vol. 29, No. 2, June 1991, (1979) 6.
6. See Y.R.K. Reddy, (1979) Cost-Benefit Analysis of Training—An Appraisal, *Long Range Planning*, Vol. 12, Dec.
7. Stephenson, T. E. (1979) Organisation Development: A Critique, *The Journal of Management Studies*, Vol. 16.
8. For illustration, see Michael McGill, (1988) American Business and the Quick Fix, Henry Holt & Company, (1989) *Excerpts in Best of Business International*, Vol. 1, No. 3.
9. This obviously is the direction of HRM itself making it distinct from the traditional personnel management. See K. Legge (1989) Human Resource

Management—A Critical Analysis, In J. Storey (Ed). *New Perspectives on Human Resource Management*, London, Routledge.
10. Alvin Toffler, (1990) *Power Shift*. New York, Bantam Books.

17

Individual Training *vs.* Group Training*

P.N. Singh

With limited resources at their disposal, trainers have always struggled to keep a balance between individual training and group training. While some individual training, specially for the acquisition of certain skills will continue to be important for the organisation, most of individual training in the behavioural area gets lost. How this happens is pictorially depicted below:

How Individual Training Gets Lost

Stage 1

One individual, out of a group, is selected for attending a behavioural course. He comes back with new knowledge, skills and attitude. He has "gray" ideas. Others of his team have not gone for the same programme. They continue to have the same attitude, which is represented by "black". As a result of training "gray" demonstrates himself a changed person. "Blacks" reactions: He will become "normal" after some time, *i.e.* he will give up "gray" and become "black" like them:

Stage 2

Team members (all blacks) distance themselves from gray.

---

* First published in IJTD in 1999.

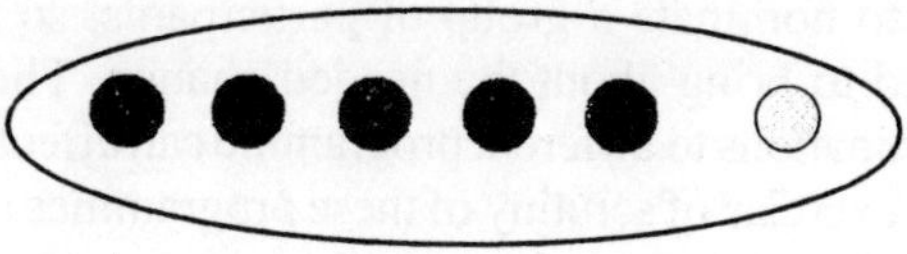

Stage 3

They gang together and isolate him.

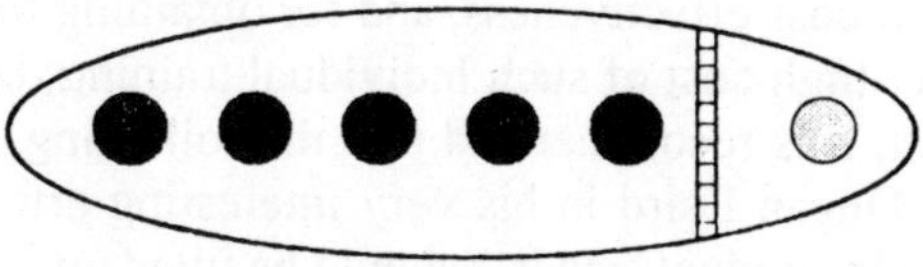

Stage 4

Gray thinks: Let me forget about his training. I have a family. I must remain in the job. Let me discard "gray" and become black. The impact of training thus gets lost.

It may so happen that "gray" is kicked out or "gray" decides to change the job by kicking himself out of his job, and taking up a new job. The impact of training gets lost here also.

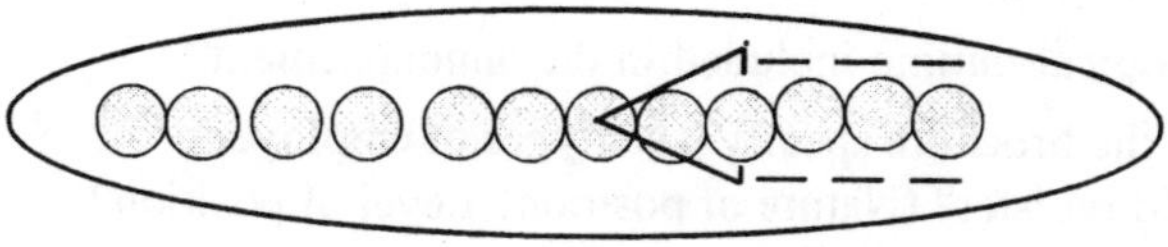

or

Lesson: Try to convert all "black" into "gray". One method can be training of the whole group, rather than individuals.

Group Training

Therefore, trainers should concentrate on group training in the behavioural areas. Ever for public seminars, it will be advisable for organisations to nominate a group of participants, so that a critical mass is created to bring about the needed change. The pressure for individual nominations to different programme can effectively resisted, by making the exercise of scrutiny of these programmes quite rigorous.

Rigorous Scrutiny of Programmes

For the sake of cost-effectiveness, and for obtaining the real benefit from relatively high cost of such individual training, because of fee and travel cost, it is recommended that the following questionnaire suggested by Dugan Laird in his very interesting article "Ideas for Responding to Individual Needs", should be filled up:

Questions to ask about the Workshop or seminar

	Yes	No
1. Does the seminar brochure publish learning objectives or "expected outcomes?"	-	-
2. Are those outcomes stated in behavioural terms?	-	-
3. Are the behaviours observable, measurable, reasonable?	-	-
4. Is a topical outline included in the announcement?	-	-
5. Does the brochure specify what types of employees should register? (Nature of position? Level of position? Experience assumed?)	-	-
6. Does the outline provide some time for participants to raise issues and ask questions?	-	-
7. Does the time schedule look flexible? (Could it possibly be completed? Can it adapt to the unique needs of individual participants?)	-	-
8. Is there provision for "process feedback" so participants can let leaders know, to what degree their need are/aren't being met?	-	-
9. Does the brochure mention the learning methods which will be employed?	-	-
10. Do those methods involve "action training"...chances for your trainees to get involved in something other than just listening and watching?	-	-

11. Is there workshop time, so your trainees can contemplate ways to apply the learnings back on the job? - -
12. Does there seem to be an opportunity for your trainees to access the leaders in small group, or one-on-one conversations? - -
13. Are the leaders well known to you or to the managers in the department in which the micro need exists? - -
14. Have the leaders published on this subject? - -
15. Have the leaders worked for, or consulted with corporate or bureaucratic organisations, or is their background entirely academic? - -

---

As per Laird, a really reliable seminar or workshop should score "Yes", on at least 10 of the above questions. It certainly should score "Yes" on five of the first six questions, if it meets the unique learning needs of your trainee.

If the programme has been offered previously, trainers can check with those who have used it. But they should be sure to ask the users how they're using the programme—not, how they liked it. Answers to the latter question will be contaminated with data about the food, the meeting site, the trip to and from the programme, other participants etc. Nobody will give a negative feedback on a programme held at Nainital, Darjeeling or Kashmir. A useful list of questions to ask previous participants at seminars and workshops would include some of these:

- Did you or your participants institute any new policies and procedures—amend or cancel any old ones—as a result of attending—the programme?
- Did participants come home with any product they could immediately put to use?
- What specific problem was solved as a result of attending this seminar?
- Have you calculated a return on investment from participation?
- If the need still existed, would you send people to this programme today?
- Did others who attended really reflect the audience appealed to in the advertising—or did they admit just anyone who paid the money?

- Should our participants make any special preparation? Was any pre-work to be done?
- In what ways did your participants get special individualized time and attention from the faculty?

When previous participants are unable to identify unique assistance or specific applications, the programme is questionable. It is always advisable to check with more than one participant from different organisations. I should also be the endeavour of the training staff to keep on locating organisations and institutions, giving similar programmes to make the best choice.

Information on Programmes

Bricker's International Directory is one of the best sources for getting details of quality executive development programmes, listed under the following 11 categories:

- General Management: 4 Weeks and Longer
- General Management: Less Than 4 Weeks
- Business Environment and Global Concerns
- Business Strategy
- Leadership
- Government and Non-profit Management
- Marketing and Sales
- Finance and Accounting
- Human Resources and Organisation
- Operations and Manufacturing
- Technology Management

This directory should help trainers in identifying quality programmes internationally and nominating their staff suitably.

Conclusion

There is need for instituting stricter controls on individual' nominations to different training programmes so that more resources could be diverted to group training for visible results in organisations.

18

Evaluation of Management Training and Development Programme of Guinness Nigeria PLC*

M.A. Ogunu

Introduction

Guinness Nigeria PLC started from small beginnings as a trading company in 1950. At that time it was engaged purely in the importation of Guinness Stout from Dublin to Nigeria for sale. The success of this business through the decade, by the encouraging embrace of Guinness Stout by Nigerians, necessitated the building of the Brewery in Ikeja, Lagos for the brewing of Guinness Stout in 1962. Ikeja Brewery was the first Guinness Brewery outside the British Isles and the third Guinness Brewery in the world.

As a result of the encouraging volume of sales of Guinness Stout the Ikeja Brewery expanded nearly ten fold by between 1973 and 1974. The company started brewing Harp Larger in 1973 with the building of a Brewery in Benin City, Edo State. This Brewery was expanded in 1978 also to produce Guinness Stout. Harp Larger was an immediate success because of its good quality. The huge growth in demand was the incentive for the construction of Ogba Brewery in 1982 also to brew Harp Larger beer.

Thus the company now has four Breweries two in Lagos and two in Benin. The product portfolio of the company was also expanded in December 1970 with the launching of a Malt drink, Malta Guinness.

* First published in IJTD in 2002.

The superb quality of this beverage made it right from the beginning, a winning brand and a household name. In 1995, the product portfolio had another boost by the launch into the market of the premium larger beer, Satzenbrau, "The final world". Brewed in the best German tradition, its very good quality ensured its wide and instant acceptance by consumers.

In compliance with the Federal Government's policy on background integration, which was enunciated in 1986, Guinness Farm was established in Kudu, Niger State. This permitted the growing and use in the brewing process of local raw materials. The farm occupies a land expanse of about 4,500 hectares where mainly maize and sorghum are cultivated. According to Igoche (1997:1-2):

Ownership of the company is 48 per cent, Nigerian and 52 per cent foreign held by Guinness Brewing Worldwide to which Guinness Nigeria is a subsidiary.

Guinness contributes to the national economy by providing direct employment to over 3,000 employees. Indirectly through suppliers, distributors and subcontractors, the company also generates employment for over 20,000 other Nigerians. In 1995, the company paid the following to Government as taxes; Excise—over 2 billion Naira, and overall taxation of above N300 million.

Statement of the Problem

Human resources development has long been recognised by many developing nations as a basic factor for socio-economic emancipation. It is a process that is concerned with the improvement and, growth of the capabilities of individuals and groups within the organisation. Schwartz (1965) observed that it was not the lack of capital or of other economic factors—land, labour and entrepreneur that constituted the greatest constraint in the development of Nigerian enterprises but the lack of managerial talents who are to help in improving training techniques.

Alfred (1960) says that for training programme to be effective, both the individual needing it and other specialists like training consultants and training managers must be involved in need identification.

King *et al.* (1977) suggest that to ensure effectiveness and efficiency of training, planners should consider, among other things, types of training most likely to attain set objectives, combination of activities to be employed, incentives for participants, appropriate media, adequacy of facilities and proper evaluation.

The brewery industry is very dynamic and competitive and is characterised by constant challenge to improve the means of producing food quality beverage. In view of its sophisticated and constantly changing technology, only brewing companies with the highest standards of efficiency and effectiveness can survive.

Every organisation, in order to survive and to be effective, should adopt the latest technology, that is, mechanisation, computerisation and automation. Technology alone, however, does not guarantee success unless it is supported by people possessing requisite skills. So organisations should train the employees to enrich them in the areas of changing technical skills and knowledge from time to time.

With the emergence of increased mechanisation and automation manufacturing of multiple products and by-products, of dealing in services of diversified lines, extension of operations to various regions of the country or in overseas countries, organisation of most modern companies has become complex. This leads to, growth in number and kind of employees and layers in organisational hierarchy. This in turn creates the problems of coordination and integration of activities at various levels. This situation calls for effective management training, especially in the skills of coordination, integration and adaptability to the requirements of growth, diversification and expansion. If training is provided by a company it is necessary to evaluate it to assess its effectiveness. This study therefore sought to examine the management training and development programme of GUINNESS NIGERIA Plc Benin City with a view to ascertaining its relevance, adequacy and effectiveness. Specifically, the study endeavoured to find answers to the following questions:

1. How adequate are the facilities for management training and development?
2. Are the training programmes relevant to the jobs performed by trainees?
3. Does the training undergone by staff improve their job performance?

Hypotheses

The following hypotheses were tested in the study:

$H0_1$: Facilities for management staff training and development are not adequate.

$H0_2$: Training programmes for management staff are not relevant to the jobs they perform.

$H0_3$: Management training undergone by management staff does not improve their job performance and effectiveness.

Significance of the Study

The quality of the human resource in an organisation is considered the most important factor that determines whether or not an organisation is going to succeed or whether it will achieve its basic objectives. In a number of pioneering studies carried out by Schultz (1961) the idea was established that expenditure on education and training is not primarily consumption but an investment which increases productive capacity of labour. Hence, as observed by Scott and Podsakoff (1985), when training is effective, its consequences produce many special advantages for the leaders and other group members. It is obvious from this statement that for an organisation to perform efficiently, the employees must be trained as to be able to perform their tasks effectively.

It was envisaged therefore that data generated from this study would enable Guinness Nigeria Plc assess its training function more critically and have a correct perception of the actual situation of management training and development in the company.

The findings of the study can motivate human resources managers to focus attention on issues critical to effective development of their workforce.

The findings of the study will be of invaluable benefit to training officers in public and private organisations as the study suggests ways of improving management training and development.

It is expected that the study will increase general understanding of strategies for effective training and development of human resources in organisations and evoke the need for evaluation of management training and development programmes in work organisations.

Methodology

The design of the research study was *ex post facto*. This is because it made use of information which had already occurred prior to the study.

Thus, there was no manipulation of variables. The variables of the study which were not manipulated were the independent variables such as type of management training and development programmes received by management staff, adequacy of the facilities and perceived relevance of the programmes. The subjects post-training job performance and effectiveness constituted the dependent variables.

Population of the Study

The population of the study was comprised of all management staff of Guinness Nigeria Plc.

Sample Size and Sampling Procedure

Owing to financial and time constraints, it was impossible to use all the management staff in the breweries of the company in Nigeria. Therefore a convenience sampling design was adopted, whereby the researcher used all the 50 management staff of the company's Benin Brewery as subjects for the study.

Research Instrument

A questionnaire titled 'Management Training and Development Questionnaire' (MTDQ) which was developed by the research was the main instrument used for data collect. The questionnaire was designed to elicit information from the subjects on the types, relevance, adequacy and effectiveness of management training and development programmes provided by the company.

The questionnaire was divided into two sections. Section A which sought information on the subjects' demographic and general background was aimed at identifying the subjects sex, age, marital status, educational qualifications, present rank and length of service.

Section B of the questionnaire gathered information from the subjects on the type of management training and development programmes they had attended and their perception of the programmes in terms of the facilities, relevance, method used and perceived impact of the training received on their job performance.

The questions were structured and open-ended with response categories. Spaces were provided for respondents to tick the appropriate category. This was to reduce the number of possible non-responses and to standardise responses to facilitate analysis.

Validity of the Instrument

The research instrument was thoroughly screened by specialists in Human Resources Training and Development in the Department of Business Administration, University of Benin. Their criticisms, suggestions and recommendations were incorporated in the final instrument. This procedure was to ensure the content and construct validity of the instrument.

Reliability of the Instrument

The Split-Half Coefficient of Reliability was used to determine the reliability of the instrument. A pretest was carried out on thirty management staff in another Brewery of the company that had the same characteristics as the sample. The thirty management staff did not participate in the actual study. In calculating the coefficient of reliability, the completed questionnaires were scored and subdivided into two parts. The division was done by placing all the odd-numbered items to form one sub-test, and all the even numbered items to form the other sub-test. The scores of the two sub-tests were then correlated.

The calculated correlation coefficient for the split half was 0.463. This value was further stepped up by using the Spearman Brown formula. The level of reliability was finally established at 0.63. The value obtained indicates that the instrument had internal consistency and was therefore reliable for use in the study.

Administration of the Instrument

The questionnaires were administered to the subjects by the researcher with the aid of a research assistant. The completed questionnaires were collected immediately. All the fifty questionnaires administered were fully completed and returned.

Method of Data Analysis

The data collected through the questionnaire (MTDQ) were analysed by use of simple percentages, mean and Chi-square.

Results and Discussion

The result of the study are presented on Tables 18.1 to 18.3.

Hypothesis One

Facilities for management staff training and development are not adequate.

To test the hypothesis, the data on Table 18.1 was analysed by use of Chi-square statistic.

Table18.1: Chi-square Analysis of the Adequacy of Training Facilities Rating

Adequacy	*Observed Frequency (o)*	*Expected Frequency (e)*	*o-e*	*(o-e)$^{2/e}$*
Very Adequate	7	10	-3	0.9
Adequate	16	10	6	3.6
Fairly Adequate	15	10	5	2.5
Not Adequate	7	10	-3	0.9
Very Indadequate	5	10	-5	2.5
Total	50	50	0	χ^2 =10.4

P>0.5

For H_0: $U_1 = U_2 = U_3 = U_4 = U_5$

H_1: At least $U_1 \# U_2$

Degree of freedom is 5 - 1 = 4.

χ^2 at 0.05 = 9.49 (Table value)

χ^2 = 10.4 (Calculated value)

Since the calculated value is greater than the table value, the null hypothesis which says that training facilities are not adequate is rejected. Facilities for staff training are adequate for effective training of management staff.

Hypothesis Two

Training Programmes for management staff are not relevant to the jobs they perform.

The above hypothesis was tested by using the Chi-square statistic. The data in Table 18.2 shows the result of the hypothesis tested.

Table 18.2: Chi-square Analysis of Rating of Relevance of Training to Job Performance

Relevance	*Observed Frequency (o)*	*Expected Frequency (e)*	*o-e*	*(o-e)$^{2/e}$*
Very Relevant	19	10	9	8.1
Relevant	15	10	6	3.6
Fairly Relevant	5	10	-5	2.5
Irrelevant	5	10	-5	2.5
Very Irrelevant	5	10	-5	2.5
No Response	1	-	-	-
Total	50	50	0	$\chi^2 = 19.2$

P>0.5

From the result of the analysis in the table above, it can be seen that the calculated Chi-square (19.2) is greater than the table Chi-square which is 9.49. The null-hypothesis which says that training programmes for supervisors are not relevant to the jobs they perform is rejected. This implies that training programmes for management staff are relevant to the jobs they perform.

Hypothesis Three

Training Programmes undergone by management staff do not improve performance and effectiveness of trainees.

This hypothesis was tested by use of Chi-square statistic as shown in Table 18.3.

Table 18.3: Chi-square Analysis of the Rating of Effectiveness of Training

Effectiveness	*Observed Frequency (o)*	*Expected Frequency (e)*	*o-e*	*(o-e)$^{2/e}$*
Very Effective	17	10	7	4.9
Effective	18	10	8	6.4
Fairly Effective	5	10	-5	2.5
Not Effective	5	10	-5	2.5
Very Ineffective	5	10	-5	2.5
No Response	-	-	-	-
Total	50	50	0	$\chi^2 = 18.8$

P>0.5

From the above result obtained, the calculated Chi-square is 18.8. The table chi-square is 9.49. Since the calculated value is greater than the table value, the null hypothesis is rejected. The training programmes undergone by staff do indeed improve their performance and effectiveness at work.

Although the null hypothesis was rejected for Hypothesis I it should be noted however that only 23 or less than 50 per cent of the respondents rated the facilities as very adequate or adequate. This shows that there is ample room for improvement in the available facilities to make training more effective than it was.

On the relevance of the programmes to the jobs manager do, it can be seen from the observed frequency figure in Table 18.2 that 35 or 70 per cent of the respondents rated the programme as very relevant or relevant. When training programmes are relevant to the jobs trainees perform, effectiveness in job performance often results. It is not surprising therefore that, as shown in Table 18.3, the same percentage of respondents agree that training programme undergone by management staff improve performance and effectiveness of trainees.

Conclusion

Management training programmes in Guinness Nigeria Plc are relevant and effective in preparing the staff for the job they do.

The training facilities were perceived by the respondents to be quite adequate. The training provided was relevant and effective in terms of the job performed by the managers.

REFERENCES

Alfred, J.M. (1960), *Personal Communication, Nigeria*, Little Brown Publication.

Igoche, J.G. (1997), *A Handy Guide to the World of Guinness Nigeria Plc.*, (Unpublished manuscript).

King, J.C. *et al.* (1977), Some requirements for successful in-service education, *The Education Digest*, Vol. XL III, No. 1.

Schwartz, S.P. (1965), *Capital Shortage Illusion: Government Lending in Nigeria*, Nigeria: Oxford University Press.

Schultz, T. W. (1961), Investment in Human Capital, *American Economic Review*, Vol. 1.

19

Women Entrepreneurs of Uttaranchal*

Padma Iyer

The Indian concept of women has been governed by two parallel currents—the visible one women in a subordinate role, the *abala* (weak sex), and underlying it, that of women as a symbol of energy, the activity principle" observes Mrs. Indira Gandhi, the third prime Minister of India. It is more true for women in Uttaranchal, who have for centuries taken up the gigantic task of earning extremely most bread-winners and home-makers of their duties. Women in Uttaranchal are endowed with that potentialities and competencies. They work extremely hard, fending for their families, which in most cases also include their husbands. However, her perpetual non-rewarding effort has only tended to bring down their motivation and self-esteem. Most of them feel broken down, anxious, depressed miserable and frustrated. This is so because the major occupation of these women is farming. A majority of the men from this hilly region have started turning away from farming, as they have started doubting its fertility Women on the other hand, have not learnt any other skill except farming and household chores. Even the very educated ones lack any kind of technical skills. Besides alcoholism is very common among the male member of Uttaranchal and this make the life of women even more miserable. The money earned after tireless striving and perseverance, which should be used for their families is spent in the supply of alcohol for their husbands. Biswas (1991) writes. "Almost all studies have carefully (?) carelessly (!!) sidelined the issue of the hill women's

* First published in IJTD in 2002.

destiny,...women in this region are deeply involved in economic management and are active partners without whose participation, survival in Himalayas may become unaccomplished.

It is thus essential that capabilities and motivations of these women need to be sustained. The only way to do this is to socially, psychologically and economically empower them. Psychological and social empowerment would tend to strengthen their confidence and economic empowerment would help them in taking independent decisions. The ideal way to economically empower these women is to inculcate entrepreneurship development in them, if they desire to take up this exciting career.

Nevertheless, commencing and managing an enterprise entails great personal, social and financial risk. However, for a woman in Uttaranchal, who has decided to take up entrepreneurship as a career, this would be a Himalayan task. This is so because she would face problems of entering a male dominated arena, having few role models, lacking confidence in her technical, managerial and entrepreneurial skills, playing a dual role of a career women and a housewife, not having any collateral and infrastructure to start and run her unit.

As shown in Table 19.1, despite the above constraints, it is indeed encouraging that of the 852 participants, who have attended Entrepreneurship Development Programmes (EDPs) conducted by the Institute of Entrepreneurship Development, Uttar Pradesh, [an apex Institute of State, (which conducts EDPs for both the States)], 321 are women. Out of these 321 women 57 (17.75%) of the total women trained, have already set up their enterprises and are running them successfully. Who are these women entrepreneurs? What are their characteristics, skills prospects and problems? What can be done by way of training, to make their lives more easy and their work less cumbersome? These are some of the questions that this paper would try to answer. The entire paper focuses on the data available at IEDUP branch office, Uttaranchal.

Table 19.1: Details of the EDPs conducted at Uttaranchal (1996-99)

Kind of EDPs Conducted	*No. of Programmes*	*No. of Women Trained*	*Total Participants*
Women	06	164	164
General	24	157	688
Total	30	321	852

EDPS conducted for women: Table 19.1 shows the types of EDPs which were organized for women during the financial years 1996-99.

Table 19.1 throws light on the following aspects of 20 per cent of EDPs conducted during the 2nd half of the decade before the advent of the millennium were exclusively for women.

On the whole 37.68 per cent of women have attended EDPs in Uttaranchal during the above period, which is extremely encouraging.

However, 688 participants, have attended to general EDPs and amongst them 157 (22.82%) are women. Since this member is less than 30 per cent more EDPs need to be conducted, exclusively for women.

Attitude and Category

The entire geographical area, where these EDPs were held, are divided into three sub-regions, according to the attitude of the residence of participants of these EDPs. These were as follows:

Higher Himalayas: These consist of the districts, Uttar Kashi, Chamoli, Rudra Prayag, Champawal, Pithoragarh.

Middle Himalayas: The middle Himalayas consist of Almora, Bageshwar, Pauri Garhwal and Garhwal.

Lower Himalayas: The lower Himalayas consist of Nainital, Udham Singh Nagar and Haridwar.

Obviously, the higher the attitudes of the hills the more problems affected it would be in terms of availability of resources.

Table 19.2 reveals the following facts:

Table 19.2: Association between Attitude of Residences of the Women Participants and their Categories

Attitude	*General*	*SC/ST*	*Total*
Higher Himalayas	82 (OF) 92.94 (EF)	35 (OF) 24.06 (EF)	117
Middle Himalayas	81 (OF) 75.46 (EF)	14 (OF) 19.53 (EF)	95
Lower Himalayas	92 (OF) 86.55 (EF)	17 (OF) 22.41 (EF)	109
Total	255	66	321

Chi Square = [{(OF-EF)^2}/EF] = 9.89

The value is significant at the 0.05 level.

The higher the altitude of the residence of the participants the lower their socio-economic status. When it comes to women, more of them from the lower category face problems which are related to their basic requirement, as compared to the general category. Thus to enjoy more social and economic independence, they attend EDPs. Thus more EDPs are to be conducted at the Higher Himalayas, for SC/ST rather than for the General Groups.

Success Rate

If Table 19.3 is analysed we get further information about the women trained at EDPs in Uttaranchal, through, follow-up of the EDPs. The analysis shows the following results:

Table 19.3: Success Rate of Women Trained in EDPs in Uttaranchal (As revealed in follow-up Camps

Kinds of EDPs	*No. of Women Participants*	*Success Rate*	
		No.	*Per cent*
Only for women	164	36	21.95
General	157	21	13.88
Total Women	321	57	17.75
Total Population	852	208	24.41

Of the 164 women trained in EDPs conducted exclusively for women, 36 (21.95%) are able to establish their units while amongst the general population, of the 157 women trained, 21(13.88%) are able to establish their units. On the whole, 57 women (17.75%) are successful in EDPs. If this percentage is compared with success of male participants in the same programmes it is seen that, 151 (24.41%) are successful, as compared to 30 per cent success EDPs all over India. In the case of women of the plains the success rate of those trained in EDPs, at IEDUP, was about 45 per cent (Iyer, 1996). The reason for their phenomenal success was attributed to the fact that women are usually not the breadwinners of their families and therefore are not affected by fear of failure. Men on the other hand have a high degree of the fear, as they are usually the breadwinners of their families.

In Uttaranchal, on the other hand, in most cases, it is women who are the bread winners, as pointed out by Bhatt (1996). Thus, women in the State are usually unable to take financial risk and commence an enterprise, because they are afraid of the fact that their units fait it would be hard to even provide food, clothing and shelter for their families. Thus these women have a higher fear of failure as compared to the women living in the plains of Uttar Pradesh. Besides, economic decisions are usually made by the male members of their families. Thus if they became successful in their career they fear that they might lose their husbands and families. Besides these women may also feel that if they spent too much time away from home their children would go into bad ways and their families would be ruined, that is, they are also usually affected by a fear of success Horner (1972) also observed the same factor with a group of successful women, who had only medium achievement level in USA. If successful women in an advanced country had such feelings, women who are on the threshold of success in India, would certainly be prone to such fear and this fear would be of greater intensity.

The Table also throws light on one other aspect, women trained in EDPs specifically conducted for them are more successful (21.95) than women trained in general EDPs (13.88). What is the reason behind this? There could be two reasons for this, which could be further examined. Firstly, that each potential woman entrepreneur in a woman EDP facilities another, thus helping the group to sustain their motivational level. Secondly, that in a general EDP, women are in a minority. The progress made by male members, who are definitely more mobile and independent, tends to probably dampen motivational level of women participating in these EDPs.

Demographic Characteristics

Demographic characteristics also play a significant role in the success of these women entrepreneurs. Let us examine some of these characteristics and how they have affected the success of these women.

Table 19.4 shows the age range of women who are successful in EDPs.

Table 19.4: Age of the Successful Women Entrepreneurs Trained at EDPs

Age Range	*Number*	*Percentage*
18-35	12	21.05
36-45	43	75.44
Above 46	02	03.51

From the above table it is seen that only 12 women (21.05) who are in the age of 18-35 years successful. These are probably the women who are extremely ambitious and also supported by their family members in the achievement of their goals or are compelled to take up a venture due to unusual circumstances. However, the age after 35 is usually the time when entrepreneurship among women develops. After 35, women are more free as their children no longer need them full-time. They are not available to them at this age, or even if are the income is only a pittance. On the other hand these women have a high need to be self-sufficient and so they take nominal and calculated and start their own enterprises.

Table 19.5: Education Level of these Successful Women Entrepreneurs

Part of Education	*Number*	*Percentage*
Intermediate	03	5.26
Graduate	22	38.60
Postgraduate	24	42.10
Technically trained	08	14.04

From Table 19.5 it is evident that the successful entrepreneurs are highly educated. Only 3 of them (5.26%) are Intermediate pass, 22 (38.60%) Post Graduate, 8 of them (14.04%) are also technically trained. It was also found that 7 of the 8 technically trained women are below the age 30. Technical skills catalyze entrepreneurship development. This could further examined.

Marital status is another factor that impairs the success. Table 19.6 reveals the marital of the 57 successful women entrepreneurs.

From Table 19.6, it is seen that most successful women entrepreneurs 43 of them (75.44%) are well settled in life. Nevertheless, 9(15.79%) are married and 5 (8.77) are divorced or widowed. The last group is the one, who is possibly settled to take up an enterprise as a means of becoming self-sufficient and earning a livelihood.

Table 19.6: Marital Status of the Successful Women Entrepreneurs

Marital Status	*Numbers*	*Percentage*
Married	43	75.44
Unmarried	09	15.79
Widowed or Divorced	05	8.77

Another factor that plays an important part in entrepreneurship development is family income.

Table 19.7: Monthly Family Income of the Successful Women Entrepreneurs before Establishment of their Units

Income Level (Rs.)	*Number*	*Percentage*
5,000-10,000	39	68.42
10,001-20,000	08	14.04
Above 20,000	10	17.54

From Table 19.7 it is seen that these successful women who are extremely educated, also tend to be extremely dissatisfied with their family income. Before the commencement of their units, 39 of them (68.42%) had a family income ranging from Rs. 5,000 to Rs. 10,000. 8 (14.04%) had family income ranging between Rs. 10,000 to Rs. 20,000 while 10 of them (17.54%) had a family income above Rs. 20,000. These women were confident that they would earn more than what was being earned in their families. Besides, they were keen on elevating their family status and thus they have taken up self-employment and entrepreneurship.

Description of their Units: An important aspect of the entrepreneurial personality of these women is the kinds of units set up by them, Table 19.8 shows the kinds of units set up by these women.

Table 19.8: Kinds of Units set up by the Successful Women Entrepreneurs

Kinds of Programmes	*Success*	*Trading*	*Service*	*Manufacturing*
Only Women	36	11	15	10
General	21	12	07	02
Total	57	23	22	12
Percentage	100	40.35	30.60	21.5

From Table 19.8 it is seen that 40.35 per cent of the women have taken to trading. This activity involves least risk and virtually no investment on machines and raw materials. It can be started with or without an infrastructure. 30.60 per cent women have taken to service industry. Women are usually good at the service industry and Uttaranchal being a place of great natural beauty, certainly, attracts tourists. Besides, to preserve its beauty and serenity, large manufacturing units cannot flourish. 12 of them (21.05%) have established manufacturing unit. These units also require very little investment as revealed in the next table. Here it is also to be noted that more women from the EDP, which catered exclusively for women, have set up units which are service and manufacturing oriented, while in those conducted for the general population, more women tended to take up trading rather than the other two sectors. Could this again reflect upon the fact that in a general EDP women's motivational level is of lesser duration than at an EDP conducted exclusively for women. This is to be further explored.

Projected cost: Beside, the kind of units, it is also essential to know about the project cost of the units. Table 19.9 gives the project cost of the units.

Table 19.9: Project cost of the Successful Units

Total Project Cost (Rs. in Lakhs)	*Number*	*Percentage*
Below 1.00	41	71.92
1.00-5.00	13	22.82
5.00-10.00	03	05.26

From the above table it is seen that all the 57 units have project costs below Rs. 10 lakh. These women have started with a low investment and have not invested and blocked their money is exorbitant plant, building, machinery and luxuries and therefore are successful. But this does not mean that everything is a bed of rose for these successful women entrepreneurs. Let us explore their thorns together with their roses.

Problems: Table 19.10 reveals the type of problems encountered by the successful women entrepreneurs.

Table 19.10: Problem Faced by the Women Entrepreneurs

Problems	*Start up*	*%*	*Problems*	*Management*	*%*
Familial	06	10.52	Lack of technical Expertise	49	85.96
Obtaining finance	51	89.47	Financial	04	71.02
Lack of experience	11	19.30	Manpower	02	13.57
Professional Disrespect	55	96.49	Marketing	33	57.89

From Table 19.10 it is seen that the most severe problems of these successful, women entrepreneurs are professional disrespect, means of obtaining finance, lack of technical expertise and marketing of their products.

Like the women entrepreneurs in the plains, in the hills also, women are harassed by the gender bias though most of them are the breadwinners of their families. It is indeed ironical that though they have the responsibility of earning money of their family, the authority of spending is vested in the male members of their families. Another problem faced by these women entrepreneurs is the means of obtaining finance. Very often, they are not given financial support from banks due to their gender. There are no technical institutions that provide technical training exclusively for women and thus though very educated they are not technically skilled. Marketing takes great effort, skills, manipulation and publicity. Women in this region need to be specially equipped in this skill also.

After analyzing the profile of women entrepreneurs, let us formulate a prescription that would help women entrepreneurs to develop and grow in Uttaranchal.

Prescriptions for Success

There are several key factors that help in the success of women entrepreneurs residing at Uttaranchal. These include the following factors:

Role models: Women EDP participants would interact with successful women entrepreneurs so that they could get an idea of the aspects started by women entrepreneurs, and feel that there are women who are successful in their enterprises and that they are not alone.

Extensive field visit: It is indeed sad that many women in the hills, especially those residing in the rural areas, have not even seen a train. They have also no idea of what a plain would look like. Besides, since enterprises have not flourished in the hills, it is essential to take the women participants to visit industrial cities like Delhi or Bombay. When they would see women running units, in those cities they would certainly be encouraged. Besides, they would also get an idea of the projects to be started. But this particular input would require more budget from the financing institutions than that received from them till now to conduct EDPs.

Extensive follow-up: When women are not successful, or face certain problems, they shirk from their coordinators. Under these circumstances it is the coordinator who should approach the participants during follow-up and motivate them once more through their counselling skills. Nevertheless, in the hills, public transport is scarce and very often coordinators cannot afford a taxi. Thus in EDPs the target of 25 people should be reduced to 10 or 15 to cater to this geographical situation.

EDPs exclusively for women: As shown in the study, women EDPs lead to greater success amongst women than general EDPs. Thus more EDPs should be conducted for women.

Support system and mentoring: Women entrepreneurs in Uttaranchal need to have a more supportive families especially husbands, friends, associates and women professional groups. Many also need mentors to guide and support as well. A mentor could be an EDP trainer, an officer from a financial organisation or an experienced women entrepreneur.

Re-orientation programmers: Short term training packages could be given for successful women entrepreneurs, so as to help their units not only survive but also grow from strength to strength.

Moratorium period: Moratorium period of loans should be extended to a year in a case of women entrepreneurs, no matter how small the loans. This would help them to overcome problems related to their gender, before their units commerce.

Technical institutions for women: ITIs, Polytechnics and other technical institutions should be open exclusively for women, with residential facilities, to attract more women into the technical and technological fields. This would catalyze their entrepreneurship development.

Professional development necessary: "Entrepreneurs, no matter what their gender, need to be determined to for the success of their endeavour and be professional in their approach. These attributes are especially important for women entrepreneurs because determination will help them succeed in establishing their business, and professionalism will contribute to their being taken seriously" (Hisrich and O'Brien, 1981). This thought also applies for a women entrepreneur in Uttaranchal.

With a revolution taking place in Information Technology, and India marching ahead in this field, many problems of women entrepreneurs seem to be automatically sorted out. Women entrepreneurs need not be very mobile to learn a particular skill, survey their markets, get their contract and these days. Personal computers with internet connections would help these women learn any skill, explore the worldwide markets and get detailed information about any project, competition in the particular sector and its marketing outlets. Thus it is vital to promote Information Technology in Uttaranchal, to provide benefits to more women entrepreneurs.

In general, the future of women entrepreneurs in this new State is optimistic. Still, promoters whether they are training or financial organisations need to strive tirelessly to achieve the goal of a male/ female ratio of 50:50 in this State. This task is hard but not impossible in a State where women are more responsible for the sustenance of their families than their male counterparts. Nevertheless this could involve the lifetime commitment of many promoters.

REFERENCES

Bhatt, Radha (Lakshmi Ashram Kosani) "Uttarakand ki Nari Shram Sadhan aur Peera", In *Uttaranchal Today*, (ed) K.S. Vaidya, pp. 191-95.

Biswas, Babul. "On being a woman", In *Strategy for development in the Himalayas*, (A profile of socio-economic change) Ed, Biswas S. K. 117-30.

Garett, H.E. *Statistics in Psychology and Education*, Vakils Fetter and Simons Pvt. Ltd., 1970, pp. 271-79.

Hisrich and O'Brien M. The woman entrepreneur Business and Sociological Perspective, In Vesper (Ed) *Frontiers in entrepreneurship research* (Wellesley Mass Bapson Centre for Entrepreneurship Studies) (1981) pp. 21-39.

Horner, M.S. "Towards understanding of achievement related conflicts in women, *Journal of Social Issues*, 20, (1972), pp. 157-75.

Iyer, P. "Gender differences between male and female entrepreneurs", Paper presented at the British Council Division, In a Seminar of Gender Issues, New Delhi.

Index